TEPS

서울대
텝스 관리위원회
최신기출
1200

문제집

SEASON

3

서울대 텝스 관리위원회 최신기출 1200 SEASON **3** 문제집

문제제공 서울대학교 TEPS관리위원회
펴낸이 임상진
펴낸곳 (주)넥서스

초판 1쇄 발행 2013년 3월 5일
초판 41쇄 발행 2025년 9월 25일

출판신고 1992년 4월 3일 제311-2002-2호
10880 경기도 파주시 지목로 5
Tel (02)330-5500 Fax (02)330-5555

ISBN 978-89-6790-212-4 18740

www.nexusbook.com

TEPS

서울대
텝스 관리위원회
최신기출
1200

How to
TEPS

서울대학교 TEPS관리위원회 기출문제 제공

문제집

SEASON
3

넥서스

PREFACE

2006년 넥서스에서 최초로 TEPS 기출문제집 〈유형별로 분석한 NEXUS 기출 800〉을 출간한 후 〈서울대 텝스 관리위원회 최신기출 1000〉〈서울대 텝스 관리위원회 제공 최신기출 시크릿〉〈서울대 텝스 관리위원회 최신기출 1200 / SEASON 2〉에 이르기까지 대표적인 TEPS 기출문제집으로 자리매김할 수 있도록 많은 사랑과 관심을 보여준 TEPS 수험생들과 학교 및 학원에서 강의를 담당하시는 선생님들께 다시 한번 감사의 마음을 전한다. 다른 영어 능력 검정시험과 달리 많은 기출문제가 공식적으로 오픈된 TEPS 시험은 그만큼 과학적인 측정 도구와 신뢰할 수 있는 콘텐츠, 뛰어난 변별력 등 테스트로서의 투명성을 이미 인정받았다. 1999년 1월 첫 TEPS 시험 시행 이후 이러한 공인된 시험에 대한 신뢰도를 바탕으로 이제는 입시 · 취업 · 승진 등 여러 분야에서 이 TEPS 시험 성적이 두루 활용되고 있는 것이 현실이다.

TEPS를 어떻게 공부해야 하느냐는 질문을 종종 받는다. TEPS 시험이 아직 한국인들에게는 만만한 시험이 아니라는 것을 너무 잘 알고 있기 때문에 제대로 된 교재와 학습법으로 TEPS 체질로 영어 공부 환경을 세팅하라고밖에 조언해 줄 수 없다. 우리가 건강한 체력을 위해 몸에 좋은 음식, 심지어는 유기농을 섭취하려고 하듯, 건강한 TEPS 체질을 갖고 싶다면 엉뚱한 TEPS 유사 문제들이 아닌 시험에 출제된 기출문제들을 많이 경험해 볼 것을 권면한다. 시중에 이미 출간된 소위 베스트셀러라는 수험서에 수록된 TEPS 문제들을 분석해 보니, TEPS 시험이 아닌 다른 영어 시험 유형 문제를 수록해 혼동을 주는 경우가 많았다. TEPS 시험에 어떤 문제가 실제로 출제되었는지만 제대로 파악해도 시험 유형을 반 이상 경험한 거라고 볼 수 있다.

이번에 출간하는 〈서울대 텝스 관리위원회 최신기출 1200 SEASON 3〉는 〈서울대 텝스 관리위원회 최신기출 1200 / SEASON 2〉에 이어 더욱 새로운 기출문제 6회분으로 구성, 학습자 편의를 위해 문제집과 해설집을 별도로 각각 제작했다. 가장 최신 기출문제들만 선별해서 수록했고, 실제 TEPS 시험장에서 접했던 문제 그대로의 디자인, 청해 방송에서 들던 MP3 음원을 모두 고스란히 그대로 가져왔다. 또한 군더더기 없이 핵심만 짚어 주는 문제 해설을 위해 끝없이 원고를 수정 보완해서 질 좋은 TEPS 기출문제를 더 잘 이해할 수 있도록 해설집을 따로 만들었다. 방대한 TEPS 문제들을 편하게 각자의 도서관이나 강의실, 집, 카페에서 경험하고 TEPS 고사장으로 향한다면 별로 긴장하지 않고 좋은 결과를 기대할 수 있을 것이다.

TEPS 기출문제집 출간을 위해 넥서스 TEPS연구소의 성가시게 많은 질문과 요구사항에도 적극적으로 도움을 주신 서울대학교 TEPS관리위원회 관계자분들께 이 자리를 통해 다시 한번 감사의 마음을 전한다. TEPS 시험이 수험생 모두의 꿈을 실현하는 데 잘 활용되기를 응원한다.

넥서스 TEPS연구소 연구원 일동

CONTENTS

FEATURE

1_ TEPS 최신기출 1,200문항

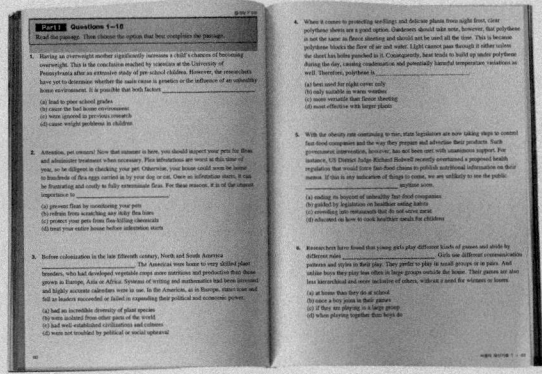

서울대학교 TEPS관리위원회가 공개한 현존 가장 최신 기출문제 1,200문항을 실제 TEPS 시험지와 동일한 디자인 환경으로 제공

2_ 수험생들에게 꼭 필요한 텝스 만점 전략

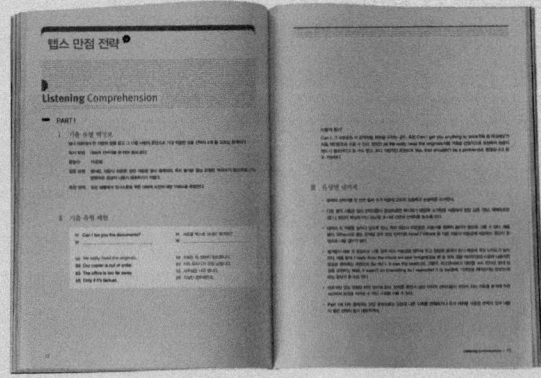

청해–문법–어휘–독해 4영역 13파트에 대한 TEPS 출제 경향 및 고득점 대비 전략을 통합적으로 분석한 출제 비밀 노트 공개

3_ 군더더기 없는 완전 해설

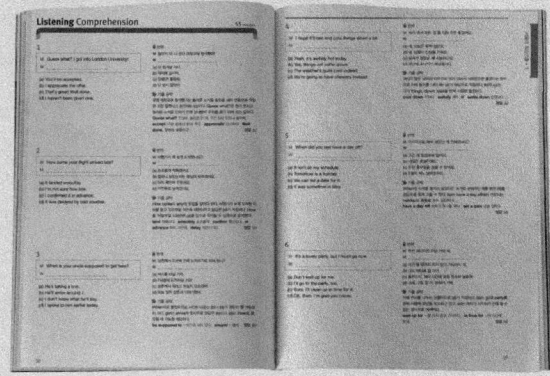

넥서스 TEPS연구소의 오랜 노하우가 녹아 있는 콤팩트한
알짜배기 해설로 오답에 대한 속시원한 해결책 제시

4_ 문제집과 해설집 별도 제작

학습자 편의를 위해 방대한 분량을 문제집과 해설집으로 별도
제작, 휴대하기 편할 뿐 아니라 학습 목적에 맞게 구매 가능

5_ 실제 고사장에서 듣던 청해 음성

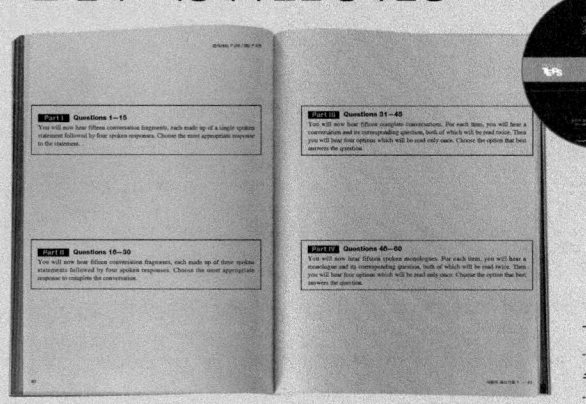

TEPS 고사장에서 청해 시간에 사용했던 MP3 음원을 그대로
수록, 생생한 청해 시험 체험

TEPS에 대하여 🤔

1_ TEPS란?

❶ Test of English Proficiency developed by Seoul National University의 약자로 서울대학교 언어교육원에서 개발하고, TEPS관리위원회에서 주관하는 국가공인 영어시험

❷ 1999년 1월 처음 시행 이후 연 12~16회 실시

❸ 정부기관 및 기업의 직원 채용, 인사고과, 해외 파견 근무자 선발과 더불어 대학과 특목고 입학 및 졸업 자격 요건, 국가고시 및 자격 시험의 영어 대체 시험으로 활용

❹ 100여 명의 국내외 유수 대학의 최고 수준 영어 전문가들이 출제하고, 언어 테스팅 분야의 세계적인 권위자인 Bachman 교수(미국 UCLA)와 Oller 교수(미국 뉴멕시코대)로부터 타당성을 검증받음

❺ 말하기 – 쓰기 시험인 TEPS Speaking & Writing도 별도 실시 중이며, 2009년 10월부터 이를 통합한 i-TEPS 실시

2_ TEPS 시험 구성

영역	Part별 내용	문항수	시간/배점
청해 **Listening** Comprehension	Part I : 문장 하나를 듣고 이어질 대화 고르기 Part II : 3문장의 대화를 듣고 이어질 대화 고르기 Part III : 6~8 문장의 대화를 듣고 질문에 해당하는 답 고르기 Part IV : 담화문의 내용을 듣고 질문에 해당하는 답 고르기	15 15 15 15	55분 400점
문법 **Grammar**	Part I : 대화문의 빈칸에 적절한 표현 고르기 Part II : 문장의 빈칸에 적절한 표현 고르기 Part III : 대화에서 어법상 틀리거나 어색한 부분 고르기 Part IV : 단문에서 문법상 틀리거나 어색한 부분 고르기	20 20 5 5	25분 100점
어휘 **Vocabulary**	Part I : 대화문의 빈칸에 적절한 단어 고르기 Part II : 단문의 빈칸에 적절한 단어 고르기	25 25	15분 100점
독해 **Reading** Comprehension	Part I : 지문을 읽고 빈칸에 들어갈 내용 고르기 Part II : 지문을 읽고 질문에 가장 적절한 내용 고르기 Part III : 지문을 읽고 문맥상 어색한 내용 고르기	16 21 3	45분 400점
총계	13개 Parts	200	140분 990점

☆ **IRT** (Item Response Theory)에 의하여 최고점이 990점, 최저점이 10점으로 조정됨.

3_ TEPS 시험 응시 정보

현장 접수
❶ www.teps.or.kr에서 인근 접수처 및 준비물(응시료, 사진) 확인
❷ 접수처 방문 : 해당 접수기간 평일 오후 12시 ~ 5시

인터넷 접수
❶ 서울대학교 TEPS관리위원회 홈페이지 접속 www.teps.or.kr
❷ 준비물 : 스캔한 사진 파일, 응시료 결제를 위한 신용 카드 및 은행 계좌

4_ TEPS 시험 당일 정보

❶ 고사장 입실 완료 : 9시 30분(일요일) / 3시(토요일)
❷ 준비물 : 신분증, 컴퓨터용 사인펜, 수정테이프, 수험표, 시계
❸ 유효한 신분증
　성인 : 주민등록증, 운전면허증, 여권, 공무원증, 현역간부 신분증, 군무원증, 주민등록증 발급 신청 확인서, 외국인 등록증
　초·중고생 : 학생증, 여권, 청소년증, 주민등록증, 주민등록증 발급 신청 확인서, TEPS 신분확인 증명서
❹ 시험 시간 : 2시간 20분 (중간에 쉬는 시간 없음, 각 영역별 제한시간 엄수)
❺ 성적 확인 : 약 2주 후 인터넷에서 조회 가능

텝스 만점 전략 🗣

Listening Comprehension

▬ PART I

I 기출 유형 핵정보

남녀 대화에서 한 사람의 말을 듣고 그 다음 사람의 응답으로 가장 적절한 것을 선택지 4개 중 고르는 문제이다.

제시 방법 대화와 선택지를 한 번만 들려 준다.

문항수 15문항

질문 유형 평서문, 의문사 의문문, 일반 의문문 등이 출제되며, 특히 평서문 응답 유형은 무리수가 많으므로 어느 방향으로 응답이 나올지 예측하기가 어렵다.

측정 영역 일상 생활에서 의사소통을 위한 대화체 표현에 대한 이해도를 측정한다.

II 기출 유형 체험

M Can I fax you the documents?	M 서류를 팩스로 보내도 될까요?
W _____	W _____
✔ (a) We really need the originals.	(a) 저희는 꼭 원본이 필요합니다.
(b) Our copier is out of order.	(b) 저희 복사기가 고장 났습니다.
(c) The office is too far away.	(c) 사무실은 너무 멉니다.
(d) Only if it's factual.	(d) 사실인 경우에만요.

이렇게 푼다!

Can I...? 의문문은 이 문제처럼 허락을 구하는 경우, 혹은 Can I get you anything to drink?(뭐 좀 마실래요?) 처럼 제안문으로 쓰일 수 있다. 정답인 (a) We really need the originals처럼 거절을 간접적으로 표현하여 원본이 반드시 필요하다고 할 수도 있고, 보다 직접적인 표현으로 Yes, that shouldn't be a problem(네, 괜찮습니다) 등 도 가능하다.

Ⅲ 유형별 대비책

- 문제와 선택지를 한 번만 들려 주기 때문에 고도의 집중력과 순발력을 요구한다.

- 다른 영어 시험과 달리 선택지들이 음성으로만 제시되기 때문에 소거법을 사용해서 정답 같은 것(o), 애매모호한 것(△), 정답이 확실히 아닌 것(x)을 표시해 가면서 선택지를 듣도록 한다.

- 대화의 첫 부분을 놓치지 않도록 한다. 특히 의문사 의문문은 의문사를 정확히 들어야 정답을 고를 수 있다. 예를 들어, When으로 묻는 문제일 경우 오답 선택지로 How나 Where 등 다른 의문사 의문문에 해당하는 응답이 함정으로 나올 경우가 많다.

- 평서문이 대화 첫 문장으로 나올 경우 여러 가능성을 염두에 두고 정답을 골라야 하기 때문에 특히 난이도가 높아진다. 예를 들어, I really liked the movie we saw tonight(오늘 밤 본 영화 정말 재미있었어) 다음에 나옴직한 응답은 동의하는 표현으로 So did I. It was the best(나도 그랬어. 최고였어)라고 대답할 수도 있지만, 반대 입장을 표현하는 Well, it wasn't so interesting as I expected it to be(글쎄, 기대만큼 재미있지는 않았는데)라는 응답이 올 수도 있다.

- 대표적인 오답 유형을 미리 정리해 둔다. 문제를 풀면서 정답 이외의 선택지들이 오답이 되는 이유를 분석해 두면 실전에서 함정을 피해갈 수 있는 스킬을 키울 수 있다.

- Part 1에 자주 출제되는 오답 유형으로는 질문에 나온 어휘를 반복하거나 유사 어휘를 사용한 선택지, 일부 내용이 틀린 선택지 등이 대표적이다.

I 기출 유형 핵정보

남녀 대화에서 세 번째 대화까지 듣고 그 다음 이어질 응답으로 가장 자연스러운 것을 4개의 선택지 중에서 고르는 문제이다.

제시 방법 대화와 선택지를 한 번만 들려 준다.

문항수 15문항

질문 유형 평서문, 의문사 의문문, 일반 의문문 등이 출제되며, 이 중 특히 평서문인 경우 어느 방향으로 응답이 나올지 예측하기 어렵다.

측정 영역 일상 대화 속 표현에 대한 이해도 측정이라는 점에서 Part 1과 동일한데, 이와 더불어 전반적인 대화 흐름의 이해도를 측정하기도 한다.

II 기출 유형 체험

M We've been invited to Amy's for dinner.	M 에이미네 저녁식사 초대를 받았어.
W What for?	W 무슨 일인데?
M I'm not sure, but we shouldn't go empty-handed.	M 무슨 일인지는 모르겠지만 빈손으론 가면 안 될 것 같아.
W _____	W _____
(a) Why don't we invite her?	(a) 그녀를 초대하는 게 어때?
(b) She's going to cook for us.	(b) 그녀가 우릴 위해 요리할 거야.
(c) I'd love to go with you.	(c) 나도 같이 가고 싶어.
✔(d) Let's bring a bottle of wine.	(d) 와인 한 병 사가자.

이렇게 푼다!

We shouldn't…/ We must…/ We have to… 등은 상대방을 강하게 설득하는 문장이다. 파티에 갈 때 빈손으로 가면 안 된다는 말에, (d) Let's bring a bottle of wine과 같이 적극적인 동의 방법을 답으로 선택해야 한다. 이렇 듯 서구 문화에서는 집으로 초대받은 경우 와인이나 케이크 혹은 꽃 등 간단한 선물을 준비해 가는 것이 예의라는 것도 기억해 두자.

Ⅲ 유형별 대비책

- 한 번만 들려 주는 세 줄의 대화를 정확하게 잘 듣도록 한다. 첫 문장을 잘 들어야 그 다음에 이어지는 두 줄의 대화를 잘 이해할 수 있기 때문에 Part 2 역시 고도의 집중력을 요한다.

- 만일 첫 줄을 놓쳤다면 당황하지 말고 그 다음 이어지는 두 줄의 대화를 잘 듣도록 한다. 가장 이상적인 청취는 세 줄을 다 알아듣는 것이지만, 혹시 그렇지 못하더라도 선택지가 나오기 직전의 말을 잘 들으면 자연스럽게 이어지는 응답을 고르는 데 도움이 된다.

- 소거법을 활용해서 정답을 고르는 것도 들려 주기만 하는 선택지에 대처할 수 있는 한 방법이다.

- 남녀 각각 어떤 말을 했는지 구분해서 들어야 오답을 피해갈 수 있다.

- 풀어본 문제의 오답을 매번 분석해서 실전에서 신속하고 정확하게 오답을 피하도록 한다.

- Part 2의 대표적인 오답 유형으로는 대화의 앞부분을 일부 놓치고 착각해서 선택할 만한 선택지, 대화에 언급된 어휘로 만든 선택지, 대화에 등장한 어휘의 또 다른 의미를 가지고 만든 선택지, 질문한 사람이 이어서 할 만한 말로 만든 선택지 등이 있다.

PART III

I 기출 유형 핵정보

남녀가 세 번씩 주고받는 대화를 듣고 4개의 선택지 중 질문에 가장 적절한 답을 고르는 문제이다.

제시 방법 대화 → 질문 → 대화 → 질문 → 선택지 순으로 들려 준다.

문항수 15문항

질문 유형 대의 파악(7문항) → 세부 내용 파악(5문항) → 추론(3문항) 순으로 나온다.

측정 영역 일상 대화에 등장하는 다양한 표현에 대한 이해도를 바탕으로 전체 대의 파악, 세부 내용 파악, 추론 능력을 측정한다.

II 기출 유형 체험

M Any special plans for your three-week vacation?	M 3주 휴가 동안 특별한 계획이 있나요?
W I think I'll visit my family and relax somewhere.	W 집에 들렀다가 어디 가서 좀 쉴 생각이에요.
M Where do you plan on relaxing?	M 어디서 쉬려고 하는데요?
W Oh, I don't know, maybe go somewhere warm.	W 글쎄요. 모르겠어요. 아마 따뜻한 곳으로 가겠죠.
M What about Thailand?	M 태국은 어때요?
W Actually, that sounds good. I'll put it on my list.	W 좋은 생각이네요. 그곳도 고려해 봐야겠어요.

Q What is the main topic of the conversation?	Q 대화의 중심 소재는?
(a) The best way to spend a vacation.	(a) 휴가를 보낼 가장 좋은 방법.
✔ (b) The woman's vacation plans.	(b) 여자의 휴가 계획.
(c) Popular holiday destinations.	(c) 인기 있는 휴양지.
(d) Setting aside time to visit family.	(d) 가족을 방문하기 위한 시간을 남겨 놓기.

이렇게 푼다!

휴가 계획은 상당히 빈출도가 높은 토픽이다. 어디로 휴가를 갈 것인지, 혹은 휴가가 어땠는지에 대해 물어보는 두 가지 내용 중 하나로 예상할 수 있다. 여자는 따뜻한 곳에서 쉬려고 하고 남자는 태국을 권하고 있으므로, 이를 간단하고 함축적으로 표현한 (b) The woman's vacation plans가 정답이다. (d)는 visiting family를 응용한 오답이다.

Ⅲ 유형별 대비책

- 처음 대화를 들을 때 전체 대화 내용을 파악한 뒤, 질문에 따라 집중할 부분에 더 집중하는 두 번째 듣기를 한다. 대화의 흐름을 파악해야 대의 파악 문제뿐 아니라 세부 내용 파악이나 추론 문제도 더 쉽게 풀 수 있다.

- 질문에 따라서 메모를 해야 하는 경우도 있다. 특히 세부 내용 파악 문제의 경우 숫자, 연도, 물건의 종류 등을 명확하게 기억하는 것이 유리하고, 남녀 각각 어떤 말을 했는지 구분해서 알아 두는 것이 오답을 피하는 데 많은 도움이 된다. 추론 능력은 대의 또는 세부 내용을 바탕으로 하기 때문에 세부 내용도 간과할 수 없다.

- 선택지를 한 번밖에 들려 주지 않기 때문에 대화 내용을 다 이해하고도 선택지를 놓쳐서 정답을 고르지 못하는 경우가 있다. 이를 방지하기 위해 소거법을 적용해서 선택지를 차례대로 표시하면서 최종 정답을 고르도록 한다.

- 질문 종류별로 오답 확률이 높은 유형을 알아 두는 것도 도움이 된다.
  - 대의 파악 오답 유형: 대화 중 일부 세부 사항만 포함한 선택지, 너무 일반적인 내용의 선택지, 대화 중 특정 키워드를 조합한 전혀 엉뚱한 내용의 선택지 등이다.

  - 세부 내용 파악 오답 유형: 대화에서 언급된 어휘를 반복한 선택지, 대화와 전혀 무관한 선택지, 일부 내용만 사실인 선택지, 남녀의 역할이 뒤바뀐 선택지, 시제가 대화 내용과 일치하지 않는 선택지 등이 있다.

  - 추론 오답 유형: 상식적으로는 맞는 진술이지만 대화 내용과는 무관한 선택지, 대화에서 언급된 어휘로 만들었지만 대화 내용과 무관한 선택지, 추론 가능한 내용과 정반대인 선택지 등이 있다.

- 대의 파악이나 세부 내용 파악 유형에 대비해 패러프레이징(paraphrasing) 연습을 하는 것이 좋다. 대화에서 언급된 어휘가 그대로 사용된 경우는 오답일 확률이 높은 반면, 언급된 어휘를 비슷한 말로 바꾸어 만든 선택지는 정답일 확률이 높으므로 paraphrasing 연습이 많은 도움이 된다.

Ⅰ 기출 유형 핵정보

담화문을 듣고 4개의 선택지 중 질문에 가장 적절한 정답을 고르는 문제이다.

제시 방법   담화문 → 질문 → 담화문 → 질문 → 선택지 순으로 들려 준다.

문항수   15문항

질문 유형   대의 파악(7문항) → 세부 내용 파악(5문항) → 추론(3문항) 순으로 나온다.

측정 영역   영어 연설, 강의, 라디오 방송 등에 나오는 다양한 표현에 대한 이해도 측정을 바탕으로 전체 대의 파악, 세부 내용 파악, 추론 능력을 측정한다.

Ⅱ 기출 유형 체험

Earlier this week, animal control officials killed a bear responsible for wounding a camper. The 21-year-old camper was sleeping when the 280-pound male black bear ripped through the side of his tent. The camper sustained bite wound and scratches but was able to scare the bear off. Earlier this month, two other bears were killed in the same area after attacking several Boy Scout members at a camp.

Q What happened to the camper who was attacked by the bear?
(a) He died from wounds.
(b) He got lost in the woods.
✔ (c) He was bitten and scratched.
(d) He was rescued by Boy Scouts.

이번 주 초에 동물 관리국 직원들은 야영하던 사람을 다치게 한 이유로 곰 한 마리를 사살했다. 280파운드의 검은 수컷 곰이 텐트 한 쪽을 찢었을 때 야영을 하던 21세의 피해자는 자고 있었다. 그는 물리고 긁혔지만 곰을 놀라게 해서 쫓아낼 수 있었다. 이달 초에는 막사에 있던 보이스카우트 회원 여러 명을 공격한 다른 두 마리의 곰이 같은 곳에서 사살됐다.

Q 곰에게 공격당한 야영객에게 무슨 일이 일어났는가?
(a) 상처 때문에 죽었다.
(b) 숲 속에서 길을 잃었다.
(c) 물리고 긁혔다.
(d) 보이스카우트에 의해 구조되었다.

이렇게 푼다!

이 문제는 질문 What happened to...?(~에게 무슨 일이 일어났는가?)에 초점을 맞춰 두 번째 들을 때 답을 골라 낼 수 있으며, The camper sustained bite wound and scratches를 바꿔 쓴 (c) He was bitten and scratched를 정답으로 선택해야 한다. 이 문제처럼 특정 사실을 묻는 문제도 출제된다.

Ⅲ 유형별 대비책

● 먼저 담화문의 전체 흐름을 파악한 뒤, 두 번째 듣기에서 질문과 연계된 부분에 집중하여 정확하게 듣는다.

● 질문 유형에 따라 맞춤식 메모를 한다. 특히 세부 사항 파악 유형 문제에 대비해서는 숫자, 연도, 물품 종류 등을 세세하게 메모해야 하고, 추론 능력은 대의 또는 세부 내용을 바탕으로 하기 때문에 세부 내용도 간과할 수 없다는 것을 기억한다.

● 질문 종류별로 오답일 확률이 높은 경우를 알아 두는 것이 도움이 된다.
  - 대의 파악 오답 유형: 담화문 내용의 일부에 해당하는 세부 사항으로 만든 선택지, 주제와 관련은 있으나 너무 범위가 넓은 일반적인 내용의 선택지, 언급된 어휘로 구성된 점 외에는 내용과 전혀 관련이 없는 선택지 등이 오답일 확률이 높다.

  - 세부 내용 파악 오답 유형: 담화문에 언급된 어휘로 만들어진 선택지나 내용과 전혀 무관한 선택지, 일부만 사실인 선택지 등이 오답으로 제시될 가능성이 크다.

  - 추론 오답 유형: 상식적으로는 맞지만 내용과는 무관한 선택지, 담화문에서 언급된 어휘로 만들었지만 내용과는 무관한 선택지, 추론 가능한 내용과 정반대의 선택지 등이 종종 사용되는 오답 유형이다.

● 대의 파악이나 세부 내용 파악 유형의 문제를 위해서는 paraphrasing 연습을 하는 것이 좋다. 언급된 어휘를 그대로 사용하면 오답일 확률이 높은 반면, 정답의 경우 언급된 어휘를 paraphrasing해서 만드는 경우가 많다.

Grammar

I 기출 유형 핵정보

두 줄의 대화문을 읽고 빈칸에 문법적으로 적절한 표현을 4개의 선택지 중에서 고르는 문제이다.

제시 방법 두 줄의 대화문이 주어진다.

문항수 20문항

측정 영역 실시간과 비슷한 시간 제약 속에서 문법적으로 정확한 영어를 대화 속에서 구사할 수 있는지 측정한다.

빈출 토픽 일상 생활 대화 중에 흔히 접할 수 있는 주제가 많이 사용되므로 청해나 어휘 영역의 대화 부분과 비슷한 내용이 나온다.

II 기출 유형 체험

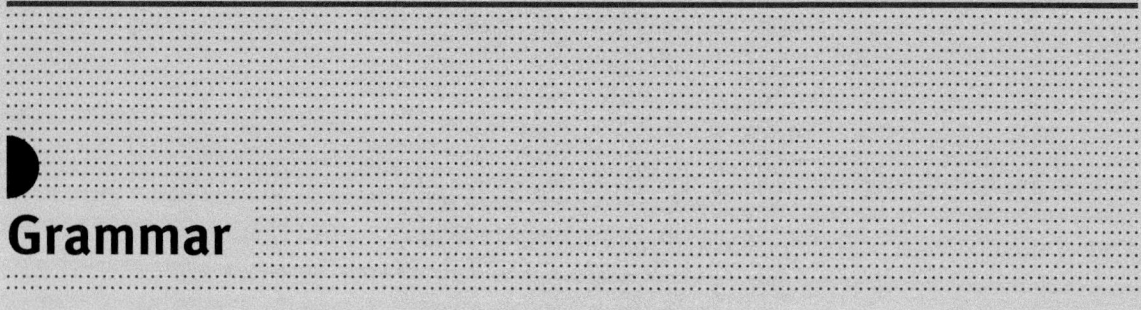

A When is the paper due?

B It _____ by Friday.

A 리포트 기한이 언제까지죠?

B 금요일까지입니다.

✔ (a) has to be done

(b) is done

(c) will do

(d) has to do

이렇게 푼다!

주어가 It이므로 수동태가 돼야 한다. 하지만 (b)를 사용해 It's done이라고 하면 '그것은 끝났다'라는 뜻이 되어 by Friday와 어울리지 않는다. 따라서, 수동태이며 by Friday와의 연결도 자연스러운 (a) has to be done이 정답이다.

III 유형별 대비책

- 정확한 영어를 적재적소에 사용하는 능력이 중요하므로 눈으로만 익히는 문법 지식을 배제한다. 대화체를 소리 내어 읽는 연습을 해서 문법이 내재화되어 상황에 맞게 즉각적으로 사용할 수 있는 수준까지 끌어올리도록 한다.

- 문법 네 가지 Part 중 비교적 평이한 난이도이기 때문에 시간 안배 차원에서 신속하게 풀고 다음 Part로 넘어가도록 한다. 단, 첫 줄은 빈칸에 올 적절한 답을 찾는 데 단서가 되므로 생략하고 넘어가면 함정에 빠지는 경우가 종종 있다. 신속하게 문제를 읽어나가되 읽지 않고 건너뛰는 일은 없어야 한다.

- 문법 문제의 빈칸은 주로 두 번째 줄에 오지만 일부 문제는 첫 번째 줄에 빈칸이 오기도 한다. 이런 유형에서는 두 번째 줄을 제대로 읽어야 출제자의 함정에 걸려들지 않는다. 즉, 빈칸 위치에 상관없이 문제에 나오는 대화는 모두 다 읽고 정확한 내용을 파악해야 오답 함정을 피해 정답을 찾을 수 있다.

- 문법 문제라고 해서 대화의 문법적인 요소만 신경 쓰면 안 된다. 상황에 적절한 어법을 고른다는 자세로 문제를 풀도록 한다. 예를 들어 대화 내용에 현재 시제가 여러 개 나온다고 무조건 현재 시제를 답으로 고르면 오히려 오답일 경우가 많다.

- 일상 대화 구문의 어법을 묻는 Part이므로 대화체의 정확한 표현을 익히는 것이 도움이 된다. 즉, 문법책의 모든 문법 요소를 처음부터 공부하는 것보다는 일상 대화 구문 표현 위주로 외울 수 있는 수준까지 익혀 두면 짧은 시간 내에 정확하게 구사할 수 있는 표현들이 많아질 것이다. 이렇게 되면 문법 Part 1도 쉽게 정복할 수 있다.

I 기출 유형 핵정보

한 개의 문장을 읽고 빈칸에 문법적으로 가장 적절한 표현을 4개의 선택지 중에서 고른다.

제시 방법 한 개의 문어체 문장이 주어진다.

문항수 20문항

측정 영역 문어체 영어의 정확한 어법 구사력을 측정한다.

빈출 토픽 학술문과 실용문 등 일상에서 접하는 문어체 문장에 언급되는 주제가 주로 사용된다.

II 기출 유형 체험

_____ David would be late was given to his boss.

데이비드가 늦을 거라는 메시지가 그의 상사에게 전달되었다.

✔ (a) The message that
  (b) A message is that
  (c) From the message
  (d) The message which

이렇게 푼다!

빈칸에는 동사 was given의 주어가 필요하므로 (b)와 (c)는 제외된다. David would be late는 완전한 문장이므로 관계대명사 which가 앞에 쓰일 수 없고, 동격절을 이끄는 that이 적절하므로 정답은 (a)가 된다.

Ⅲ 유형별 대비책

- 구어체 문장보다 문어체 문장은 의미 파악이 힘들 수 있으므로 평상시 문어체 문장의 직독직해 연습을 충분히 한다. 특히 관계사들로 연결된 문장, 절 안에 또 다른 절이 있는 문장 등 복잡한 문장을 평상시에 많이 접해 보도록 하자. 난해한 문장을 만났을 때 바로 의미를 파악할 수 있어야 문법 Part 2 문제를 신속하게 해결할 수 있다.

- 주어와 동사가 여러 개 나오는 긴 문장은 주절의 주어와 동사를 파악한 후, 다른 문법 사항들을 따져 보도록 한다. 특히 가장 빈출되면서도 기본이 되는 주어–동사 수 일치 문제는 주절의 주어와 동사를 파악해야만 풀 수 있는 문제 이다.

- 영어를 외국어로 사용하는 한국인을 위한 TEPS 시험에서는 한국인이 특히 취약한 관사와 문장 구조 등에 대해 묻는 문제가 다수 출제된다. 이를 대비하기 위해서는 문장 내 쓰임새를 익혀 두는 것이 낱낱의 문법 지식을 알고 있는 것보다 신속하고 정확하게 문제를 푸는 데 많은 도움을 줄 것이다. 영어 활용 능력 수준 측정을 위해 TEPS가 고안된 점을 염두에 두고, 평소에 정확한 영어 구사 능력 함양에 집중하도록 한다.

- 문법 Part 1과 마찬가지로 정확한 어법을 익히려면 청해 Part 4 긴 담화문 속에 나오는 문장이나 어휘 Part 2 문장을 익혀 두는 것도 좋다. 각 분야별 어휘와 구문에 익숙해질수록 읽고 이해하는 속도가 자연히 빨라지게 되고, 아울러 문장 안에서 정확한 쓰임새도 익힐 수 있기 때문이다.

I 기출 유형 핵정보

네 줄의 대화문을 읽고 문법적으로 이상한 부분이 있는 문장을 고르는 유형의 문제이다.

제시 방법   네 줄의 대화문이 주어진다.

문항수   5문항

측정 영역   길어진 대화에서 비문법적 요소를 가려내는 능력을 측정한다.

빈출 토픽   일상 생활에서 접하는 대화에 나오는 주제가 주로 사용된다.

II 기출 유형 체험

(a) A You said you had something to discuss with me.

(b) B Yeah, I have been debating whether to go back to work or not.

(c) A Are you actually thinking about becoming a full-time mom?

✔ (d) B That's which I want to discuss with you.

(a) A 나와 의논할 게 있다고 했지.

(b) B 응, 다시 일을 시작할지 고심 중이야.

(c) A 정말 전업 주부가 될 생각이야?

(d) B 그게 바로 의논하고 싶은 점이야.

이렇게 푼다!

관계대명사 용법을 물어보는 문제이다. (d)에서 discuss의 목적어가 없고, which는 관계대명사인데 선행사가 없으므로 선행사를 포함하는 관계대명사 what으로 고쳐야 한다.

Ⅲ 유형별 대비책

- 주어진 선택지가 따로 없어서 어떤 문법에 관한 문제인지 전혀 알 수 없고 주어진 대화 내용을 읽으면서 틀린 부분을 골라야 하기 때문에 보다 적극적인 태도로 문제에 임해야 한다. 즉, 각 대화에서 어느 문법 요소가 틀렸는지 모르는 상태에서 틀린 부분을 찾아야 하기 때문에 대화 내용을 파악함과 동시에 모든 품사와 구문 요소가 정확한지도 일일이 확인하는 습관을 평소에 들여야 당황하지 않고 실전에서 실력 발휘를 할 수 있다.

- 주어진 시간 내에 틀린 문법 사항을 골라야 하기 때문에 즉각적으로 비문법적인 부분을 찾아내는 훈련이 평상시에 필요하다. 이렇게 하기 위해서는 다른 문법 Part의 문제 대비와 마찬가지로 일상 대화 및 학술문과 실용문을 많이 접해서 다양한 문장에 익숙해져야 한다.

- 모든 문법 학습 요소들이 다 출제되는 것이 아니라 단골로 출제되는 문법 사항이 있음을 알자. 문장 구조, 시제, 수 일치, 관사 등에 해당하는 문법 요소들을 집중해서 훈련하는 것도 단기간에 Part 3을 정복할 수 있는 길이다. 하지만, Part 3 역시 제한된 문법 사항에만 국한해 다른 문법 요소를 무시했다가 낭패를 볼 수 있다는 것을 유의하자.

- Part 4에 비해 짧은 대화체라 약간 수월하게 보일 수 있겠지만 선택지가 주어진 Part 1과 2보다는 고난이도인 경우가 많다. 특히 재빨리 읽으면서 틀린 문법 사항도 찾아내야 하므로 평상시 대화문의 정확도를 분석하는 것도 실전에서 틀린 부분을 파악하는 데 도움이 될 것이다. 즉, 정답을 찾는 데에만 급급하지 말고 한 문제를 풀더라도 문법적으로 옳고 그른 부분들에 대한 분석을 자세히 하다 보면 실전에서 당황하지 않고 틀린 부분을 찾아낼 수 있다는 것이다.

I 기출 유형 핵정보

4개의 문어체 문장을 읽고 문법적으로 어색한 부분이 있는 문장을 고르는 유형의 문제이다.

제시 방법   4개의 문어체 문장이 하나의 지문으로 주어진다.

문항수   5문항

측정 영역   문어체 문장으로 구성된 지문에서 비문법적인 요소를 가려내는 능력을 측정한다.

빈출 토픽   신문, 잡지, 교재 등 일상 생활에서 문어체로 접하게 되는 주제가 사용된다.

II 기출 유형 체험

(a) Major League Baseball will begin mandatory testing for steroids. (b) From next March, each player will be tested and samples thoroughly analyzed. (c) The penalty for a first positive test will submit to treatment. (d) After their fifth positive test, players will receive a one-year suspension.

(a) 메이저리그 야구에서 의무적으로 스테로이드 검사를 시작할 것이다. (b) 내년 3월부터, 모든 선수들이 검사를 받을 것이며, 혈액 샘플들은 철저히 분석될 것이다. (c) 첫 양성 반응에 대한 처벌은 치료를 받는 것이다. (d) 양성 반응을 다섯 차례 보인 선수들은 1년 동안 출전 정지된다.

이렇게 푼다!

(c)에서 서수(first) 앞에는 정관사 the가 오는 것이 원칙이다. 물론 이 원칙이 깨지는 경우도 있지만, the first positive test가 올바른 형태이다.

Ⅲ 유형별 대비책

- Part 3 대화체에 비해 Part 4는 지문 길이도 더 길고 문어체라서 내용 파악이 훨씬 더 어렵고 시간도 가장 많이 걸린다. 그렇기 때문에 비문법적인 요소를 찾기가 특히 더 어려울 수 있으므로 신속하게 문어체 문장들을 읽고 직독직해를 통해 내용을 즉시 파악할 수 있는 능력을 평상시에 훈련하도록 한다.

- 지문 내용은 물론 문제에서 요구하는 문법 사항 예측이 어렵기 때문에 더욱 적극적인 문제 풀이 전략이 필요하다. 4개의 문장을 읽으면서 내용 파악을 하는 동시에 모든 가능성을 열어 두고 비문법적으로 보이는 부분을 찾아 나가야 하는데, 이때 가능성이 있는 부분을 일단 밑줄 그어 놓은 뒤 신속하게 다시 그 부분들을 재확인하는 것도 정확도를 높이는 한 방법이 될 수 있다.

- 주어진 시간 내에 틀린 문법 사항을 골라야 하기 때문에 즉각적으로 비문법적인 부분을 찾아내는 훈련이 필요하다. 이를 위해서는 정확한 표현을 즉각적으로 사용할 수 있을 정도로 알고 있어야 한다. 즉, Part 3 대비를 위해서 대화체를 많이 익혀 둠으로써 신속하게 비문법적인 대화 부분을 알아차리는 훈련을 하듯이, Part 4 대비책으로 학술문과 실용문을 접하면서 거의 암기할 정도로 정독하는 것도 문법 내재화를 도울 것이며, 이런 훈련 과정을 거치고 나면 자연스럽게 틀린 부분이 눈에 잘 띌 것이다.

- Part 2에 나오는 문장 네 개가 한꺼번에 출제된다고 생각하면 좀 부담이 덜어질 것이다. Part 2 문장들에서 문법적 오류를 찾는다고 생각하면 이제 마음이 편해질 것이다.

  - 시제 문제: 각 문장마다 여러 시제가 혼합되어 있는 경우가 대부분이기 때문에 시제의 형태만 참고해서 틀린 시제를 찾는 것은 거의 불가능하다고 봐야 한다. 내용 파악이 선행되어야만 시제가 잘못 쓰인 곳을 찾을 수 있다.

  - 관사 문제: a와 the의 쓰임 여부는 4개 문장에서 어떤 명사가 이미 앞서 언급된 것이고 아닌지를 이해한 후에 결정되므로 내용 파악이 우선되어야 한다.

Vocabulary

Ⅰ 기출 유형 핵정보

두 줄의 대화문을 읽고 빈칸에 가장 잘 어울리는 어휘를 고르는 문제이다.

제시 방법 두 줄의 대화문이 주어진다.

문항수 25문항

측정 영역 대화에서 사용하는 구어체 표현을 적소에 활용할 수 있는지 측정한다.

빈출 토픽 일상 생활과 관련 있는 주제가 많이 출제된다.

Ⅱ 기출 유형 체험

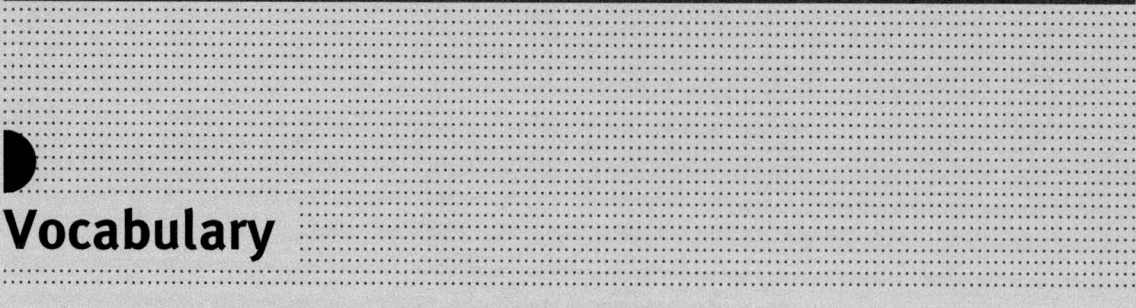

A How did Beth hurt her leg so bad?

B I heard she _____ coming down the mountain yesterday.

(a) faltered
(b) limped
(c) lingered
✔(d) tripped

A 베스는 어쩌다 그렇게 다리를 심하게 다쳤니?

B 어제 산을 내려오다가 걸려 넘어졌대.

(a) 흔들리다
(b) 절뚝거리다
(c) 버티다
(d) 발을 헛디디다

이렇게 푼다!

다리를 다친(hurt her leg) 이유로는 산을 내려오다(coming down the mountain) '넘어졌을' 가능성이 가장 크다. '넘어지다'는 표현에는 (d)에 사용된 trip 외에 fall, tumble down 등이 있다.

Ⅲ 유형별 대비책

- 짧은 시간 내에 문맥에 어울리는 어휘를 골라야 하기 때문에 많은 어휘를 알고 있는 것뿐만 아니라 문맥(context)에 적절한 어휘를 사용할 수 있는 능력을 키우는 것도 중요하다. 따라서 어휘를 처음 접할 때엔 참고 자료를 동원해서 문장 내에서 쓰이는 다양한 예문을 동시에 익혀 두어야 한다. 시간 내에 모든 어휘 문제를 잘 풀기 위해서는 특히 문맥 속에서 각 어휘의 쓰임을 거의 외우다시피 알고 있어야 시간 낭비 없이 즉각적으로 빈칸에 올 정답을 고를 수 있을 것이다.

- 해당 어휘의 우리말을 단순하게 암기하는 것은 별 도움이 안 된다. 우리말로는 그럴듯해도 쓰임이 어색한 어휘의 뉘앙스 차이를 구분할 줄 알아야 하므로 문장 전체로 어휘를 이해하는 것이 장기적으로 유리하다.

- 청해의 대화 파트뿐만 아니라 문법 Part 1과 3에 언급된 대화들도 어휘 실력 향상을 위해 활용될 수 있음을 기억하고 어휘 영역 이외의 빈출 표현도 문맥 속에서 익혀 두도록 한다.

- 대화를 신속히 읽고 즉각적으로 빈칸을 채워 넣어야 하기 때문에 실제 대화를 하면서 적절한 어휘를 사용할 수 있을 정도의 실력이 되도록 많은 표현을 통째로 익혀 두어야 한다.

- 일상적인 대화 속에서 자주 등장하는 어휘뿐만 아니라 이어동사, 이디엄 등도 출제되므로 숙지해 두도록 한다.

- 형태상 · 의미상 혼동되는 어휘, 의미 덩어리로 사용되는 연어 등의 정확한 활용법도 아울러 알아 둔다.

Ⅰ 기출 유형 핵정보

한 개의 문어체 문장을 읽고 빈칸에 가장 잘 어울리는 어휘를 고르는 문제이다.

제시 방법   한 개의 문어체 문장이 주어진다.

문항수   25문항

측정 영역   일상 생활에서 접할 수 있는 문어체 표현을 즉각적으로 사용할 수 있는지 측정한다.

빈출 토픽   학술문뿐만 아니라 실용문에 이르기까지 매우 다양한 주제를 다룬다.

Ⅱ 기출 유형 체험

The management has decided to _____ a complex strategy to resolve the crisis.

(a) breach
(b) withdraw
(c) alternate
✔ (d) implement

경영진은 위기를 해결하기 위해 복합적인 전략을 이행하기로 결정했다.

(a) 위반하다
(b) 철수하다
(c) 번갈아 나오게 만들다
(d) 시행하다

이렇게 푼다!

전략을 수행하다'에 해당하는 동사를 골라야 한다. 위기 해결을 위해선(to resolve the crisis) 다양한 전략을 세우거나(establish)나 수행(implement)해야 한다. 선택지 중 이와 가장 어울리는 동사는 (d) implement이다.

Ⅲ 유형별 대비책

- 학술문과 실용문의 주제별 빈출 어휘를 익혀 둔다. 빈출 어휘는 정답 선택지뿐만 아니라 오답 선택지에 나오는 어휘도 포함한다. 주제별로 자주 출제되는 어휘는 한정되어 있기 때문에 기출 어휘가 다시 출제될 확률이 높다.

- Part1과 마찬가지로 각 어휘의 쓰임새를 알아야 하기 때문에 전체 문장을 익히도록 한다. 그래야만 문법적으로도 정확한 어휘 활용 능력을 키울 수 있기 때문이다.

- 미묘한 뉘앙스 차이가 있는 쉬운 어휘의 용례 예문을 적극적으로 활용해야 한다. 의미가 비슷해 보이는 어휘들끼리 묶어서 따로 정리하면 도움이 될 것이다.

- 신문 기사, 잡지, 광고, 학술지, 비평 등의 실용문과 전문적인 학술문에서 다양하게 출제되므로 평상시 이런 종류의 글을 많이 접하는 것이 도움이 된다. 15분이라는 짧은 시간 내에 50문항이나 되는 문제를 무리 없이 풀기 위한 대비법 중 하나가 주제별로 다양한 문장을 평소에 자주 읽는 것이다. 이렇게 함으로써 필수 어휘를 자주 접할 수 있을 뿐만 아니라 문장 이해 속도도 향상될 수 있다.

- 대화체 문제와 마찬가지로 주제별 어휘뿐만 아니라 연어 및 형태상·의미상 혼동되는 어휘를 잘 알아 두도록 한다.

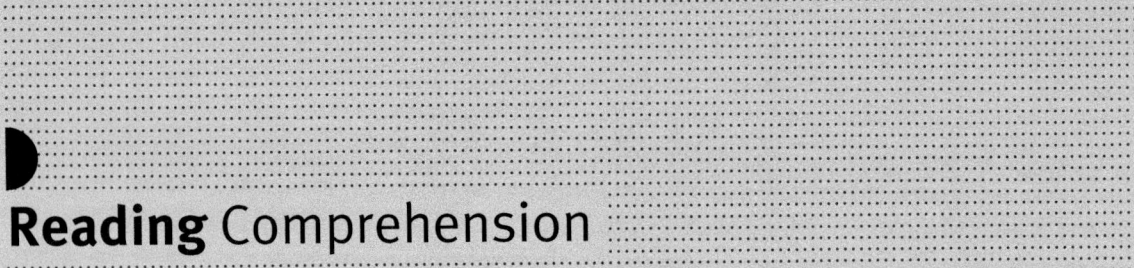

Reading Comprehension

■ PART I

Ⅰ 기출 유형 핵정보

100단어 내외의 단일 지문을 읽고 빈칸에 들어갈 적절한 선택지를 고르는 문제이다. 14문항은 구나 절을 고르는 문제이고, 나머지 2문항은 문장과 문장 사이를 이어주는 연결어를 찾는 문제이다.

제시 방법　지문의 처음 문장이나 마지막 문장, 드물게 중간 문장에 빈칸이 있는 한 개의 글이 주어진다.

문항수　16문항

측정 영역　글의 전반적인 이해 능력 및 논리적인 흐름 파악 능력을 평가한다.

빈출 토픽　학술문과 실용문에서 골고루 출제된다.

Ⅱ 기출 유형 체험

The idea that people live according to how others will perceive them has been established as the rule, not the exception. The real question now lies in the reasons for this way of life. It was hypothesized by C. S. Lewis that this desire to belong and to fit in is a natural human characteristic. He believed that people have _____.

(a) a tendency to regard themselves as normal
(b) no idea how to deal with human nature
(c) a need to distinguish themselves as unique
✔ (d) an instinctive drive to belong to a group

다른 사람이 자신을 어떻게 인식하느냐에 따라 인간의 행동이 결정된다는 개념은 예외가 아닌 법칙으로 굳어졌다. 이런 상황에서의 현실적인 물음은 왜 그렇게 사느냐이다. C. S. 루이스는 어딘가에 소속되고 맞춰지고 싶은 욕망은 인간의 본능적인 특성이라고 가정했다. 그는 사람들은 특정 그룹에 소속되고자 하는 본능적 욕구를 갖고 있다고 믿었다.

(a) 자신을 평범하다고 여기는 성향을
(b) 인간의 본성을 어떻게 다룰지에 대해 아무런 생각도 없는
(c) 자신을 특별한 존재로 여기고자 하는 욕구를
(d) 특정 그룹에 소속되고자 하는 본능적 욕구를

이렇게 푼다!

첫 문장에서 people live according to how others will perceive them이라는 내용과 세 번째 문장의 desire to belong and to fit in이라는 표현에서, 사람들에게는 집단에 소속되고자 하는 욕구가 있다는 (d)를 추론할 수 있다.

III 유형별 대비책

- 모든 지문을 자세히 읽겠다는 생각을 접는다. 1분에 한 문제씩 풀어야 하기 때문에 정독을 하기에는 절대적으로 시간이 부족하므로 주요 어휘 위주로 대의 파악 및 흐름 파악에 주력해야 시간 내에 문제를 다 풀 수 있다.

- 주제별 어휘를 평소 많이 알아 둔다. 청해, 문법, 어휘 등 TEPS의 다른 영역과 마찬가지로 방대한 어휘 지식을 갖추고 있어야 독해 속도도 빨라지고 정확한 이해가 가능하다.

- 빈칸의 위치에 따라 독해의 목적이 달라져야 한다. 빈칸이 첫 문장에 있는 경우 대의 파악만 해도 되지만 마지막 문장에 올 때에는 대의 파악뿐만 아니라 논리적 흐름도 염두에 두면서 독해를 해야 한다.

- 오답 함정 선택지 유형을 연습해 둔다.
  - 지문에 나오는 어휘로 만들었지만 문맥과 전혀 상관없는 선택지
  - 너무 일반적인 내용으로 만든 선택지
  - 상식적으로는 괜찮아 보이지만 내용과는 무관한 선택지
  - 지문 내용의 일부처럼 보이기는 하지만 논리적인 흐름 면에서는 어울리지 않는 선택지

I 기출 유형 핵정보

100단어 내외의 단일 지문을 읽고 주어진 질문에 적절한 답을 4개의 선택지에서 고르는 유형이다.

제시 방법   한 개의 지문에 한 개의 질문이 주어진다.

문항수   21문항

측정 영역   단일 지문에 대한 전체 및 세부 내용 이해 및 추론 능력을 측정한다.
대의 파악(6문항) → 세부 내용 파악(10문항) → 추론(5문항) 순으로 나온다.

빈출 토픽   학술문과 실용문에서 모두 골고루 출제된다.

II 기출 유형 체험

After years of negotiations, an agreement on ownership of five islands off of Queensland, Australia, has been finalized. The state government has finally agreed that the islands should become private property. For the past two years, it had argued that the islands belonged to the government rather than the natives of the islands. The agreement ends years of anguish. Native Don Banu, who has been following the debate for many years, said, "It's a great relief for all of us. Now we can start to move forward." The government is currently consulting islanders and expects to hand over the deeds of ownership in December.

Q What can be inferred about the decision made by the government?

(a) It was about who can own the island businesses.

✔ (b) It favored the local inhabitants of the islands.

(c) It could result in widespread disagreements.

(d) It was made sooner than expected.

수년간의 협상 끝에, 호주 퀸즐랜드 근해의 다섯 개 섬에 대한 소유권 협정이 체결되었다. 주 정부는 결국 섬을 개인 소유로 하는 데 동의했다. 정부는 지난 2년 동안 섬이 원주민 소유가 아닌 정부 소유라고 주장해 왔다. 이번 협정으로 인해 수년 간 지속된 고통도 끝이 났다. 많은 세월 동안 논쟁을 지켜본 원주민 돈 바누는 "이번 일은 우리 모두에게 커다란 안심이 됩니다. 이제 우리는 새로운 일을 시작할 수 있게 되었습니다"라고 말했다. 정부는 현재 섬 주민들과 논의 중이며, 12월 소유권 이양을 할 작정이다.

Q 정부가 내린 결정에 대해 추론할 수 있는 것은?

(a) 누가 섬 사업을 소유할 수 있는가에 관한 것이었다.

(b) 섬 지역 주민들을 지지했다.

(c) 광범위한 반대를 야기할 수 있었다.

(d) 예상보다 일찍 이루어졌다.

이렇게 푼다!

두번째 문장에서 섬이 개인 소유(private property)가 되었다는 것은 결국 섬이 원주민의 소유임을 의미하며, 세 번째 문장의 natives가 local inhabitants of the islands와 같은 의미임을 파악할 수 있으면 쉽게 정답이 (b)임을 찾을 수 있다.

Ⅲ 유형별 대비책

- 직독직해하는 습관을 들인다. 우리말로 번역하려 하지 말고 신속하게 영어 지문을 읽으면서 내용을 이해하는 습관을 들여야 한다.

- 지문을 다 읽겠다는 생각을 버려라. 대의 파악 문제의 경우 주요 내용어 중심으로 읽고, 세부 내용 파악 문제는 질문에 따라 선택지의 진위 여부를 한 개씩 확인해 가며 읽거나, 육하원칙 문제는 질문 내용을 제대로 파악하고 해당 부분을 신속히 찾아서 그 부분을 자세히 읽는다. 추론 문제는 대의 파악 및 세부 내용 파악이 선행되어야 하기 때문에 좀 더 시간을 할애해야 할 것이다.

- 오답 함정을 각 문제 유형마다 미리 알아 두고 잘 피하도록 한다.
  - 대의 파악 오답 유형: 세부 사실을 대의로 혼동하게 하는 오답이 자주 출제된다.
  - 세부 내용 파악 오답 유형: 일부 내용만 사실인 경우, 지문에서 언급된 어휘로 만들었지만 내용과는 상관없는 선택지를 주의하자.
  - 추론 오답 유형: 그럴듯해 보이지만 지문 내용과는 상관없는 오답. 정답과 정반대 진술이 선택지로 제시되기도 한다.

I 기출 유형 핵정보

5개의 문장으로 구성된 100단어 내외의 단일 지문을 읽고 글의 흐름상 어색한 문장을 찾는 유형의 문제이다.

제시 방법 주제문에 이어 4개의 문장이 제시된다.

문항수 3문항

측정 영역 지문의 응집력 파악 능력을 측정한다.

빈출 지문 토픽 학술문과 실용문 모두 골고루 출제된다.

II 기출 유형 체험

In 1871, American Indians were placed on federal land reservations. (a) Today, American Indian tribes must be understood as nations within the nation of the United States. (b) The Indians had no control of their communities and no power to affect federal polices over them. (c) They were under the jurisdiction of the Bureau of Indian affairs, which decided what they would eat, where they would live, and ultimately how they would live. (d) Thus, they were stripped of their political rights and even their cultural heritage.

1871년 미국의 인디언들은 연방정부가 정한 거주지로 옮겨졌다. (a) 오늘날 인디언 부족은 미국이라는 나라 안에 존재하는 별개의 나라로 이해되어야 한다. (b) 인디언들은 공동체에 대한 지배권도, 그들에 대한 연방정부의 정책에 영향을 미칠 힘도 없었다. (c) 무엇을 먹을지와 어디서 살지, 그리고 궁극적으로 어떻게 살 것인지를 결정하는 것도 인디언 사무국의 관할이었다. (d) 이런 식으로 그들은 정치적 권리와 심지어 문화적 유산마저 빼앗겼다.

이렇게 푼다!

첫 문장(주제문)과 (b), (c), (d)는 1871년 이래 인디언들이 미국에서 겪어온 박해와 수탈에 대해 언급하고 있다. 그러나 (a)는 인디언 부족을 미국 안에 존재하는 별개의 국가로 인정해야 한다는 내용으로, 미국과 인디언 부족을 동등한 위치에서 언급하고 있으므로 개연성이 없다.

III 유형별 대비책

- 처음 제시되는 주제문에서 벗어난 문장을 찾는 것이므로 4개의 선택지 문장을 읽을 때에 항상 주제문과의 연관성을 염두에 두고 읽도록 한다. 문법 Part 4의 경우 각 문장 간의 연관성까지 염두에 두고 내용을 파악할 필요는 없으나 독해 Part 3에서는 주제문과의 연관성이 문제 풀이의 핵심이다.

- 주제문과 연관성은 있으나 문장의 위치가 잘못되어 흐름을 깨는 유형도 있으니 흐름상 잘 어울리는지도 살피도록 한다.

- 글의 어조가 갑자기 바뀌는 경우도 어색한 문장에 해당하므로 어조의 변화에도 주의하도록 한다.

- 주어진 주제문에 대한 문장이 3개 나온 뒤 새로운 주제문이 4번째 문장으로 나오게 되면 어색한 문장이 된다는 것도 기억한다.

서울대 최신기출 1

Listening Comprehension

Grammar

Vocabulary

Reading Comprehension

TEPS

LISTENING COMPREHENSION

○ Scripts P 266 / 정답 P 326

Part I Questions 1—15

You will now hear fifteen conversation fragments, each made up of a single spoken statement followed by four spoken responses. Choose the most appropriate response to the statement.

Part II Questions 16—30

You will now hear fifteen conversation fragments, each made up of three spoken statements followed by four spoken responses. Choose the most appropriate response to complete the conversation.

Part III Questions 31—45

You will now hear fifteen complete conversations. For each item, you will hear a conversation and its corresponding question, both of which will be read twice. Then you will hear four options which will be read only once. Choose the option that best answers the question.

Part IV Questions 46—60

You will now hear fifteen spoken monologues. For each item, you will hear a monologue and its corresponding question, both of which will be read twice. Then you will hear four options which will be read only once. Choose the option that best answers the question.

TEPS

GRAMMAR

G

RAMMAR

Part I Questions 1—20

Choose the best answer for the blank.

1. A: How long does it take Bill to drive to work?

   B: I have no idea. I don't know

   _____.

   (a) where he lives
   (b) where lives he
   (c) does he live where
   (d) where does he live

2. A: Why are you selling lottery tickets?

   B: We're trying _____ money for charity.

   (a) raise
   (b) raised
   (c) to raise
   (d) to be raising

3. A: I can't believe you bought that painting.

   B: _____. It was a waste of money.

   (a) Either I can't
   (b) Either can't I
   (c) Neither I can
   (d) Neither can I

4. A: I wish I had a window seat. I hate sitting in an aisle seat when I fly.

   B: Well, I wouldn't mind _____ seats with you.

   (a) changes
   (b) changing
   (c) to change
   (d) to be changed

5. A: How about taking a break?

   B: I'd _____, but I'm too busy.

   (a) like
   (b) like to
   (c) like to do
   (d) like to take

6. A: What time can you come tomorrow?

   B: I'm not sure. _____ you know tonight.

   (a) I let
   (b) I'll let
   (c) I've let
   (d) I had let

7. A: What are you smiling about?

   B: I got an "A" _____ my math exam.

   (a) at
   (b) to
   (c) on
   (d) with

8. A: Mom, do you know what happened to my sneakers?

   B: Just a minute. I'm on _____.

   (a) phone
   (b) a phone
   (c) the phone
   (d) some phone

9. A: Sorry I haven't contacted you for so long.
    B: That's all right. I understand _____.

    (a) how you are busy at work
    (b) how are you busy at work
    (c) how busy are you at work
    (d) how busy you are at work

10. A: Is Judy single?
    B: No, _____ for about a year.

    (a) she's married
    (b) she was married
    (c) she'll be married
    (d) she's been married

11. A: Will you be free on Saturday?
    B: I don't know. I _____ be, but I'll have to check my calendar.

    (a) can
    (b) must
    (c) might
    (d) would

12. A: Hello. Can I speak to Mr. Arthur?
    B: There's nobody here _____ that name.

    (a) to
    (b) in
    (c) by
    (d) for

13. A: Have you read my term paper yet?
    B: Yes, and I'm afraid it isn't as well-written _____.

    (a) I'd like to be so
    (b) I'd like it to be as
    (c) as I'd like it to be
    (d) as so I'd like it to be

14. A: What exactly will be my duty as a judge in this contest?
    B: You'll decide who among the contestants _____ the best candidate.

    (a) were being
    (b) was being
    (c) are
    (d) is

15. A: Do you think it's OK to take medication with orange juice?
    B: _____ your doctor recommended a specific drink, take it with water.

    (a) If
    (b) As
    (c) Since
    (d) Unless

16. A: It's a miracle Steve won the match.
    B: Well, he deserved it. I've never seen anyone _____ for perfection.

    (a) so hard to work
    (b) to work hard so
    (c) work hard so
    (d) work so hard

17. A: How's the yoga class you joined?

B: Oh, it turned out to be _____ more interesting than I had expected.

(a) far
(b) that
(c) such
(d) very

18. A: How is your teaching going?

B: Not so great. _____ it would be.

(a) I thought it than harder
(b) I thought it's harder than
(c) It's harder I thought than
(d) It's harder than I thought

19. A: I can't decide what to get Ann.

B: I'm sure she'll be pleased with _____ you choose.

(a) whichever
(b) whatever
(c) which
(d) that

20. A: It's annoying to have to lock up everything even for a short break.

B: Yeah, but there's _____ since that's the rule here.

(a) about it nothing we can do
(b) nothing about it we can do
(c) it we can do nothing about
(d) nothing we can do about it

Part II **Questions 21—40**

Choose the best answer for the blank.

---

21. Most of the surviving literature about China's fabled first Emperor _____ during the Han Dynasty.

(a) is written
(b) was written
(c) is being written
(d) has been written

22. On August 25, 1944, Paris _____ by Allied forces after four years of Nazi occupation.

(a) has been liberated
(b) was liberated
(c) has liberated
(d) liberated

23. Although they are refreshing and their taste is _____, soft drinks contain much sugar.

(a) appealed
(b) to appeal
(c) appealing
(d) being appealed

24. The boy's handwriting was like _____ of a much younger child.

(a) it
(b) his
(c) one
(d) that

25. With this rental service, you can have your favorite DVDs _____ to your door.

    (a) delivering
    (b) to deliver
    (c) delivered
    (d) deliver

26. If the ambulance _____ any later, the accident victim would not have made it.

    (a) will arrive
    (b) has arrived
    (c) had arrived
    (d) were arriving

27. _____ on actual events, the film tells the story of a political scandal that involves the President.

    (a) Base
    (b) Based
    (c) Basing
    (d) To base

28. Most students seemed to find _____ test fair and challenging.

    (a) written
    (b) the written
    (c) few written
    (d) other written

29. It is not easy to meet someone with _____ you can explore a serious relationship.

    (a) that
    (b) which
    (c) whom
    (d) whose

30. Last summer, my friend Saunders and I _____ looking forward to the freedom of university life.

    (a) am
    (b) are
    (c) was
    (d) were

31. Hinduism is one of the world's major religions, _____ it does not have a single founder or a central religious organization.

    (a) yet
    (b) for
    (c) as
    (d) so

32. In August 1998, the value of the Russian ruble was a fraction of _____ it had been a few months before.

    (a) that
    (b) how
    (c) what
    (d) which

33. The teenager was told that he _____ his stereo so loud at night.

    (a) not better play
    (b) better not to play
    (c) had not better play
    (d) had better not play

34. Historians agree that by 1000 BC, the horse _____ an integral part of many ancient civilizations.

    (a) become
    (b) has become
    (c) had become
    (d) will become

35. Mars is tinted red because _____ .

(a) its soil being iron oxide up to 14 percent

(b) of its iron oxide soil is up to 14 percent

(c) of up to 14 percent its iron oxide soil

(d) its soil is up to 14 percent iron oxide

36. _____ a desire to be independent, adolescents often come into conflict with their parents.

(a) Have

(b) Having

(c) To have

(d) They have

37. In India, the excrement of cows is used _____ .

(a) either fuel or fertilizer

(b) either fuel or as fertilizer

(c) as fuel or either fertilizer

(d) as either fuel or fertilizer

38. In _____ , people learned information and stories by heart so that they could pass them on orally.

(a) the ancient times

(b) the ancient time

(c) an ancient time

(d) ancient times

39. A brand name or trademark _____ through advertising.

(a) may become famous overnight almost

(b) may become famous almost overnight

(c) almost famous overnight may become

(d) almost overnight may famous become

40. Some scientists _____ humans by religious groups and view human development differently.

(a) attributing of the status reject

(b) reject the status attributed to

(c) attributed to reject the status

(d) reject attributing status of

Part III Questions 41—45

Identify the option that contains an awkward expression or an error in grammar.

41. (a) A: The movie starts at 5:30, and it's already 5:20!
(b) B: We should've taken the subway instead of the bus.
(c) A: Yes. By the time we get there, the movie has started.
(d) B: I'd hate to miss the beginning. Let's see it tomorrow instead.

42. (a) A: Tim is working long hours to get a promotion.
(b) B: He'll never get promoted no matter how hardly he tries.
(c) A: Really? Why? Do you know something I don't?
(d) B: Yeah, I heard that his supervisor doesn't like him.

43. (a) A: My husband and I have decided to adopt a baby.
(b) B: How wonderful! What could your daughters say when you told them?
(c) A: They were thrilled with the idea of a new brother or sister.
(d) B: Well, I hope it works out. Let me know how it goes.

44. (a) A: If I have the money, I would probably invest in the stock market.
(b) B: Stocks can be a risky investment. You have to be careful.
(c) A: Yeah, I guess you're right. Then what kind of investment do you think is best?
(d) B: I think I'd just open a term deposit at my bank.

45. (a) A: Well, see you tomorrow. I'm going home.
(b) B: OK. I'm leaving myself as soon as I finish this paperwork.
(c) A: Have safe commute. Don't stay too late.
(d) B: Don't worry. It shouldn't take too much longer.

Part IV Questions 46−50

Identify the option that contains an awkward expression or an error in grammar.

46. (a) Throughout history, the moon has often been viewed as embodying feminine qualities. (b) The way it swells up and shrinks has been seen as a symbol of pregnancy and birth. (c) Its four phases of "new," "waxing," "full," and "waning" have been with the life cycle associated of birth, growth, maturity, and death. (d) Even the moon's pale rays have been linked to feminine softness, contrasting with the harsh rays of the sun.

47. (a) Many scientists preceded Darwin in their support for the idea that species somehow evolve. (b) However, they proposed unworkable theories, many of which strike us now as quite outlandish. (c) No explanation more neater than Darwin's had been posited on the subject before. (d) His ideas alone have stood the test of time and are now supported by conclusive scientific evidence.

48. (a) Even if humankind stopped producing greenhouse gases today, global warming would continue for decades. (b) The latest research suggests that the global mean temperature will be 1 to 2 degrees higher by 2030. (c) If this prediction is correct, rainfall runoff could be 3% higher and sea levels could rise by 20 centimeters or more. (d) Extreme weather events such as floods, droughts, and storms expected to increase.

49. (a) Comets are huge frozen lumps of gas, ice, and dust that orbit the sun at the outer reaches of our solar system. (b) Now and then a lump is pulled out of its peaceful orbit and into the solar system by the gravity of a star or planet. (c) As the comet is drawn closer to the sun, its surface heats up, and it starts evaporating. (d) Jets of gas explode from inside its nucleus, spit out tons of material per minute to form a tail millions of miles long.

50. (a) At least 1 million Americans are asked to take a lie detector test every year. (b) Most people think a lie detector test involves defendants, plaintiffs, or witnesses in legal cases. (c) However, the test is sometimes used by companies to screen potential employees. (d) On some other occasions, it is used on officials in government agencies that requires periodic loyalty checks.

This is the end of the Grammar section. Do NOT move on to the next section until instructed to do so. You are NOT allowed to turn to any other section of the test.

TEPS

Vocabulary

Directions

This part of the exam tests your vocabulary skills. You will have 15 minutes to complete the 50 questions. Be sure to follow the directions given by the proctor.

Part I **Questions 1—25**

Choose the best answer for the blank.

1. A: Excuse me, but is Dr. Stanley free now?
   B: I'm afraid not, but you can make a(n) _____ for tomorrow.

   (a) appointment
   (b) settlement
   (c) opening
   (d) promise

2. A: Is it possible to book a double room for tonight?
   B: I'm afraid all our rooms are _____.

   (a) paid
   (b) filled
   (c) closed
   (d) checked

3. A: Hi, my name's Ed Lee. And yours is?
   B: Oh, I'm Catherine Anderson. Just _____ me Cathy.

   (a) tell
   (b) call
   (c) greet
   (d) name

4. A: I don't know which dress to buy.
   B: Yes, it's difficult to _____.

   (a) decide
   (b) accept
   (c) seek
   (d) wear

5. A: Excuse me, sir, did you _____ green tea?
   B: No, I asked for coffee.

   (a) offer
   (b) order
   (c) require
   (d) inquire

6. A: I like your new hairstyle, Jessica.
   B: Thanks for _____.

   (a) viewing
   (b) noticing
   (c) minding
   (d) searching

7. A: What should I draw a picture of?
   B: Anything that _____ you, I suppose.

   (a) delivers
   (b) interests
   (c) wonders
   (d) imagines

8. A: Do you think I should enter the competition?
   B: Sure, you should _____.

   (a) go for it
   (b) look it up
   (c) take it over
   (d) push through it

9. A: I think a bottle of red wine would go nicely with this meal.

B: That _____ me.

(a) suits
(b) places
(c) equals
(d) matches

10. A: You seemed to be daydreaming in class today.

B: Sorry. I was _____ about the upcoming festival.

(a) hearing
(b) thinking
(c) speaking
(d) complaining

11. A: Hi, do you have women's gym shoes?

B: Sorry. We don't _____ those.

(a) carry
(b) wear
(c) stack
(d) trade

12. A: Robert's parents give him anything he wants.

B: No wonder he's such a(n) _____ kid.

(a) avid
(b) spoiled
(c) obedient
(d) disciplined

13. A: Would you like to join us for dinner after work?

B: No thanks. I'm going to _____ home.

(a) head
(b) clear
(c) make
(d) bring

14. A: Have you made up your mind about joining the firm?

B: No, I can't give you a(n) _____ answer yet.

(a) definite
(b) original
(c) solidified
(d) unyielding

15. A: Are you sure it's wise to put all your savings into starting a business?

B: I know it's _____, but I want to do it.

(a) threatening
(b) exposed
(c) telling
(d) risky

16. A: I hope we have enough time between our flights.

B: Don't worry. The _____ is two hours.

(a) layover
(b) interlude
(c) transport
(d) intermission

17. A: I heard you lost your wallet.

 B: Yes, it's so _____.

(a) irritating
(b) elevating
(c) gratifying
(d) disgusting

18. A: Is it true Carl was tricked into buying fake jewelry?

 B: Yeah, he was really _____.

(a) taken for a ride
(b) dead on his feet
(c) a fly in the ointment
(d) pushing up the daisies

19. A: Where can I get information about enrolling here?

 B: Here is a brochure for _____ students.

(a) migrating
(b) impending
(c) prospective
(d) anticipatory

20. A: The exam was very tricky, wasn't it?

 B: Yeah. I might have _____ it.

(a) bloated
(b) flunked
(c) wrecked
(d) stumped

21. A: Are my travel expenses covered?

 B: Yes, they'll be _____ after you submit all the receipts.

(a) surmised
(b) permitted
(c) reimbursed
(d) accumulated

22. A: Amy is distraught about her job.

 B: Yes. I've tried to _____ her, but nothing seems to help.

(a) diminish
(b) console
(c) lighten
(d) abate

23. A: Hi, Joe's Garage? I'd like to bring my car in for an oil change.

 B: No problem, I think we can find a _____ for you on our schedule.

(a) slot
(b) core
(c) tally
(d) billet

24. A: Is this path right? We should be going east.

 B: Actually, the path _____ eastward up ahead.

(a) veers
(b) spans
(c) pivots
(d) arches

25. A: Bobby, do the kids at school tease you?

 B: Yeah, they've all been _____.

(a) telling me off
(b) picking on me
(c) taking after me
(d) chewing me out

Part II Questions 26—50

Choose the best answer for the blank.

26. The plot in the novel was hard to follow because it was very _____.

(a) complex
(b) ordinary
(c) direct
(d) firm

27. We would like to _____ customers that our summer sale will last only two more days.

(a) lead
(b) remind
(c) suggest
(d) memorize

28. Many people were late for work because traffic was _____ on the Golden Gate Bridge due to an accident.

(a) filtered
(b) tracked
(c) jammed
(d) confused

29. This all-purpose steam iron will completely _____ wrinkles in curtains, pants, and dress shirts.

(a) refuse
(b) cancel
(c) crunch
(d) remove

30. Throughout Africa, the poor are _____ from schools and universities and are thus unable to obtain a proper education.

(a) altered
(b) opposed
(c) excluded
(d) converted

31. A significant _____ of the test will be from the homework given this semester.

(a) angle
(b) portion
(c) discord
(d) compound

32. The cobra's bite is _____ and has been known to kill a person in 15 minutes.

(a) vital
(b) lethal
(c) stable
(d) steady

33. Your account will no longer be in good standing if any payment is past _____ for 30 days or more.

(a) due
(b) end
(c) time
(d) limit

34. Humankind's _____ to reach the moon was finally achieved in 1969.

(a) utilization
(b) product
(c) appeal
(d) quest

35. The suspect of the shooting was _____ outside the mall, and the police were called.

(a) deferred
(b) conveyed
(c) pointed
(d) spotted

36. As a staunch _____, the husband refused to attend the church services.

(a) zealot
(b) atheist
(c) nemesis
(d) moralist

37. Rather than giving a straight answer to the reporter's questions, the mayor continued to make _____ statements.

(a) lucid
(b) evasive
(c) ingenious
(d) repressive

38. Alice _____ her boss about the pay and conditions she was working under, and she convinced him that changes were needed.

(a) confronted
(b) authorized
(c) regulated
(d) imposed

39. Caffeine is addictive, and it may cause headaches and other symptoms in those who _____ stop consuming it.

(a) usually
(b) abruptly
(c) officially
(d) continually

40. Any forecast about what the economy will be like a year from now would be nothing more than a _____ guess, since it's so unpredictable.

(a) wild
(b) frilly
(c) brute
(d) cordial

41. The nation's tenth straight year of high unemployment has led economists to wonder why the problem is so _____.

(a) abundant
(b) persistent
(c) restrained
(d) hazardous

42. In a job interview, appropriate attire is _____ because it is a major part of one's first impression.

(a) valid
(b) subtle
(c) crucial
(d) pressing

43. The use of _____ to purchase influence over greedy public officials is as old as government itself.

(a) bribes
(b) creeds
(c) deficits
(d) statutes

44. Due to budget constraints, no more company credit cards will be _____ to department heads.

(a) opted
(b) issued
(c) elicited
(d) disclosed

45. The committee needs to _____ the program until such time as our budget allows for it.

(a) shelve
(b) placate
(c) augment
(d) resurrect

46. Boats _____ supplies to desperate residents of Indonesia's flood-stricken towns.

(a) rallied
(b) ferried
(c) conjured
(d) garnered

47. The point made by Mr. Foster may be _____ to the main topic of this meeting, but it is still worth considering.

(a) adhesive
(b) illustrious
(c) peripheral
(d) rudimentary

48. Even when greatly outnumbered, Alexander the Great always managed to _____ the enemy.

(a) rout
(b) coax
(c) slander
(d) appease

49. Osteoporosis, or bone thinning, is linked to calcium _____, as calcium constitutes a large percentage of bone mass.

(a) asperity
(b) severity
(c) deficiency
(d) proficiency

50. Because the lives of the characters in the novel were so _____, the actions of one affected all others.

(a) disparate
(b) engrossed
(c) coextensive
(d) intertwined

This is the end of the Vocabulary section. Do NOT move on to the Reading Comprehension section until instructed to do so. You are NOT allowed to turn to any other section of the test.

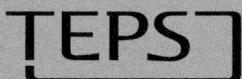

Reading
comprehension

Part I **Questions 1—16**

Read the passage. Then choose the option that best completes the passage.

1. Having an overweight mother significantly increases a child's chances of becoming overweight. This is the conclusion reached by scientists at the University of Pennsylvania after an extensive study of pre-school children. However, the researchers have yet to determine whether the main cause is genetics or the influence of an unhealthy home environment. It is possible that both factors _____.

(a) lead to poor school grades
(b) cause the bad home environment
(c) were ignored in previous research
(d) cause weight problems in children

2. Attention, pet owners! Now that summer is here, you should inspect your pets for fleas and administer treatment when necessary. Flea infestations are worst at this time of year, so be diligent in checking your pet. Otherwise, your house could soon be home to hundreds of flea eggs carried in by your dog or cat. Once an infestation starts, it can be frustrating and costly to fully exterminate fleas. For these reasons, it is of the utmost importance to _____.

(a) prevent fleas by monitoring your pets
(b) refrain from scratching any itchy flea bites
(c) protect your pets from flea-killing chemicals
(d) treat your entire house before infestation starts

3. Before colonization in the late fifteenth century, North and South America _____. The Americas were home to very skilled plant breeders, who had developed vegetable crops more nutritious and productive than those grown in Europe, Asia or Africa. Systems of writing and mathematics had been invented and highly accurate calendars were in use. In the Americas, as in Europe, states rose and fell as leaders succeeded or failed in expanding their political and economic power.

(a) had an incredible diversity of plant species
(b) were isolated from other parts of the world
(c) had well-established civilizations and cultures
(d) were not troubled by political or social upheaval

4. When it comes to protecting seedlings and delicate plants from night frost, clear polythene sheets are a good option. Gardeners should take note, however, that polythene is not the same as fleece sheeting and should not be used all the time. This is because polythene blocks the flow of air and water. Light cannot pass through it either unless the sheet has holes punched in it. Consequently, heat tends to build up under polythene during the day, causing condensation and potentially harmful temperature variations as well. Therefore, polythene is _____.

(a) best used for night cover only
(b) only suitable in warm weather
(c) more versatile than fleece sheeting
(d) most effective with larger plants

5. With the obesity rate continuing to rise, state legislators are now taking steps to control fast-food companies and the way they prepare and advertise their products. Such government intervention, however, has not been met with unanimous support. For instance, US District Judge Richard Holwell recently overturned a proposed health regulation that would force fast-food chains to publish nutritional information on their menus. If this is any indication of things to come, we are unlikely to see the public _____ anytime soon.

(a) ending its boycott of unhealthy fast-food companies
(b) guided by legislation on healthier eating habits
(c) crowding into restaurants that do not serve meat
(d) educated on how to cook healthier meals for children

6. Researchers have found that young girls play different kinds of games and abide by different rules _____. Girls use different communication patterns and styles in their play. They prefer to play in small groups or in pairs. And unlike boys they play less often in large groups outside the home. Their games are also less hierarchical and more inclusive of others, without a need for winners or losers.

(a) at home than they do at school
(b) once a boy joins in their games
(c) if they are playing in a large group
(d) when playing together than boys do

7. The sixteenth-century Renaissance architect Andrea Palladio has long been
_____. Although he designed buildings almost
exclusively in and around Venice, his works, known for their harmony and beauty,
had a great impact throughout Europe and beyond. For example, in London, the great
eighteenth-century English architect Christopher Wren used the Palladian style for his
triumphant St. Paul's Cathedral. In America, the classical style of Thomas Jefferson's
buildings at Monticello and the University of Virginia also owe a debt to Palladio.

(a) a tremendous influence on Western architecture
(b) celebrated for his scholarship on the Renaissance
(c) the man credited for the dome on St. Paul's Cathedral
(d) mistaken as the designer of Venice's famous buildings

8. We at Miracle Springs Health Spa hereby announce that we
_____. A recent full-spectrum test revealed that the
source feeding our baths has been poisoned due to the negligence of Remand-Haps,
a manufacturer of industrial chemicals. Remand-Haps has violated a number of State
and Federal regulations on water pollution, causing our business to shut down for the
duration of two weeks. If you are one of our customers and are willing to testify, please
come to the Town Hall on June 10th at 8 pm.

(a) have put our facilities up for sale
(b) have not deliberately misled the court
(c) are opening new operations to the public
(d) are filing a lawsuit over contaminated water

9. Frederick the Great, who ruled Prussia from 1740 until 1780, epitomized the enlightened
German ruler. He was a highly cultured monarch, a kind of philosopher-king. He
supported the arts, wrote poetry and scholarly essays, played the flute, composed concertos
and sonatas, and regularly corresponded with the French philosopher and writer Voltaire.
Because of such accomplishments, Frederick was regarded as a role model by artists and
intellectuals throughout Europe. To this day, he is _____.

(a) respected as a great conqueror
(b) admired for his philosophical works
(c) considered the founder of modern Germany
(d) famous for his enthusiasm for the arts and humanities

10.

Dear Andrew,

I am writing to update you on the selection process to fill the position of vice president. As it stands, I have narrowed my choices down to you and Ms. Diana Hudson. You are both exceptionally qualified, and I want you to know that the services both of you have provided to this company have been beyond comparison. I also want to make it clear that the person who is not selected is in no way lacking. Regardless of the outcome, both of you are _____.
I expect to make my final decision sometime this week.

Yours sincerely,
Justin Blake
President, Brokk Tech

(a) going to be dearly missed by the company
(b) promising candidates for company president
(c) exceptions to the rule in this kind of situation
(d) considered indispensable assets to this company

11. At Simpsons, our gas-steam power stations _____.
That is because we know our business of harnessing natural resources also depends on conserving them. In addition, the environment and future generations depend on how efficiently we use our natural resources today. When it comes to producing more energy from raw materials with less waste, our power stations are unmatched. Moreover, we will continue to work for even higher efficiency levels. Simpsons—the company for the future.

(a) have been made with the most advanced components
(b) give you more for your dollar than our competitors do
(c) offer an environment-friendly workplace for employees
(d) are consistently the most energy-efficient in the industry

12. A new study shows that Arctic Ocean sea ice is _____.
The basis of the study was to retroactively predict the rate at which sea ice would melt
from 1953 to 2006 using governmental models of climate change. The predictions were
then measured against actual data about sea ice conditions recorded during that span
of time. The results of the comparison revealed that 18 of the climate change models
used by the government underestimated the rate of melting by a significant margin. The
current situation turned out to be thirty years ahead of the predictions of the models.

(a) slowly recovering due to conservation efforts
(b) not actually melting because of global warming
(c) melting faster than climate change models predict
(d) disappearing at a pace predicted over fifty years ago

13. Rock art emerged among humans about 35,000 years ago. Since that time, people have
consistently decorated rock surfaces. Thus, the study of rock art can reveal aspects of
human evolution and technological change. Indeed, its longevity makes it especially
useful in providing sociocultural information not generally available to the archaeologist.
For example, it shows the oldest depictions of religious behavior. Because of its nature,
rock art can account for _____.

(a) a number of different interpretations of its meaning
(b) people's innate desire to decorate their surroundings
(c) the reason why religions in an area suddenly died out
(d) a major proportion of a region's archaeological record

14. Much of what we know about Mars and its potential for harboring water and supporting
life was culled by the Mars rover, *Opportunity*, and its twin, *Spirit*. Evidence indicates
that early in Mars's existence its environment was wet and host to hot springs and high
concentrations of dissolved minerals. The development or survival of microbes was
likely stymied by these minerals, which act much in the same way that salt acts as a
preservative. Indeed, *Opportunity* confirmed in a recent examination the exceedingly
high salinity of ancient Martian water. From this, scientists conjecture that
_____.

(a) life can adapt to very inhospitable conditions
(b) less water existed than was formerly believed
(c) mineral deposits on Mars are expected to keep rising
(d) the chances of finding evidence of life on Mars look slimmer

15. Some of history's greatest composers were misunderstood in their own day. Not everyone could relate to the compositions of Beethoven, Brahms, Mahler, Strauss, Debussy, Stravinsky, or Ives when their music was first heard. Their works were considered shocking—in some cases, even appalling—because they shattered the conventions governing musical forms and ideas. _____, these composers were innovators, and as such, they advanced the art of music and further enriched human culture.

(a) Still
(b) Thus
(c) Likewise
(d) Moreover

16. Long lines, irritable flight attendants, cramped quarters, and questionable food have all made traveling by air less than a pleasure. On top of this, consider that in one four-month period in 2007, 30% of flights arrived late, creating a nuisance for nearly 20,000 passengers. In July of that year, thousands of flights were cancelled—50% more, in fact, than the previous year. _____, the airlines themselves are not faring well. The industry suffered a huge setback because of 9/11, and now it is having to contend with skyrocketing fuel prices.

(a) Hence
(b) For example
(c) What is more
(d) Notwithstanding

Part II **Questions 17—37**

Read the passage and the question. Then choose the option that best answers the question.

17. Most families in the neighborhood where I grew up suffered from desperate poverty. However, if you looked beyond that, they had a desire that was just like that of the wealthy. These poor families, who often could not afford decent clothes for their children, accumulated mountains of junk in their backyards: rusted wheelbarrows, pots, broken swing-sets, and sofas. It was as if, despite their poverty and the uselessness of their trashy belongings, the poor are still driven by the same instinct as the rich to acquire more than they possess or need.

    Q: What is the passage mainly about?
    (a) A childhood in a poor neighborhood
    (b) A reason why some families remain poor
    (c) A similarity between the poor and the rich
    (d) A junkyard found in a poor neighborhood

18. Want an insider tip that could save you a bundle on diapers? Switch to generic store brands instead of the pricier name-brand ones. Research performed at three local daycares—involving several thousand diaper changes—shows that you probably won't detect any difference. With generic store brands doing their best to duplicate the improvements their brand-name counterparts are incorporating into their diapers, there is virtually nothing to distinguish one brand from the other.

    Q: What is the main idea of the passage?
    (a) Research on diapers was done at individual homes.
    (b) Little difference in quality exists among diaper brands.
    (c) Brand-name diapers have recently come down in price.
    (d) Store brand diapers are better than brand-name diapers.

19. If you are looking for family events that will also teach your children about nature and the outdoors, look no further! Our community center has activities for the whole family. Here are some of the things we have planned: a bug-finding night, an astronomy evening, a night hike, a herpetology adventure (looking for frogs, toads and snakes), a night of crafts, and much more! In cases of severe weather, we will crank up the popcorn machine, watch a great nature film, and then have a special animal presentation.

Q: What is the advertisement mainly about?
(a) Fun family activities at a community center
(b) Organized sports events for young children
(c) Courses on animals in the local community area
(d) Community center exercise programs for families

20. Post-traumatic stress disorder (PTSD) is common among Israel's combat-wounded veterans and is an affliction that entitles them to disability benefits. With 15% of veterans, roughly 3,000 people, suffering from some variety of PTSD, the nation's treasury is sure to be impacted in no small way. Although the exact numbers are not known, one veteran who fought in 1973 in Israel's Yom Kippur War said he takes home $2,000 every month in government benefits.

Q: What is the passage mainly about?
(a) Various health problems faced by Israeli veterans
(b) The impact of the Yom Kippur War on Israel and its veterans
(c) The high medical costs paid by Israeli veterans who have PTSD
(d) The financial burden imposed on Israel by PTSD-suffering veterans

21. Stresses in today's business world may cause some supervisors to become abusive to subordinates. They might shout or use other forms of verbal intimidation. While this behavior may motivate employees to temporarily perform well, it could cause the company to suffer financially in the long run. A study has found that employees who have suffered verbal abuse from superiors tend to do less to promote their company. They speak disparagingly about the company to outsiders and will often seek work elsewhere.

Q: What is the main idea of the passage?
(a) Supervisors are sometimes justified in becoming abusive.
(b) Intimidation of employees helps efficiency in the short term.
(c) Verbal intimidation of employees ultimately hurts a company.
(d) Abused employees are more likely to be unhappy in the workplace.

22. The republican ideal of Rome had been sufficient at a time when Rome was merely the preeminent city on the Italian peninsula. By the middle of the first century BC, however, Rome had become a multi-continent empire stretching from Spain to Iraq and ruling over 50 million subjects. It was plagued by civil unrest and required a strong ruler. Accordingly, when Augustus gained power in 27 BC, he made himself "Princeps," or "first among equals," establishing a monarchical system that would govern the empire for centuries.

Q: What is the main topic of the passage?
(a) Rome's transformation from a republic into a monarchy
(b) The expansion of the Roman Empire in the first century BC
(c) The reason the Roman republic survived for so many centuries
(d) Imperial Rome's response to civil unrest in the first century BC

23.

Hi Luis!

I can't believe that my Hawaiian trip is coming to a close. Only one day left. Time has passed so quickly! Hawaii is such a beautiful place with lush plants and trees, wonderful scenery, and exotic flowers. My whole vacation was spent at a spa in Koloa, Kaui. Every day for a week I exercised, did yoga, meditated, and ate vegetarian food and tropical fruits. I also went swimming and hiking. I feel so refreshed! Wish you were here!

Love,
Sue

Q: Which of the following is correct about Sue according to the letter?
(a) She has been traveling around Hawaii.
(b) She has spent two weeks in Hawaii.
(c) She exercised while on vacation.
(d) Her vacation has been tiring.

24. Economic policies since 2000 appear to have left the middle class no better off than it was in the late 1990s. In fact, an analysis of Census Bureau data shows that middle-class levels of wealth are slightly lower. The analysis compared income data from the 2000 census with data from an experimental Census Bureau survey done in 2007. However, further analysis of data from sources other than the Census Bureau will be required to confirm this finding.

Q: Which of the following is correct according to the passage?
(a) The middle class may have been wealthier in the 1990s.
(b) The analysis involved census data from 1990 through 2007.
(c) Economic policies since 2000 have benefited the middle class.
(d) The Census Bureau data has been confirmed by other sources.

25. The main purpose of this course is to develop your ability to think like an economist. You will come to grips with fundamental concepts like opportunity cost, rational choice, scarcity, and marginal cost. You will learn to understand partial equilibrium analysis and the strengths and weaknesses of a market economy. The course will necessarily expand your knowledge and understanding of various economic theories. Michael Blurton's book *Modern Economist* will be an essential component of this endeavor.

Q: Which of the following is correct about the course according to the passage?
(a) It helps participants to learn economic basics.
(b) It focuses on the failings of market economies.
(c) It consists of an in-depth analysis of one theory.
(d) It does not require students to use a class textbook.

26. Jonas Mekas is a pioneer in the history of cinema. The Lithuanian immigrant invigorated New York City's independent film scene as the first film critic for *The Village Voice* in 1958 and as co-founder of *Film Culture* magazine. A longtime champion of experimental cinema, Mekas founded the Anthology Film Archives and the Filmmakers' Coop in Manhattan, creating two seminal institutions for avant-garde cinema. Mekas has also been a prolific experimental filmmaker for decades. His most recent film, *A Letter from Greenpoint*, was screened at festivals across the globe.

Q: Which of the following is correct about Mekas according to the passage?
(a) He has lived and worked in New York City all his life.
(b) He established *Film Culture* magazine on his own.
(c) He publicly criticized modern avant-garde films.
(d) He has made many experimental movies.

27. Language domination and loss has occurred throughout history, and it is still taking place. It usually occurs when a smaller ethnic group adopts another language in the process of being assimilated within a larger or more dominant group. That is the situation seen recently, with languages disappearing at an unprecedented rate from North America, Brazil, Australia, Indonesia, and parts of Africa. No one knows how many languages have been lost since humans began to speak—perhaps thousands—and the number is steadily growing.

Q: Which of the following is correct about language loss according to the passage?
(a) It was a rare phenomenon before modern times.
(b) It usually results from the isolation of an ethnic group.
(c) It is now happening faster than at any other time in history.
(d) It has probably affected thousands of languages in recent years.

28. One of the first genetically engineered products available to farmers was bovine somatotropin, a growth hormone used to increase a cow's milk yield by up to 20%. The hormone occurs naturally in cattle and helps promote growth in calves and regulate milk production. The synthetic version of the hormone, however, is manufactured by using DNA technology and administered by injection. Opponents of its use claim that it causes health problems in both cows and humans. Although this claim has not been substantiated, bovine somatotropin is now banned in many countries.

Q: Which of the following is correct about the growth hormone according to the passage?
(a) Its use can double a cow's milk production.
(b) It is not produced naturally in animals like cows.
(c) It has not been proven to be harmful to human health.
(d) Its opponents claim it is safe for cows but not for humans.

29. Using people's race as a basis for restricting them from accessing public spaces, institutions, and areas of residence constitutes racial segregation. It is a tactic often used by a ruling class to protect its politically and economically dominant position. Recent examples in history include European colonists and American settlers, for whom racial segregation was the foundation of slavery and was also a general means of maintaining social superiority. Further back in history, comparable examples exist in such conquerors as Asian Mongols, African Bantus, and American Aztecs, who employed racial segregation to similar effect.

Q: Which of the following is correct about racial segregation according to the passage?
(a) It is a way for one race to exercise power over another race.
(b) It threatens a ruling class's ascendant position in society.
(c) It is a fairly recent means of maintaining dominance.
(d) It was against the Asian Mongols' ideals of integration.

30. After half a century of state-enforced atheism, relaxed policies in China have prompted millions to flock to traditional faiths. A recent poll by Shanghai University found that 31% of Chinese 16 or older are religious, putting the number of believers at 400 million. Still, the Chinese government continues to restrict religious practice to state-sanctioned groups and registered places of worship. Also, only five religions are officially recognized: Buddhism, Taoism, Roman Catholicism, Protestantism, and Islam.

Q: Which of the following is correct according to the passage?
(a) China has recently banned religious worship.
(b) Over one-third of Chinese adults are Catholics.
(c) Religious worship must be done at home in China.
(d) The Chinese government has authorized five religions.

31. This week, HMA Classical will release a brand-new recording of pianist Glenn Gould's 1955 recording of "Goldberg Variations" by Bach. It is not a digital remastering but a "re-performance" of the original, created by a company called Zenph. Great performances like Gould's were often encumbered by the limits of audio technology in the past. Now, at Zenph, they can be rerecorded using a Yamaha Disklavier Pro, an acoustic piano controlled by a computer, which duplicates an original recording with scientific accuracy and timing. Zenph's recordings match the originals, yet they are of superior sound quality.

Q: Which of the following is correct about HMA Classical's new release?
(a) It is written by pianist Glenn Gould.
(b) It was performed by musicians hired by Zenph.
(c) It was recently rerecorded using special equipment.
(d) It corrects errors in Glenn Gould's accuracy and timing.

32. Recently, the environmental endocrinologist David Norris of the University of Colorado discovered alarming changes in the white sucker fish population of Boulder Creek. Upstream, where the water flows pure and clear out of the Rocky Mountains, the ratio of males to females is 50 to 50, which is what would be expected. Downstream, however, below a wastewater treatment plant, the females outnumber the males by 5 to 1. Of even more concern, Norris found that about 10% of the fish were not clearly male or female but had sexual characteristics of both.

Q: Which of the following is correct about white sucker fish according to the passage?
(a) They had not previously been found in Boulder Creek.
(b) A large majority of those living upstream are female.
(c) Males are more numerous below the treatment plant.
(d) Some living downstream have no distinct gender.

33.

To the Editor:

As reported in yesterday's edition, the lovely fountain at Governor's Park has been turned off to conserve water. Well, if the city council turns it back on, I will come to the council's building every Friday with my own water to make up for the water used. Here is another suggestion: instead of washing all of the city council members' vehicles every week, how about washing them every 10 days? This will save much more water than turning off the fountain.

Yours sincerely,
Susan Jones

Q: What can be inferred about the writer?
(a) She often goes to Governor's Park to complain.
(b) She thinks the city council's priorities are wrong.
(c) She believes water restrictions should be increased.
(d) She has recently been unable to visit Governor's Park.

34. The information for the member's email directory of the Texas KOHL Committee was compiled by our staff from the handwritten data provided by members on their membership application forms. If your contact information is incorrect, please contact Jeffery Utz so he can update it. Also, if you use the directory to send emails to other members, please confine yourself to committee-related matters; do not post solicitations, garage-sale notices, etc. Thank you for your continued support of Texas KOHL.

Q: What can be inferred from the passage?
(a) Jeffery Utz is the current president of Texas KOHL.
(b) People have not been using the list to sell personal items.
(c) Memberships of the committee cannot be obtained online.
(d) Most of the membership details were not recorded correctly.

35. Regardless of how qualified you may be for a job and how well you fit a company's requirements, most interviewers will be reluctant to hire you if they are not convinced you are genuinely enthusiastic about the job. They have to be certain that you will be a committed, long-term employee, rather than someone who is going to decide two weeks after being hired that the position is not what he or she really wanted.

Q: What will most likely follow the passage?
(a) Tips on how to best organize a résumé
(b) Stories about unsuccessful job interviews
(c) Fast ways to adapt to employer requirements
(d) Advice on showing enthusiasm at an interview

36. Jonathan Hauser's book on the oil and energy industries in developing nations is a stunning portrait of greed, environmental damage, repression, and violence. Hauser, a journalist for the *Washington Post*, spent 11 years working on this book in his spare time, and it was worth the wait. Thoroughly researched and very readable, *Ravaged Earth* pulls no punches, which is perhaps why it has already come under fire from oil executives and leaders in developing nations. If you are concerned about the future of our planet, you must read this book.

Q: What can be inferred about Jonathan Hauser from the book review?
(a) He portrays oil companies negatively in his book.
(b) He worked in the energy industry before becoming a journalist.
(c) He interviewed politicians from developing nations for the book.
(d) He dislikes critics of his book that support environmental conservation.

37. Graduation rates might seem like a logical way to gauge the quality of a college. However, the reality is not that simple. Graduation rates may vary depending on how easy courses are or on whether teachers give high or low grades. Colleges can also improve graduation rates by raising admission standards. Also, low graduation rates might reflect a high number of economically disadvantaged students who are forced to drop out to earn a living, rather than the competence of a college.

Q: What can be inferred about the writer of the passage?
(a) He was able to graduate because of financial assistance.
(b) He attended a college with unusually high admission standards.
(c) He believes that most colleges manipulate their graduation rates.
(d) He is skeptical about using graduation rates to evaluate colleges.

Part III   Questions 38—40

Read the passage. Then identify the option that does NOT belong.

38. Come and enjoy the variety and quality of food at Country Steakhouse! (a) Steak-lovers' choices range from a 7-ounce bacon-wrapped fillet to a whopping 24-ounce T-bone. (b) It will come as no surprise that Americans are eating more T-bone steaks than they were last year. (c) Non-beefeater options include pork spare ribs with a spicy sauce or a roasted rack of lamb. (d) For those who like seafood, a choice of lobster, grilled fish, crab cakes, and oysters awaits you.

39. I like reading speculations from the past about what life would be like in the future. (a) It is possible that future generations will be affected immensely by the inventions being developed today. (b) Think of those futuristic fantasies from the 1950s, for example, showing robots doing housework in the year 2000. (c) In a way, those predictions actually came true, although with human-operated machines rather than with talking androids. (d) Past generations predicted watches with small TVs on them too, but of course none of them foresaw the digital technology involved.

40. People in early photographs often look strange or stiff. (a) Part of the reason is the dated fashions and furnishings, or the faded quality of the pictures. (b) Also, early photographic technology obliged people to remain motionless for several minutes, sometimes with awkward results. (c) Moreover, it was not until the late 1800s that film was invented to replace photographic plates, leading to the development of cameras. (d) However, the main reason may simply be that in a world not yet used to photography, people had not learned how to adopt photogenic poses.

This is the end of the Reading Comprehension section. Please remain seated until the proctor has instructed otherwise. You are NOT allowed to turn to any other section of the test.

서울대 최신기출 **2**

Listening Comprehension

Grammar

Vocabulary

Reading Comprehension

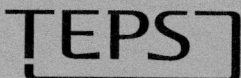

LISTENING
COMPREHENSION

Part I Questions 1—15

You will now hear fifteen conversation fragments, each made up of a single spoken statement followed by four spoken responses. Choose the most appropriate response to the statement.

Part II Questions 16—30

You will now hear fifteen conversation fragments, each made up of three spoken statements followed by four spoken responses. Choose the most appropriate response to complete the conversation.

Part III **Questions 31—45**

You will now hear fifteen complete conversations. For each item, you will hear a conversation and its corresponding question, both of which will be read twice. Then you will hear four options which will be read only once. Choose the option that best answers the question.

Part IV **Questions 46—60**

You will now hear fifteen spoken monologues. For each item, you will hear a monologue and its corresponding question, both of which will be read twice. Then you will hear four options which will be read only once. Choose the option that best answers the question.

TEPS

GRAMMAR

DIRECTIONS

This part of the exam tests your grammar skills. You will have 25 minutes to complete the 50 questions. Be sure to follow the directions given by the proctor.

Part I Questions 1—20

Choose the best answer for the blank.

1. A: My apartment is so messy.

B: Yeah, _____. Don't worry about it.

(a) mine is so
(b) so mine is
(c) so is mine
(d) mine so is

2. A: Did you hear that Tom left the company?

B: No. I wonder what _____ him decide to do that.

(a) made
(b) makes
(c) is making
(d) will make

3. A: What's in the bag?

B: Oh, it's _____.

(a) just a little something I bought
(b) just something little I bought it
(c) a little something I just bought it
(d) this something little I just bought

4. A: Did you just hear the alarm?

B: Yes. Somebody _____ have pulled it.

(a) can
(b) must
(c) would
(d) should

5. A: Hey, how did you do on your presentation?

B: Oh, I think it was _____ a success.

(a) way
(b) very
(c) quite
(d) much

6. A: Let's go see a play tomorrow.

B: I _____, but I promised to babysit.

(a) would like
(b) would like to
(c) would like to do
(d) would like to do to

7. A: A good job is so hard to find!

B: Don't worry. You'll find _____.

(a) soon enough the right job
(b) the job right enough soon
(c) the right job enough soon
(d) the right job soon enough

8. A: Should I throw out this manual?

B: No. It tells us _____ to do if the printer malfunctions.

(a) that
(b) how
(c) what
(d) which

9. A: I wish I had an espresso machine.
   B: But it would just take up space _____ your kitchen.

   (a) at
   (b) in
   (c) of
   (d) to

10. A: What are you doing later tonight?
    B: Nothing much. I'll _____.

    (a) just hang out at probably home
    (b) hang out just probably at home
    (c) probably just hang out at home
    (d) at home probably just hang out

11. A: This report is full of errors!
    B: I know. The statistics in there _____ incorrect.

    (a) is
    (b) are
    (c) has been
    (d) have been

12. A: What did you do after you found a hotel?
    B: I went straight to bed, _____ from the long trip.

    (a) exhaust
    (b) exhausted
    (c) to exhaust
    (d) exhausting

13. A: Will the director retire this month?
    B: No, he _____ until next month.

    (a) hasn't left
    (b) hadn't left
    (c) didn't leave
    (d) isn't leaving

14. A: Did you decide not to take that job you _____ in New York?
    B: Yes. It's too far away from my family.

    (a) offer
    (b) offered
    (c) are offered
    (d) were offered

15. A: Did this man rob your store?
    B: Yes. He's _____.

    (a) who did
    (b) who it did
    (c) the one who it did
    (d) the one who did it

16. A: Where does Billy work?
    B: At _____. I forgot the name of it.

    (a) restaurant
    (b) restaurants
    (c) a restaurant
    (d) the restaurant

17. A: Thomas can read and he's only four!
    B: Yes, he's very advanced _____ his age.

    (a) in
    (b) for
    (c) with
    (d) around

18. A: I don't feel like I need regular medical check-ups.
    B: But you should have them to catch _____.

    (a) illness at a stage early
    (b) illness at an early stage
    (c) at the early stage illness
    (d) at the stage early in illness

19. A: Will Judy finish the project on time?

B: I doubt it. She's so _____ behind.

(a) more
(b) right
(c) too
(d) far

20. A: The prices of gas and oil have gone through the roof.

B: Yeah, _____ so high.

(a) they're hard to believe to have gotten
(b) it's hard believing them having gotten
(c) it's hard to believe they've gotten
(d) hard believing they've gotten

Part II   Questions 21—40

Choose the best answer for the blank.

---

21. Not many students enrolled in the course, _____ the teacher became concerned it would be cancelled.

(a) but
(b) yet
(c) so
(d) if

22. Sally found _____ which charities to donate money to very complicated.

(a) determines
(b) determined
(c) determining
(d) to determine

23. On average, people spend about a third of their lives _____ .

(a) slept
(b) to sleep
(c) sleeping
(d) having slept

24. Various German communities in Poland _____ their separate identity for centuries.

(a) is retained
(b) are retained
(c) has retained
(d) have retained

25. In his inaugural address, Kennedy described the vision _____ would guide the new generation.

(a) that
(b) what
(c) of which
(d) for whom

26. _____ problems with the school's pool, the maintenance staff discovered a crack in its filtration system.

(a) To investigate
(b) Investigating
(c) Investigated
(d) Investigate

27. Expecting two manuscripts, the publisher decided to read _____ arrived first.

(a) that
(b) which
(c) whichever
(d) whomever

28. The girl offered _____ by volunteering at the orphanage.

(a) to be helping
(b) for helping
(c) helping
(d) to help

29. Philip was a freshman and was easily recognized as _____ because of his naive look.

(a) it
(b) one
(c) him
(d) them

30. As it _____ last night, the flowers Jack planted yesterday will need to be watered.

(a) has not been raining
(b) has not rained
(c) is not raining
(d) did not rain

31. _____ of being at the scene of the robbery, the woman kept having nightmares.

(a) The experience was traumatic so
(b) Traumatic was the experience so
(c) Was so traumatic the experience
(d) So traumatic was the experience

32. _____ you have taught the same lesson before, thorough preparation for every class is important.

(a) Until
(b) Even if
(c) Whereas
(d) As though

33. _____ for the preliminary competition.

(a) Showed up not all the contestants
(b) The contestants not all showed up
(c) All the contestants not showed up
(d) Not all the contestants showed up

34. A million dollars today is not as impressive an amount as it once _____.

(a) is
(b) was
(c) has been
(d) was being

35. Your body can absorb _____ better if you eat foods that have plenty of vitamin C in them.

(a) iron
(b) an iron
(c) the irons
(d) a few irons

36. Betero started to sculpt in the 1970s, after his reputation as a painter _____.

(a) well already had been established
(b) already well had been established
(c) had already been well established
(d) had been established already well

37. It is imperative that an institution conducting federally-funded research _____ an internal review board.

(a) create
(b) created
(c) is creating
(d) be created

38. Guus Hiddink is a good soccer coach because he teaches his players that a true professional _____.

(a) gives his all the score no matter what
(b) no matter gives his all to the score
(c) the score no matter gives his all
(d) gives his all no matter the score

39. The aspects of experience that psychology takes as its province _____ an enormous range.

(a) cover
(b) covers
(c) was covering
(d) were covering

40. Moving out of London is particularly attractive to public sector workers, whose salaries tend to be _____.

(a) lower than of private firms
(b) private firms lower than them
(c) lower than those at private firms
(d) those lower than at private firms

Part III **Questions 41—45**

Identify the option that contains an awkward expression or an error in grammar.

41. (a) A: Look at all these cars lined up outside the department store!
    (b) B: There must be a big sale today or something.
    (c) A: Parking is definitely going to be a huge problem.
    (d) B: Hmm. It would have been better if we take a cab.

42. (a) A: Mr. Glazer, could you tell me how Joey is doing in Spanish class?
    (b) B: His work is fine, but his class participation could stand some improvement.
    (c) A: Well, I think he's withdrawn because his last teacher punished the kids for making mistakes.
    (d) B: Really? That surely explains why he's too intimidating to speak up in class.

43. (a) A: There seem to be more students absent than usual in my class.
    (b) B: There's a flu going around. Half of my second period students have it.
    (c) A: I heard Alison is away, too. Maybe she's caught the same thing.
    (d) B: I couldn't be surprised. I feel flu symptoms coming on myself.

44. (a) A: Do you think we'll have enough dessert for our guests tonight?
    (b) B: I was also wondering about that, so I went out and bought some donuts just in case.
    (c) A: What a relief! Thanks. How many did you get?
    (d) B: A dozen of donut of assorted varieties that everyone should like.

45. (a) A: You look really upset. What happened, a bad day at work?
    (b) B: Well, waiting for a taxi near work, my purse got stolen.
    (c) A: You're kidding! You mean it was a snatch and run?
    (d) B: Yeah, a guy came by me on a motorbike and just pulled it off my shoulder.

Part IV Questions 46—50

Identify the option that contains an awkward expression or an error in grammar.

46. (a) Satisfaction is guaranteed through our convenient and hassle-free online gift service. (b) We ensure that every gift is beautifully wrapped and delivered promptly in perfect condition. (c) Simply select from our online catalog and we are confirming your order within 24 hours. (d) If you do not receive confirmation, please contact us again to ensure that your order has been received.

47. (a) Type 2 diabetes, the most common form of diabetes, are sometimes called adult-onset diabetes. (b) Excessive weight and a stressful lifestyle are major risk factors for this condition. (c) There is also a genetic link, as the disease often runs in families. (d) While most sufferers are people over 40, more and more children are now being diagnosed with type 2 diabetes.

48. (a) Miguel Hidalgo was a priest and revolutionary leader who fought for Mexico's independence from Spain in the early 19th century. (b) His study of revolutionary writings and the injustices he saw helped him convince that Mexico should be free from colonial rule. (c) Therefore, in 1810, Hidalgo and a group of revolutionaries formed an army and led an uprising against the Spanish authorities. (d) They were victorious initially, but within a few months the Spanish defeated them, and Hidalgo was caught and executed.

49. (a) Every autumn, Monarch butterflies return to Mexico after spending the summer in Canada and the US. (b) The Mexican people welcome back the returning butterflies, which they believe bear the spirits of their departed. (c) These spirits are honored on the Day of the Dead, a traditional Mexican holiday. (d) Holiday is on November 1st and is a time not of sadness, but of celebration.

50. (a) Fossil records actually exist for only a relatively small number of ancient creatures. (b) This is because many creatures had no skeletons or other hard parts and rotted away entirely. (c) Others simply lived in an environment where fossilization was unlike to occur. (d) In fact, most fossil records are for creatures that lived in seas, lakes and rivers.

This is the end of the Grammar section. Do NOT move on to the next section until instructed to do so. You are NOT allowed to turn to any other section of the test.

TEPS

VOCABULARY

Part I   Questions 1—25

Choose the best answer for the blank.

1.   A: I'm glad you could come to my party.
   B: Well, thanks for _____ me.

   (a) taking
   (b) noting
   (c) having
   (d) getting

2.   A: Dinner is on me tonight. Enjoy.
   B: No, this is my _____.

   (a) bet
   (b) job
   (c) treat
   (d) right

3.   A: These shoes I'm wearing are very uncomfortable.
   B: Mine too. They're tight and _____ my feet.

   (a) hurt
   (b) drill
   (c) chop
   (d) break

4.   A: This tax return form is too confusing.
   B: You should _____ a professional to do it, then.

   (a) fix
   (b) hire
   (c) catch
   (d) apply

5.   A: Pat, could you drive the kids to their piano lessons today?
   B: But it's your _____ to take them.

   (a) care
   (b) turn
   (c) order
   (d) action

6.   A: Excuse me, is only one carry-on bag allowed?
   B: Yes, and there is a _____ to the size as well.

   (a) case
   (b) limit
   (c) matter
   (d) burden

7.   A: Jerry, can you fix my computer today?
   B: Sorry. My schedule is too _____.

   (a) full
   (b) active
   (c) blocked
   (d) complete

8.   A: I'd like to pay in cash.
   B: Sure, whatever is _____ for you.

   (a) useful
   (b) ordinary
   (c) convenient
   (d) worthwhile

9. A: T-Mart. How may I help you?

    B: Hi, I'm calling to _____ about any job openings.

    (a) enlist
    (b) adjust
    (c) inquire
    (d) question

10. A: The violin is just too hard to learn!

    B: It can be _____ at first, but it'll get easier.

    (a) preventive
    (b) frustrating
    (c) resistant
    (d) delicate

11. A: Any word on our pay increases?

    B: A meeting will be held _____ that this afternoon.

    (a) issuing
    (b) noticing
    (c) excepting
    (d) concerning

12. A: Have you given up red meat?

    B: Yes, I'm taking my doctor's _____.

    (a) advice
    (b) thought
    (c) demand
    (d) statement

13. A: How about seeing a movie tonight?

    B: Sorry, but I have a(n) _____ engagement.

    (a) latter
    (b) former
    (c) intended
    (d) previous

14. A: Have you told the staff about the layoffs?

    B: No. I don't know how to _____.

    (a) get it out
    (b) call it out
    (c) bring it up
    (d) cough it up

15. A: This salad dressing has gone bad.

    B: But it's not past its _____ date.

    (a) rejection
    (b) objection
    (c) expiration
    (d) production

16. A: I don't think I'll ever play tennis well.

    B: Keep practicing and you'll _____.

    (a) make off with it
    (b) get the hang of it
    (c) have a way with it
    (d) take my word for it

17. A: Excuse me, can I transfer to the green line at this stop?

    B: Yes, actually three lines _____ here.

    (a) elapse
    (b) concur
    (c) intersect
    (d) transgress

18. A: Did your assistant update your files without even being asked?

B: Yes. I like how she shows
_____.

(a) reliance
(b) initiative
(c) command
(d) sufficiency

19. A: Should I tip the room service person when our meal arrives?

B: No, the bill includes a(n)
_____.

(a) invoice
(b) deposit
(c) penalty
(d) gratuity

20. A: You never talk to Jim these days.

B: We're not on _____ terms.

(a) speaking
(b) traversing
(c) expressing
(d) commuting

21. A: Harry? I didn't expect to run into you at this conference!

B: Alexis? Well, this certainly is a(n)
_____ meeting!

(a) chance
(b) offhand
(c) reckless
(d) doubtful

22. A: Could I ask you something about parenting?

B: Of course. That's a subject that never _____ to interest me.

(a) fails
(b) defies
(c) eludes
(d) condemns

23. A: I've been so unhappy since breaking up with Denise.

B: You need to _____ your depression.

(a) iron out
(b) cheer up
(c) snap out of
(d) muscle in on

24. A: Did you find that book as affecting as I did?

B: Yes, I did. It left a(n) _____ impression on me.

(a) indelible
(b) eradicable
(c) clairvoyant
(d) miscognizant

25. A: I'm surprised Korea has become such an economic _____.

B: I know. Even though the country's small, it sure is powerful.

(a) pugilist
(b) cession
(c) alcove
(d) titan

Part II **Questions 26—50**

Choose the best answer for the blank.

26. For a nation to develop quickly, it must encourage high literacy _____ among young people.

    (a) rates
    (b) units
    (c) talents
    (d) markers

27. Participants are _____ to pay their fees one month before the conference.

    (a) given
    (b) asked
    (c) differed
    (d) considered

28. Fax machines _____ information from one location to another through telephone lines.

    (a) transmit
    (b) capture
    (c) enter
    (d) push

29. Without government _____, the school will not be able to purchase new library books.

    (a) profits
    (b) entries
    (c) funding
    (d) substance

30. For generations, France felt _____ and angry about the Franco-Prussian War because they lost a lot of land.

    (a) lofty
    (b) bitter
    (c) riddled
    (d) obedient

31. _____ in young Korean adults has increased sharply due to unhealthy diets and lack of exercise.

    (a) Obesity
    (b) Tenacity
    (c) Reluctance
    (d) Immensity

32. Retailers are obligated to _____ the risks of using lead-based paints for the sake of public health.

    (a) betray
    (b) disclose
    (c) excavate
    (d) undertake

33. Under stress, headache pain worsens and soon becomes _____.

    (a) concise
    (b) insinuating
    (c) excruciating
    (d) monotonous

34. The ultimate goal of this conference is to strengthen international ties and _____ world peace.

    (a) promote
    (b) enlarge
    (c) submit
    (d) imply

35. Aborigines were the first _____ of Australia, reaching the continent some 60,000 years ago.

    (a) species
    (b) entities
    (c) personas
    (d) inhabitants

36. _____ copyrighted material such as websites, music and software can lead to legal troubles.

    (a) Pirating
    (b) Framing
    (c) Breaking
    (d) Downing

37. The increase in productivity should lead to a _____ from the current economic downturn.

    (a) recovery
    (b) review
    (c) retreat
    (d) repair

38. The vast majority of the European peasant population in the Middle Ages wore simple clothing made from coarse, homespun _____.

    (a) loaves
    (b) fabrics
    (c) segments
    (d) ingredients

39. Throughout history, people have _____ their bodies with jewelry and makeup.

    (a) savored
    (b) adorned
    (c) polished
    (d) renovated

40. Just a _____ of our skin cream once a day leaves skin looking radiant.

    (a) dab
    (b) rap
    (c) nip
    (d) jot

41. Although _____ by art historians, the painter Adam Elsheimer has few admirers among the lay public.

    (a) scaled
    (b) altered
    (c) revered
    (d) diversified

42. Smoothie Lip Balm makes _____ lips a thing of the past with its new and improved moisture-rich formula.

    (a) etched
    (b) frosted
    (c) chapped
    (d) sprained

43. This movie presents a very realistic _____ of mountain climbing.

    (a) portrayal
    (b) outlook
    (c) venture
    (d) range

44. Universities become top-tier by
_____ respected scholars to
become faculty members.

(a) jostling
(b) courting
(c) bundling
(d) modifying

45. Committee members are _____
toward each other despite their
differences.

(a) irate
(b) ample
(c) morose
(d) congenial

46. The prosecutor's questions _____
the witness, who became confused and
upset.

(a) rattled
(b) vibrated
(c) placated
(d) assuaged

47. Former first lady of the Philippines
Imelda Marcos had a(n) _____
for shoes and was rumored to own over
a thousand pairs.

(a) penchant
(b) solipsism
(c) aspersion
(d) insurgence

48. The candidates' ridiculous antics are
disgraceful and have turned the
campaign into a(n) _____ of
democratic politics.

(a) epitome
(b) soliloquy
(c) rudiment
(d) burlesque

49. All vehicles built after 2001 must
be checked annually to ensure
_____ with emissions standards.

(a) permission
(b) retardation
(c) compliance
(d) temperance

50. States are complaining that they have
to _____ in vital areas like
education in order to meet soaring
health care costs.

(a) ebb
(b) gnaw
(c) bloat
(d) scrimp

This is the end of the Vocabulary section. Do NOT move on to the Reading Comprehension section until instructed to do so. You are NOT allowed to turn to any other section of the test.

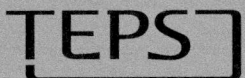

READING
COMPREHENSION

Part I Questions 1—16

Read the passage. Then choose the option that best completes the passage.

1. In the 1950s, the schooling environment in Maine was not very accepting of French-American children. Many were forced by teachers to conceal their French-American origins by taking English names, and children that were caught speaking French at school were given harsh punishments. It is therefore no wonder that many French-American parents at that time decided not to teach their children their mother tongue. They realized that _____.

    (a) the only way to get ahead was to speak English
    (b) studying hard was important in language learning
    (c) the schools had too many French-language teachers
    (d) becoming bilingual would give their kids an advantage

2. The primary trigger of allergies during springtime is pollen. Pollen is a microscopic powder-like material consisting of the male fertilizing grains of grass, trees and flowers. Tree pollen is the leading cause of allergies in early spring, while grass and flower pollens are more common in late spring. Grass and flower pollens are worse in areas where there are many lawns and gardens, like city suburbs. So with the continuing expansion of suburban areas, we can expect to see a

    _____.

    (a) reduction in pollen during spring
    (b) steady increase in allergic reactions to pollens
    (c) decrease in spring allergies among suburbanites
    (d) further rise in the amount of untouched greenery

3. The state government is finally getting serious about _____.
    As a first step, it will provide $20 million to school boards to open up school gyms after hours for use by students. These extra hours, it believes, will offer much-needed additional opportunities for physical activity. Second, the government will require that schools give students 20 minutes of daily exercise during school hours. Finally, it will ban junk foods from being sold in vending machines on school property.

(a) creating a healthier environment for students
(b) assisting students with sports scholarships
(c) supporting organized athletics programs
(d) developing nutritious cafeteria menus

4.

Dear Jack,

Hawaii has been wonderful so far with one exception. We stayed at a place called the Mango Shack last night, and were woken up all night long by mangoes falling from 30 feet above on the metal roof. It sounded like someone was hitting the roof with a baseball bat! That is how loud it was! We started thinking that maybe the Mango Shack was not as fun as we thought it would be. Oh well, we learned our lesson. Next time we will definitely _____.

Your friend,
Sandy

(a) learn more about the Mango Shack
(b) be more careful when walking on the beach
(c) book a reservation there as soon as we arrive
(d) think twice before staying at oddly-named places

5. Aldous Huxley's *Brave New World* warns of the dangers of _____.
In the novel, the rigid government controls reproduction through technological and medical intervention, rendering marriage and family obsolete. The government also uses complicated entertainment machines to occupy leisure time. Soma, a psychotropic-hypnotic drug created by the state to pacify citizens, is another example of the kind of "advances" the novel sharply criticizes.

(a) governments clinging to outdated methods of regulating people
(b) giving the state control over new and powerful technologies
(c) citizens leading the technological progression of society
(d) outside influences infiltrating weak governments

6. Some spiders of the species *Argiope aemula* make webs with X-shaped patterns, which scientists believed attracted prey more effectively. However, what scientists could not understand was why the design was not universal among *aemulas*. To solve the mystery, they installed cameras in front of 56 webs with patterns and 59 without. While the patterned webs attracted 60% more prey, they also attracted more predators: 70% of wasp attacks were on spiders in patterned webs. Scientists hope these findings shed light on why _____.

   (a) patterned webs fail to trap more prey
   (b) webs do little to prevent predator attacks
   (c) predators prefer non-patterned *aemulas* webs
   (d) not all *aemulas* pattern their webs with X-shapes

7. China's Spring-Autumn and Warring States periods, marked by disunity and civil strife, were also _____. The atmosphere of reform and openness to new ideas can be attributed to competition among warring regional lords, each of whom wanted his region to achieve preeminence in every area—especially the arts. As a consequence, many of China's cultural feats in painting, poetry, music and dance originated from this time.

   (a) times of cultural expansion outside China
   (b) troubled times of broad cultural ignorance
   (c) neglected times in China's cultural history
   (d) times of unprecedented cultural excellence

8. After touring the US in the 1930s, Alexis de Tocqueville, a French historian, wrote about his experiences, pointing out _____. He observed that Americans had a keen desire for conveniences and this reflected not so much a leisurely lifestyle as a busy one. Americans, Tocqueville wrote, became more restless and busier the richer they got. He found it ironical that they spent their time working to acquire comforts and conveniences but then lacked the leisure time to actually enjoy them.

   (a) a tendency among Americans to neglect propriety
   (b) the untapped potential of America's workforce
   (c) a curious paradox in the American character
   (d) the benefits of the American work ethic

9. Mark Twain wrote the novel *Huckleberry Finn* when America was _____. The novel was published in 1885, some two decades after Lincoln's formal emancipation of slaves and the end of the Civil War. America was still undergoing a period of reconstruction—rebuilding communities and trying to integrate freed slaves into normal society. The process did not go smoothly, for while integration was not failing outright, race relations were still strained. These ongoing social tensions are reflected in Twain's novel.

(a) enjoying a period of wealth and optimism
(b) busily rebuilding what the war had destroyed
(c) confident in the strengthening of race relations
(d) still struggling with racism and the aftereffects of slavery

10. The bright lights of New York are not what they used to be. New building restrictions, sensor-based lighting, and moves to reduce energy costs have all conspired to give Manhattan's skyline a fainter glow. Fewer office towers are lit up all night long, turning the cityscape into a patchwork pattern of sparsely lit buildings, with exterior decorative lighting often restricted to the top floors. Indeed, the nightly spectacle of tall towers with their illuminated floors is _____.

(a) a sign of success and power
(b) definitely a thing of the past
(c) a beautiful and inspiring sight
(d) sure to continue into the future

11. The countries of sub-Saharan Africa predominantly rely on agriculture for economic survival and thus are deeply impacted by world trade agreements and globalization. Presently their agricultural industries are forced to compete with those of developed countries that receive exorbitant subsidies and are able to produce cheap products. Compounding this problem is the failure of the international financial system to relieve sub-Saharan economies of their unsustainable debts, which would allow for future development. As far as this region is concerned, globalization _____.

(a) has been a boon for its agricultural industries so far
(b) is proving to be more a scourge than a blessing
(c) has convinced governments to give subsidies
(d) remains a project for the distant future

12. The water table used to be _____, but not so much anymore. One reason for this is that now most rainwater enters streams, is then channeled into storm sewers, and then is swiftly emptied into waterways. From there it is flushed out too quickly into lakes and coastal waters, and as a result, never has an opportunity to become groundwater. This has led to extreme depletion of the water table and drought in many countries around the world.

(a) replenished by a good heavy rain
(b) depleted from abuse and overuse
(c) considered an unusable water source
(d) restored through eco-friendly methods

13. Business tourism represents a new way of rethinking fundamental assumptions and of apprehending the real-world applications of your business's products. Basically, it involves employees touring businesses related to their business. For example, staff from a medical equipment company might tour hospitals where they can actually see the devices they make in use, or a software firm's programmers might tour businesses and tech support centers that deal with their software. This is not about networking or recreation or adventures in character building. It is about

_____.

(a) rewarding employees for their consistent hard work
(b) contemplating one's work from a fresh perspective
(c) reducing workplace alienation among co-workers
(d) holistically assessing staff productivity

14. Storytelling is a universal human activity that transcends culture and history. Its widespread appeal is due to a story's ability to link audience emotions to those of the story's characters, a process referred to as "narrative transport." Researchers have found that the degree to which audiences experience narrative transport depends on how closely their knowledge and life experiences parallel those of a story's characters. It is also facilitated more easily in people with greater empathy. In essence, narrative transport _____.

(a) circumvents negative audience reaction to certain stories
(b) plays a major role in developing empathy in the audience
(c) hinges on audience identification with the characters in the story
(d) maintains psychological distance between the audience and characters

15. The discovery of electricity was quickly followed by the invention of a stream of devices that enhanced communications. The first of these was the single-wire electric telegraph, a concept developed by Samuel Morse in the 1830s. Then in the 1870s two inventors, Alexander Graham Bell and Elisha Gray, independently designed devices that could transmit speech electronically—the telephone. Bell was the first to patent it, and the telephone soon became essential for business. _____, an Italian named Guglielmo Marconi was experimenting with radio telegraphy. He broadcast his first message in 1897 and had sent a message across the Atlantic by 1901.

(a) For instance
(b) Meanwhile
(c) As a result
(d) Indeed

16. InvitingPapers.com was conceived and developed to assist scientists, corporate researchers, professors, and research students who are seeking publication opportunities for their research papers. Our database of information on calls for papers in all disciplines is considered in academic circles to be not only the most exhaustive on the Web, but also the most intelligently presented and organized. _____, our advanced search function enables you to refine your searches according to specialization, abstract deadline, acronyms and keywords. Keep abreast of the publication events in your discipline: become a member of InvitingPapers today.

(a) In brief
(b) Otherwise
(c) What's more
(d) Notwithstanding

Part II **Questions 17—37**

Read the passage and the question. Then choose the option that best answers the question.

17. After writing the first draft of an assignment, try to forget about it for a few days or even a week. When you return to it, read the draft critically, assessing whether it all makes sense. Make sure that the draft focuses on a single idea and that you have presented clear and sufficient evidence to persuade your readers of this idea. Once it accomplishes these things, start thinking about how to tighten the paper's organization and polish its style.

Q: What is the best title for the passage?
(a) How to Write about Literature
(b) Putting Unique Touches on a Paper
(c) How to Begin Writing an Assignment
(d) Evaluating an Assignment's First Draft

18.

Dear Mr. Jones,

As per our agreement in our phone conversation yesterday, I have sent the defective computer monitor I bought from you—in all its original packaging—by overnight delivery service. When you receive it, I expect you will hold up your end of the agreement and promptly deposit the full cost of the monitor, as well as the shipping fee, in my bank account. I would also appreciate it if you would confirm receipt of this email.

Sincerely,
David White

Q: What is the email mainly about?
(a) A new monitor that will arrive by overnight delivery
(b) The various defects discovered in a computer monitor
(c) An agreement about reimbursement for a faulty monitor
(d) The personal information required to ship a new monitor

19. Researchers at the aerospace and defense firm called BAE Systems have created a new super-sticky material that mimics the adhesive properties of the gecko lizard's feet. Known as "Synthetic Gecko," the adhesive is made of polymer and is covered in millions of tiny mushroom-shaped stalks for grip—similar to those on geckos' foot pads. It can stick to any surface, even dirt-covered ones, is entirely reusable and residue-free, and is strong enough to hold a family car to a roof. But while Synthetic Gecko is a breakthrough glue, researchers say it is still no match for the powerful sticking capabilities of the actual gecko.

Q: What is the news report mainly about?
(a) A scholarly investigation of different kinds of glues
(b) A gecko lizard that is being studied by BAE systems
(c) A new type of glue originating from natural ingredients
(d) An adhesive material inspired by the gecko lizard's feet

20. Although email is a great invention, you need to be careful when using it—especially when it comes to emails you receive. Be suspicious of any messages you get that contain requests for personal information. No reputable company will ask you for credit card or banking information or social security numbers through email. Do not supply such information if requested to do so by email. And do not trust emails requesting money, stating that you have won a prize, or giving you the chance to make money. These should just be deleted.

Q: What is the writer's main advice?
(a) Delete all spam emails immediately.
(b) Be wary of what emails request from you.
(c) Do not try to read every email you receive.
(d) Do not ask for personal information through email.

21. Phoebe is an outer satellite of Saturn whose origin was a mystery to scientists for many years. This changed somewhat in 2004, however, when the Cassini spacecraft obtained highly detailed images of the celestial body. From the images, scientists were able to surmise that Phoebe may be a frozen artifact of a bygone era—a primordial mixture of ice, rock and carbon-containing compounds, similar in many ways to material seen on Pluto. Scientists believe bodies like Phoebe were plentiful in the outer reaches of the solar system about four and a half billion years ago.

Q: What is the best title for the passage?
(a) Phoebe Inspires Technological Breakthroughs
(b) Cassini Images Fail to Shed Light on Phoebe
(c) Images Provide Clues to Phoebe's Origins
(d) Phoebe Considered Entirely Unique Body

22. All Financials Management (AFM) is your best choice for debt negotiation, loan restructuring and fiscal dispute resolution. We can save you from the complexities of litigation or bankruptcy by liaising with creditors to help you reduce debt. First we assess your situation and then counsel you on the practical strategies available. In this way, you can resolve your financial problems rapidly and without fuss. Our cost-effective process saves you money to pay your debts, rather than spending that money on lawyers. Call AFM now—we give you choices.

Q: What does AFM mainly do?
(a) It provides legal representation at bankruptcy courts.
(b) It identifies the means to solve financial problems.
(c) It lends money to financially troubled creditors.
(d) It advises people on how to claim bankruptcy.

23. Brighten up any room of your house with Home Emporium pillows! Our new imported pillows come in an assortment of beautiful colors—tan, pink, red, violet, lime and blue. You can also choose from a wide variety of shapes. All pillows are made of thick cotton and finished with piped edges and a hidden zipper. They are also machine-washable. Add beautiful touches to your home today with help from Home Emporium.

Q: Which of the following is correct about Home Emporium pillows according to the passage?
(a) They are available in yellow.
(b) They are imported products.
(c) They come in very limited shapes.
(d) They cannot be cleaned in a laundry machine.

24.

Dear Uncle Ed,

We are giving my sister Jennifer and her husband a party in honor of their 25th wedding anniversary next month. It will be held at one in the afternoon on Saturday the 11th, at the Green Oaks Country Club in Overton. There will be a formal lunch, followed by music and dancing. I hope you and Aunt Ann will be able to join us in the celebration. Remember, it is a surprise party, so please RSVP to me, not to Jennifer!

Love,
Rhonda

Q: Which of the following is correct about the party according to the invitation?
(a) It is in honor of Ed and his wife.
(b) It will be held in the evening.
(c) It will be a casual gathering.
(d) It is intended as a surprise.

25. In the 1830s in England, two pivotal historical events occurred that improved the lives of the English people. The first was the opening of the Liverpool and Manchester Railway—the first railway line in the world. The train transformed England's physical landscape and supported the growth of its commerce. The second was the opening of the country's Reform Parliament. The new governing system reapportioned representatives in government in a way fairer to the growing cities of the industrial north. These two events greatly affected England's society for the better.

Q: Which of the following is correct according to the passage?
(a) The Liverpool and Manchester Railway was the last built in Europe.
(b) The train altered the way England looked and benefited its economy.
(c) The new system discriminated against England's northern cities.
(d) The events had a negative impact on England and its citizens.

26. The Yagua Indians of the Amazon rainforest are renowned for their skill at using blowpipes for hunting. The blowpipes are made from the materials of different trees and plants and can take several days to make. The darts blown from the pipes are made of wood, and their tips are coated with a deadly poison called curare, which is prepared by cooking and mixing certain forest roots and leaves together. The blowpipe skills of the Yagua became more widely known through the growth of tourism in the Amazon basin. In fact, these days Yagua make money by selling blowpipes to tourists.

Q: Which of the following is correct about the Yagua according to the passage?
(a) They carry spears tipped with a fatal poison.
(b) They can make a blowpipe within one day.
(c) They no longer live in the Amazon basin.
(d) They sell model blowpipes to outsiders.

27. Elite Cars has been authorized to sell vehicles from a rental fleet and now we've got more inventory than we can handle. Over 75 vehicles of all kinds must be sold! So we're holding an amazing 10-hour sale. From 10 am to 8 pm tomorrow, all rental cars, trucks, minivans, SUVs, and 4x4s will be sold at extremely discounted prices. These prices will be so low that there will be no need to even negotiate! Not to be missed!

Q: Which of the following is correct about Elite Cars according to the advertisement?
(a) It is looking for more rental cars to sell.
(b) It is selling a variety of vehicle types.
(c) Its sale will last for about 10 days.
(d) Its sale includes new cars.

28. Yesterday I was reminded of when the Chicago Cubs last won a Major League Baseball World Series. It was when the automobile was still a new and untrustworthy invention and the electric light was not yet 20 years old. In the many losing years that followed that win, most of the European monarchies collapsed, two World Wars were fought, and disco came and went. It sure has been a long, losing road for the Cubs since their moment of glory so many years ago. And yet, the team's diehard fans cling to the belief that this will be the year that things turn around.

Q: Which of the following is correct about the Chicago Cubs according to the passage?
(a) They have failed in all attempts to win the World Series.
(b) They lost the World Series the year the car was invented.
(c) Their wins coincided with several key historical events.
(d) Their fans maintain faith in the team's ability to win.

29. The University of California AIDS Research Laboratory is currently conducting research on why some people with HIV can remain healthy for years, while others usually progress to AIDS within ten years on average. The research team is particularly interested in the experiences of Kay Simpson, a long-term carrier of HIV who has yet to become ill. She has not been on medication but stays healthy. If researchers can answer the question of how this is possible, it could greatly help in the development of a vaccine for the virus.

Q: Which of the following is correct about the laboratory according to the passage?
(a) It is investigating why some HIV-positive people remain healthy.
(b) It has determined that HIV progresses to AIDS within 15 years.
(c) It is studying Kay Simpson's strange reaction to AIDS drugs.
(d) It has developed a vaccine that successfully prevents AIDS.

30. The Group of Eight major industrialized countries (G8) and leading developing countries have reached a general agreement on the need to combat climate change. A meeting of the 17 major economies produced a consensus on the necessity for drastically reducing carbon emissions, but the details of implementation remain unresolved. The US has long championed the idea of broadening talks on climate change from the G8 to big polluting countries in the developing world, insisting that it will only sign a replacement for the 1997 Kyoto Protocol if those countries are involved.

Q: Which of the following is correct according to the passage?
(a) The G8 and major developing countries have agreed to address climate change.
(b) How and when carbon emissions will be reduced was settled at the meeting.
(c) The US thinks only G8 countries should be involved in climate change talks.
(d) The agreement reached at the meeting has replaced the Kyoto Protocol.

31. Edouard Manet's famous painting *The Lunch on the Grass* created a scandal in Paris when it was first exhibited in 1863. The painting depicted two fashionably dressed men seated by an undressed woman. But as the writer Emile Zola wrote, it was ironic it created a scandal because the Louvre had long displayed paintings of nudes without any controversy. Also, Manet had drawn inspiration from Marcantonio Raimondi's engraving called *The Judgment of Paris* (c. 1515), a respected artwork which itself features nudes. Manet had simply painted modern versions of them in *The Lunch on the Grass*.

Q: Which of the following is correct about *The Lunch on the Grass* according to the passage?
(a) Manet was lauded by the public when it was first exhibited.
(b) It became the center of a scandal after Zola wrote about it.
(c) Manet modeled it on several nude paintings in the Louvre.
(d) Its composition was inspired by an engraving by Raimondi.

32. In the year 2000, the Syrian government freed Lebanese political prisoners in the hope of placating a growing anti-Syrian movement in Lebanon. The prisoners were predominately Christians who had been captured in 1991 towards the end of the Lebanese civil war. At that time, the Syrian regime was systematically crushing a revolt by Christian Lebanese and other minor political factions in Lebanon. Human rights groups say that the Syrian regime captured hundreds of political prisoners at the time, and many of them are still thought to be languishing in Syrian jails.

Q: Which of the following is correct about the Syrian government in 2000 according to the passage?
(a) It freed prisoners in response to Lebanese pressure.
(b) It crushed a revolt by hostile political factions in Syria.
(c) It backed a Christian uprising during Lebanon's civil war.
(d) It is known to retain several thousand Christian prisoners.

33. Spring has been great, but now here at L. Crew Fashion we're clearing out stock to make room for incoming summer merchandise! For a limited time only you can pick up items from our spring collection at an amazing 65% off! And if you are not completely satisfied with your purchase, you can either return it and get your money back or exchange it for another item. Visit L. Crew Fashion now and take advantage of the kind of deals you have to see to believe!

Q: What can be inferred about L. Crew Fashion from the passage?
(a) It is going out of business.
(b) It rarely offers spring sales.
(c) It is holding an end-of-season sale.
(d) Its spring stock was badly damaged.

34. Tapio Rautavaara of Finland was a talented athlete, actor, and singer. He won a gold medal in the javelin event at the 1948 Summer Olympics and acted in a score of Finnish movies. He also recorded a total of 310 songs in his lifetime. But Rautavaara's life was cut short in 1979 when he slipped and fell, hitting his head on the floor. Although he was immediately rushed to a hospital, staff there mistakenly thought he was drunk and simply bandaged his head and sent him home. The next night, tragically, he died from a cerebral hemorrhage.

Q: What can be inferred about Tapio Rautavaara from the passage?
(a) He took up athletics after a successful movie career.
(b) His songs are what he is primarily remembered for.
(c) He was not able to compete in athletics after 1948.
(d) His injuries were not taken seriously after his fall.

35. Are you worried that the computer age is passing you by? Confused when people start talking about online apps, forums and blogs? Worry no more! Crest Ridge Community College offers adult courses that will open up the world of computers to you. Our highly qualified instructors will take you through all the basics you need to know to become computer literate. Courses start at only $100 for four classes a month. For more information, call Crest Ridge Community College at 555-9191.

Q: What can be inferred about the courses from the advertisement?
(a) They are for adults with little experience using computers.
(b) They are specially designed for children's computer education.
(c) They are offered both on campus and online for the same price.
(d) They are taught by college students majoring in computer science.

36. The symptoms of strep throat include fever, sore throat, swollen neck glands, problems with digestion and headaches. It is usually transmitted person-to-person through direct contact with nasal secretions. If your child has these symptoms, consult a doctor. To prevent transmission, children with strep throat should be kept out of school for at least 24 hours after antibiotic treatment begins. Furthermore, make sure that they cover their mouths and noses when coughing and sneezing and that they wash their hands thoroughly several times a day.

Q: What can be inferred about strep throat from the passage?
(a) It does not respond well to antibiotic treatment.
(b) It usually requires a lengthy stay in the hospital.
(c) It is a more serious illness in adults than in children.
(d) It remains contagious for a day after treatment starts.

37. My biggest pet peeve is when I make a business phone call and the secretary of the person with whom I want to connect tells me, in intimate detail, why his or her boss is unavailable. As a boss myself, I certainly would not appreciate my secretary revealing to anyone who calls that the reason I can't come to the phone is because I'm getting my gall bladder removed, or the like. Frankly, that is being both insensitive and unprofessional. So I always test my new secretaries by calling them myself to hear the reason why I am unavailable.

Q: What can be inferred about the writer from the passage?
(a) He is critical of the rules and regulations of the business world.
(b) He is impressed with the level of professionalism of secretaries.
(c) He believes discreetness is called for when explaining absences.
(d) He thinks phone etiquette is given too much priority in business.

Part III **Questions 38—40**

Read the passage. Then identify the option that does NOT belong.

38. World War I was very bloody and destructive because it was the very first war in which new industrial-era weapons were utilized. (a) For example, tanks and huge cannons were used for the first time in battle, resulting in unprecedented casualties. (b) Commanders failed to develop tactics for breaking through entrenched positions without heavy losses. (c) Airplanes dropped bombs and were also fitted with machine guns and cannons. (d) And submarines were armed with torpedoes, which were used to blow up battleships and supply ships.

39. The American Dream is defined as the freedom to attain wealth through hard work. (a) More realistically, however, it is accomplished through being successful in capitalist business. (b) Evidence of this is the fact that all the great private fortunes in America were built by people who ran their own businesses. (c) Businesspeople must continually compete for advancement, so they work hard and put in long hours. (d) Thus, capitalistic enterprise, not just hard work, is what delivers the American Dream—an assertion that many underpaid employees would agree with.

40. The human body has a number of means by which it can effectively protect itself from the cold and preserve warmth. (a) Shivering, which is a rapid contraction and expansion of the muscles, can help the body create internal heat. (b) Also, when the body is in cold surroundings, blood flow to the surface is restricted, which lowers the skin's temperature. (c) This decreases heat transfer to the outside since the difference in temperature between the body and its surroundings is reduced. (d) But if the body's core temperature drops below 93 degrees Fahrenheit, you can get hypothermia, which can be fatal.

This is the end of the Reading Comprehension section. Please remain seated until the proctor has instructed otherwise. You are NOT allowed to turn to any other section of the test.

서울대 최신기출 3

Listening Comprehension

Grammar

Vocabulary

Reading Comprehension

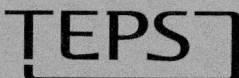

LISTENING COMPREHENSION

LISTENING COMPREHENSION

Part I Questions 1—15

You will now hear fifteen conversation fragments, each made up of a single spoken statement followed by four spoken responses. Choose the most appropriate response to the statement.

Part II Questions 16—30

You will now hear fifteen conversation fragments, each made up of three spoken statements followed by four spoken responses. Choose the most appropriate response to complete the conversation.

Part III **Questions 31—45**

You will now hear fifteen complete conversations. For each item, you will hear a conversation and its corresponding question, both of which will be read twice. Then you will hear four options which will be read only once. Choose the option that best answers the question.

Part IV **Questions 46—60**

You will now hear fifteen spoken monologues. For each item, you will hear a monologue and its corresponding question, both of which will be read twice. Then you will hear four options which will be read only once. Choose the option that best answers the question.

TEPS

GRAMMAR

Part I   **Questions 1—20**

Choose the best answer for the blank.

1. A: How did you end up staying at this hotel?

    B: There were very _____ choices in this area.

    (a) few
    (b) little
    (c) fewer
    (d) lesser

2. A: Do you think it's going to rain?

    B: It _____, though I can't say for sure.

    (a) will
    (b) does
    (c) might
    (d) would

3. A: Can you help me with the dishes?

    B: OK, _____ wait until this movie is over.

    (a) so
    (b) yet
    (c) but
    (d) and

4. A: Oh, no! Someone has painted graffiti on our building.

    B: I hope they find _____ is responsible.

    (a) that
    (b) what
    (c) whoever
    (d) whichever

5. A: What did you do on the weekend?

    B: I spent most of my time _____ for exams.

    (a) prepare
    (b) preparing
    (c) to prepare
    (d) to have prepared

6. A: I don't like the clothes in the stores these days.

    B: Me neither. Fashion these days _____ too extreme.

    (a) were being
    (b) was being
    (c) are
    (d) is

7. A: What do you think of your new cell phone?

    B: Honestly, it's not as good _____ as I thought it would be.

    (a) device
    (b) a device
    (c) the device
    (d) such device

8. A: Will your puppy grow into a big dog?

    B: Actually, I don't know _____ when he's fully grown.

    (a) like what he will be
    (b) like what will he be
    (c) what will he be like
    (d) what he will be like

9. A: Where should I put this delivery?
   B: Just put it _____ you like.

   (a) whatever
   (b) wherever
   (c) whenever
   (d) whichever

10. A: Don't you jog these days?
    B: No. I have arthritis, and my doctor told me _____.

    (a) not
    (b) not to
    (c) not to do
    (d) to not to do it

11. A: Which drink would you like to have?
    B: Just _____ for me, thank you.

    (a) apple cider
    (b) apple ciders
    (c) apples ciders
    (d) an apples cider

12. A: How did the get-together with your college friends go?
    B: It _____ much better if one of them hadn't been so disagreeable.

    (a) had been
    (b) would be
    (c) will have been
    (d) would have been

13. A: Oh no, I think I left the oven on!
    B: Don't worry, I remembered _____ it off before we left.

    (a) turning
    (b) to turn
    (c) turned
    (d) turn

14. A: Kevin must be devastated over the death of his parents.
    B: Yeah, he's finding _____.

    (a) it hardly to accept it
    (b) accepting it hardly
    (c) it to accept hard
    (d) it hard to accept

15. A: How about going on a picnic this weekend?
    B: I'm sorry, but I'm _____ behind in my work.

    (a) that
    (b) way
    (c) such
    (d) much

16. A: How long has Alex been away?
    B: By tomorrow, he _____ for a month.

    (a) was gone
    (b) has been gone
    (c) is going to be gone
    (d) will have been gone

17. A: Do you have anything more to tell us?
    B: No, nothing _____ what I have already said.

    (a) above
    (b) amidst
    (c) beyond
    (d) between

18. A: Steak would have been better than pasta for dinner last night.

  B: Yeah, but then _____ pay more for the meal.

  (a) we had to
  (b) we'll have to
  (c) we'd have to
  (d) we'd have had to

19. A: I heard Rob suffered a burglary.

  B: Yes, but fortunately no valuables in his house _____ stolen.

  (a) is
  (b) are
  (c) was
  (d) were

20. A: Our stock price went down again.

  B: I know, and there's no telling _____.

  (a) when will it ever go up back
  (b) will it ever go back up when
  (c) when it will ever go back up
  (d) it will when go ever up back

Part II **Questions 21—40**

Choose the best answer for the blank.

---

21. _____ regularly is fairly easy to do and inexpensive.

  (a) Jog
  (b) Jogged
  (c) Jogging
  (d) Having jogged

22. The noise _____ by his neighbors woke him up every night.

  (a) made
  (b) makes
  (c) was made
  (d) having been made

23. When the student asked what was wrong with his essay, the _____.

  (a) problem the teacher to him explained
  (b) teacher explained the problem to him
  (c) problem to him the teacher explained
  (d) teacher the problem explained to him

24. _____ the condition of his home after the flood, James began looking for another place to live.

  (a) Give
  (b) Given
  (c) Giving
  (d) Having given

25. Since starting in the car business a decade ago, the man _____ about 20 cars a month.

(a) sold
(b) sells
(c) has sold
(d) is selling

26. A bite from a cobra can be deadly if not _____ quickly.

(a) was treated
(b) treating
(c) to treat
(d) treated

27. _____ that all mountain roads were closed to traffic.

(a) Became so bad the weather
(b) The weather became so bad
(c) The weather had so bad become
(d) Had so bad the weather become

28. Music has an amazing ability to _____.

(a) affect our moods
(b) affecting our moods
(c) our moods to affecting
(d) moods of ours to affect

29. By the time Mr. Coleman retires next year, he _____ at this company for 35 years.

(a) worked
(b) is working
(c) will be working
(d) will have worked

30. Karl Marx postulated that capitalism would prove incapable of producing _____.

(a) a distribution acceptable of income
(b) acceptable income of a distribution
(c) income acceptable of a distribution
(d) an acceptable distribution of income

31. Eels and _____ fish swim by moving their bodies in a wave motion.

(a) of other varieties snake-like
(b) other of snake-like varieties
(c) varieties snake-like of other
(d) other snake-like varieties of

32. Children who see disturbing images on TV may worry not only about their own safety but also about _____ of the people they love.

(a) it
(b) that
(c) such
(d) those

33. Peer advisors were selected, and _____ about six incoming students.

(a) responsibility for them each is
(b) to them each responsibility is
(c) responsible will each be for
(d) each will be responsible for

34. It is not often easy to turn down an invitation to dinner without giving _____.

(a) excuse
(b) an excuse
(c) the excuse
(d) all excuses

35. _____ the phone than Bob knocked at the door.

    (a) Sue hung up no sooner
    (b) Sooner had Sue hung up
    (c) Had Sue hung up sooner
    (d) No sooner had Sue hung up

36. Years ago, unlike today, the oceans were free of engine noise and sonar, _____ a quiet and more natural environment for marine life.

    (a) provided
    (b) providing
    (c) to provide
    (d) they provided

37. The boss said the work needs to be done no matter _____.

    (a) how it takes many hours
    (b) how many hours it takes
    (c) how many its hours take
    (d) how its hours take many

38. The boy _____ the piano until his mother comes home.

    (a) played
    (b) was playing
    (c) will be playing
    (d) had been playing

39. Some argue that the Roman conquest of Britain did not and _____ not possibly have resulted in the immediate demise of native artists.

    (a) should
    (b) would
    (c) could
    (d) must

40. After being scammed once, the young man quickly developed the habit _____ car salesmen tell him.

    (a) of suspicious of whatever the
    (b) to be of suspicion of whatever
    (c) of being suspicious of whatever
    (d) to have whatever suspicion about

Part III Questions 41–45

Identify the option that contains an awkward expression or an error in grammar.

41. (a) A: Do you remember Mr. Barker? He used to be our history teacher.
    (b) B: Mr. Barker? Was he the old teacher with the gray beard?
    (c) A: No, Mr. Barker was quite young, but he didn't have a beard.
    (d) B: Oh, yeah, the teacher that I was thinking of was Mr. Jameson.

42. (a) A: Hi, this is Sam. I'm calling about our trip on Saturday.
    (b) B: Can I call you back a bit later? I just sat down to dinner.
    (c) A: I'm sorry. I thought you have finished dinner by now.
    (d) B: No, I got back home late, so I just started.

43. (a) A: Have you been dieting? You seem to have lost a lot of weight.
    (b) B: Yeah, I decided to try a new diet program, and I lost 12 kg.
    (c) A: Wow, that much! Is this one of those clubs or something?
    (d) B: No, I just read about it by a book. I'll lend it to you if you want.

44. (a) A: Wow, it's really clouding over. It looks like rain this afternoon.
    (b) B: Yeah, the forecast was for heavy showers all evening.
    (c) A: Terrible! Well, I'd better buy the umbrella, then.
    (d) B: No, just use this extra one of mine.

45. (a) A: I can't believe you've had four donuts already!
    (b) B: But they taste so good! Maybe I'll have just one more.
    (c) A: I think four are more than enough, don't you?
    (d) B: No, not really. Besides, I'm not on a diet.

Identify the option that contains an awkward expression or an error in grammar.

46. (a) Salt enhances flavor, that is why it is in so many food products. (b) In fact, about three quarters of the salt we eat is already in the food we buy. (c) However, too much salt is bad for your health. (d) For this reason, you should always check food labels to see how much salt the food contains.

47. (a) In the late 1800s in the US, there was mass outrage against big business, political corruption, and class inequalities. (b) Everything from best-selling books to popular magazines blasted the greed of the super-rich and the fecklessness of politicians. (c) People felt that the "monopolists" and "plutocrats" were plundering the hardworking majority, not just in the US, but in Europe, too. (d) In 1892, for example, writer Ignatius Donelly stated that a "vast conspiracy has been organized and is rapid taking possession of the world."

48. (a) Even talented writers put their essays through many revisions so that everything reads correctly. (b) This is especially necessary for beginners who sometimes forget their "audience," the readers. (c) So when revising your essays, take your readers into account, anticipated how they will see your work. (d) Think about their interpretation of your words and clarify potential misunderstandings.

49. (a) Some people hold the view that obese people should be taxed for the burdens by them put upon society. (b) They argue that the obese use up more resources, such as healthcare services and government assistance. (c) And they say that since the obese use more, they should be obligated to pay more for things like health insurance. (d) In this way, they assert, obese people can be held accountable for their excess weight.

50. (a) The desire for healthier and more economical foods has led many people to grow their own. (b) As many as 2% of households now estimated to have their own fresh supply of healthy, organically-grown vegetables. (c) Growing their own also allows people to save money, a huge benefit in a shaky economy with soaring food prices. (d) So with society's double focus on healthy eating and saving money, it is clear why many have awakened to the benefits of the simple backyard vegetable garden.

This is the end of the Grammar section. Do NOT move on to the next section until instructed to do so. You are NOT allowed to turn to any other section of the test.

TEPS

Vocabulary

Part I **Questions 1—25**

Choose the best answer for the blank.

1. A: You know what? I was 87 kilograms the last time I checked.
   B: Really? I didn't think you _____ that much. You look so thin.
   (a) filled
   (b) weighed
   (c) balanced
   (d) measured

2. A: This is really great coffee. Thanks.
   B: Sure. I'm glad you like the _____ of it.
   (a) cup
   (b) taste
   (c) style
   (d) grade

3. A: Hello. Is this the Jones' residence?
   B: No, sorry, you've got the _____ number.
   (a) bad
   (b) faulty
   (c) wrong
   (d) unsure

4. A: Let's have something _____ for dinner tonight.
   B: OK, I'll make some curry for a change.
   (a) same
   (b) equal
   (c) various
   (d) different

5. A: How about taking a rest from cleaning?
   B: OK. We'll have a _____ in 10 minutes.
   (a) break
   (b) base
   (c) case
   (d) clue

6. A: You work too much these days. We never go out and have fun.
   B: Sorry, I'll _____ you soon.
   (a) make fun of
   (b) make it up to
   (c) watch out for
   (d) come around to

7. A: Is all our luggage in the car?
   B: Yes, everything is _____ to go.
   (a) set
   (b) built
   (c) mailed
   (d) reached

8. A: Is there a special waiting area for first-class passengers?
   B: Yes, our first-class _____ is on the second floor.
   (a) loft
   (b) lounge
   (c) lodging
   (d) location

9. A: Did you have an exciting weekend?

   B: No, it was _____. I didn't do much.

   (a) dull
   (b) vague
   (c) unclear
   (d) crowded

10. A: I'm going to confront the boss about our ridiculous work load.

    B: Be tactful. Don't _____ your career.

    (a) scrutinize
    (b) jeopardize
    (c) discriminate
    (d) misrepresent

11. A: Can you break a 20 dollar bill?

    B: Sorry, I only have _____ for a ten.

    (a) means
    (b) matter
    (c) change
    (d) content

12. A: Why didn't you go to Mary's party?

    B: I just wasn't in the _____.

    (a) tone
    (b) mood
    (c) feeling
    (d) emotion

13. A: Do you know how to use this new juicing machine?

    B: No. Have a look at the _____.

    (a) elements
    (b) instructions
    (c) orientations
    (d) fundamentals

14. A: Does your hotel offer discounts to business travelers?

    B: Yes, corporate clients receive special _____.

    (a) tabs
    (b) rates
    (c) costs
    (d) wages

15. A: I can't believe you told Melissa about her surprise party.

    B: But I didn't realize it was _____ to be a secret.

    (a) imitated
    (b) prepared
    (c) supposed
    (d) explained

16. A: I'm amazed that the man doesn't feel sorry for his crimes.

    B: I know. He hasn't shown any _____.

    (a) malice
    (b) remorse
    (c) acquittal
    (d) fortitude

17. A: Are you free to help with this report?

    B: Sorry, I'm _____ other work.

    (a) hooked on
    (b) tied up with
    (c) putting aside
    (d) holding out on

18. A: We should make a formal complaint about our overtime hours.

    B: Right. Let's go and _____ one together.

    (a) lodge
    (b) instill
    (c) press
    (d) enact

19. A: Tim is such a sociable guy, isn't he?

    B: Yes, he's very _____.

    (a) lenient
    (b) careless
    (c) hesitant
    (d) outgoing

20. A: This wine tastes stronger than usual.

    B: Yes, it's a(n) _____ wine.

    (a) fortified
    (b) magnified
    (c) discharged
    (d) emphasized

21. A: I read that book you recommended. It was great.

    B: Yes, it's very _____.

    (a) infusing
    (b) excising
    (c) conniving
    (d) engrossing

22. A: Would you care for some peanuts?

    B: No. I'm allergic to them. I _____ all over.

    (a) slip up
    (b) wind up
    (c) chill out
    (d) break out

23. A: Hi, George. So, you're back from France already?

    B: Yeah, it was just a week long _____.

    (a) sojourn
    (b) chasm
    (c) locus
    (d) ebb

24. A: Should I take 3rd street or keep driving and turn at 4th?

    B: Turn at 4th. You'll _____ heavy traffic on 3rd.

    (a) exert
    (b) detour
    (c) confront
    (d) apprehend

25. A: This meat is hard to chew.

    B: I guess I should've _____ it more.

    (a) crushed
    (b) sanitized
    (c) tenderized
    (d) fragmented

26. Blast Off is an energy drink that _____ double the caffeine to help you stay awake longer.

    (a) puts
    (b) makes
    (c) contains
    (d) presents

27. The government should _____ taxes so people can have more money to spend.

    (a) lower
    (b) value
    (c) flatten
    (d) involve

28. A ten-mile-long traffic jam occurred after police _____ the highway.

    (a) closed
    (b) kept
    (c) quit
    (d) led

29. Although the Internet is useful for finding a job, do not _____ other important avenues such as newspapers and networking.

    (a) judge
    (b) relieve
    (c) neglect
    (d) suspect

30. The two secret agents attacked each other over the course of the movie, each in turn _____ the upper hand.

    (a) standing
    (b) fighting
    (c) making
    (d) gaining

31. With an account at our online store, payment is made _____ with one simple click.

    (a) suitable
    (b) optional
    (c) unlimited
    (d) convenient

32. The meal was not as good as _____ and nor was the service, which was disappointing after a tiring day of sightseeing.

    (a) granted
    (b) realized
    (c) expected
    (d) subjected

33. In American law, everyone is innocent until _____ guilty.

    (a) chosen
    (b) proven
    (c) reasoned
    (d) exhibited

34. The company's upcoming events are _____ on the bulletin board.

(a) posted
(b) folded
(c) packed
(d) fastened

35. Those who commit credit card fraud must be brought to _____ for their crime.

(a) justice
(b) utility
(c) denial
(d) vice

36. The war _____ the male labor force so greatly that women had to staff factories.

(a) depleted
(b) debriefed
(c) disbursed
(d) discharged

37. This pet store _____ in rare tropical fish and other creatures.

(a) interacts
(b) mediates
(c) diversifies
(d) specializes

38. The research team discovered a cave that ancient artists had _____ with a variety of drawings.

(a) scuffed
(b) revered
(c) adorned
(d) varnished

39. Deserts are home to a fascinating variety of plants and animals that have adapted to the _____ environment.

(a) harsh
(b) crude
(c) absent
(d) dented

40. The computer network has backup systems so that hardware malfunctions do not _____ work in the office.

(a) irritate
(b) predict
(c) disrupt
(d) reclaim

41. Some parents have the attitude that children should be allowed their freedom and therefore rarely _____ them.

(a) match
(b) soothe
(c) lighten
(d) discipline

42. Scientists remain _____ about alleged sightings of the ivory-billed woodpecker, as it has been extinct for over 60 years.

(a) stable
(b) uncertain
(c) unsuitable
(d) sympathetic

43. The hurricane _____ the town, leaving few houses standing intact.

(a) delayed
(b) reversed
(c) restricted
(d) destroyed

44. The term "Orientalism" is not _____ by some specialists today because it suggests the perspective of European colonialism.

(a) used
(b) shown
(c) gathered
(d) obtained

45. Corporate restructuring and layoffs are still _____ and will be dealt with at the next board meeting.

(a) sullen
(b) ornate
(c) fiddling
(d) pending

46. Long walks in the park help people empty the mind and return home replenished and _____.

(a) revived
(b) disgraced
(c) subsumed
(d) congregated

47. The band's performance so thrilled the crowd that it would not be _____ with a mere three encores.

(a) jilted
(b) sated
(c) wielded
(d) apprised

48. The unanticipated side effects of drug interactions can sometimes cause medical _____ worse than the illness itself.

(a) compounds
(b) constituents
(c) commodities
(d) complications

49. Joe was a(n) _____ basketball fan who always bought season tickets to watch his favorite team.

(a) dire
(b) avid
(c) abject
(d) potent

50. The crash of a Comair jet on Sunday ended the company's longest safety _____ in aviation history.

(a) streak
(b) channel
(c) terminal
(d) segment

This is the end of the Vocabulary section. Do NOT move on to the Reading Comprehension section until instructed to do so. You are NOT allowed to turn to any other section of the test.

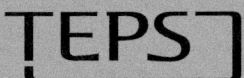

READING
COMPREHENSION

Part I   Questions 1—16

Read the passage. Then choose the option that best completes the passage.

1. There are many ways that you can get involved in _____.
    Even small steps can make a big difference. You can do little things like recycling all
    you can. Take public transport or even walk rather than use your car. Make a small
    donation to organizations working to save threatened species. Even if it is small, do
    something today to help the Earth and the life it supports.

    (a) being a global citizen
    (b) protecting our planet
    (c) helping needy children
    (d) saving near-extinct animals

2. Many kids would love a pair of the latest air pump running shoes, but parents
    question whether they are really worth their hefty price tag. They might look good,
    but there is no evidence that air pump runners make kids jump higher or give
    any more support than other good-quality athletic shoes. It seems hard, then, to
    _____, especially when the shoes actually offer no
    special advantages.

    (a) justify their price
    (b) criticize their design
    (c) export them worldwide
    (d) get kids to really like them

3. Results from surveys conducted on tobacco use in Sri Lanka from 1999 to 2007 indicate
    that young people are _____. Over the survey period, a
    number of changes could be identified. The percentage of students aged 13-15 who were
    smokers dropped from 4.0% to 1.2%. Also, the percentage of non-smokers in this group
    who said they might start smoking fell from 5.1% to 3.7%. These results reflect the
    effect of tobacco-control measures and a growing public recognition of the dangers of
    smoking.

    (a) turning away from tobacco
    (b) advocates of tobacco's pleasures
    (c) resisting anti-smoking campaigns
    (d) ignorant of smoking-related diseases

4. In Europe, people began to eat with utensils during medieval times. At first, utensils accompanied hand-eating: that is, people would bring their own knives to dinner parties and the host would supply a spoon, but hands were still used. By the 14th century, the fork was introduced and commonly used among the wealthy in Italy, who carried it in a special case. Following this change, people began to consider eating with the hands as uncivilized, and so _____.

(a) more table rules were introduced
(b) they stopped the spread of germs
(c) utensils replaced hands for eating
(d) they switched back to using spoons

5.

Dear Ann,

Why is it that after a couple has dated for two years, everyone assumes that they are ready to get married and that the woman is anxiously waiting for the ring? I am 31 years old and have been in a relationship for three years. I'm happy with things as they are. _____ when family and friends pity me because I haven't been so "lucky" as to get engaged. What should I do?

Sincerely,
Marsha

(a) I get very hesitant
(b) I have no problem
(c) It really annoys me
(d) It often humors me

6. _____ has come from piecing together their prehistoric migratory patterns. Researchers have established that approximately 11 million years ago the cat family emerged in Asia. Two million years after that, cats advanced from Siberia into Alaska, across the ancient Beringian land bridge, and spread across North America. Over time, several American cat lineages migrated back to Asia, and in the process different cat species evolved, such as lynxes, lions, leopards, as well as what we know as the common house cat.

(a) Insight into the evolution of cats
(b) Evidence for the loss of tiger numbers
(c) Knowledge on the predatory habits of cats
(d) Proof that cats originated in North America

7. The following report outlines progress made in 126 countries around the world to combat the HIV/ AIDS crisis. Some countries have greatly reduced instances of HIV/ AIDS with sophisticated prevention programs, but they have been slow in making treatments available. Other countries have widespread treatment programs, but their HIV/ AIDS prevention programs are still in their infancy. Thus,

    _____.

    (a) further data is needed to provide more conclusive results
    (b) the global HIV/ AIDS crisis is worse than previously thought
    (c) a disparity exists in different countries' responses to HIV/ AIDS
    (d) efforts in fighting HIV/ AIDS are proving remarkably successful

8. My 75-year-old father was confined to a wheelchair following a stroke three years ago, and my mother was too frail to look after him. She tried but just did not have the capability, so he had to be admitted to a nursing home. Both he and Mom found separation extremely stressful. So after a few months, we brought him home. By that time I had organized some part-time homecare at a reasonable rate and had some modifications done to their home. After sorting out a few other issues, they now enjoy _____. Dad does copper enameling, and Mom potters around in the garden.

    (a) a healthy marriage without the conflicts of the past
    (b) a new home similar to the one they had left behind
    (c) a relatively comfortable home life that suits them
    (d) a busy lifestyle with plenty of outdoor activities

9. The fan was an essential part of female dress for several centuries, and it served as more than just a fashion accessory. Women at the time could not easily speak their minds without breaking social rules, but by holding the fan in a special way they could convey anything from a flirtatious invitation to a declaration of love. In other words, women

    _____.

    (a) had a variety of different types of fans
    (b) flirted with men from wealthy families
    (c) were more socially liberated in that period
    (d) used the fan as a means of secret communication

10. Scientists predict that _____ because of global warming. They assert that some areas will experience increasingly more powerful storms and rising sea levels, and they point out that even now areas only slightly above sea level—like the Louisiana shoreline—are seeing their protective fringe of ocean marshes and barrier islands being swallowed up. In fact, since the 1930s, some 1,900 square miles of Louisiana's coastal wetlands have vanished beneath the Gulf of Mexico.

(a) some US coastlines are at risk of disappearing
(b) weather patterns throughout the US could fluctuate
(c) thousands of ocean-front properties will be damaged
(d) fragile coastal water ecosystems will get contaminated

11. In *Florence Nightingale: Her Life and Work*, biographer Mark Bostridge explores the life of a woman that many know only from her work. He argues that the common perception of Florence Nightingale as a pioneering nurse and heroine of hospital reform is far too one-dimensional. It overlooks her human qualities and personal life, such as how she was torn between a desire for fame and a sense of duty to her family. Indeed, few know that her chosen career conflicted with her family's wishes and the social demand for marriage. Thus, Bostridge _____.

(a) gives us a more balanced assessment of Nightingale's life
(b) fails in this biography of Nightingale because of his biases
(c) holds nothing back in revealing Nightingale's personal flaws
(d) shows the exceptional qualities that made Nightingale a heroine

12. Marion Worldwide has a proven track record of providing advertising and marketing communication services to internationally renowned businesses and organizations. We have the creativity and the technological know-how to give you the best integrated print and digital marketing solutions for leveraging your market position. Regardless of whether you require expert help with an isolated communications strategy or a turnkey product campaign, you can depend on Marion Worldwide. Contact us now

_____.

(a) to schedule your online legal consultation
(b) to book a seat at this latest marketing seminar
(c) for the best in innovative promotional solutions
(d) for more information on our publishing services

13. The economic council is against the mandating of government-controlled price levels for wheat. Artificially regulated wheat prices will only burden the economy and promote inefficient production. In contrast, allowing free market forces to prevail would give efficacious producers the advantage they rightly deserve. Free market competition would also keep prices down and benefit consumers. Therefore, the council believes the state should _____.

(a) shelve the mandate to regulate wheat prices
(b) allow the dispute with local farmers to escalate
(c) reward producers unable to support themselves
(d) decrease import duties on wheat and other grains

14. Bacteria propel themselves forward by using tail-like appendages called flagella. They stop moving by disengaging the flagella with a molecular "clutch." When Bacteria stop, they form colonies on objects, and this creates a greater infection risk to humans. So scientists are hoping to work out a way to prevent bacteria from being able to disengage their flagella. So far they have identified the gene responsible for the molecular clutch. This could help them find a way of _____.

(a) detecting the presence of bacteria on various objects
(b) keeping bacteria on the move and unable to colonize
(c) developing a new antiseptic treatment to kill bacteria
(d) preventing bacteria from tricking the immune system

15. In 1918, Russia's Czar Nicholas II and his family were shot and buried by revolutionaries. Later, their remains were uncovered, except for those of Crown Prince Alexei, the Czar's son. People pondered what had become of the 13-year-old. Some thought he had survived. Others believed his remains were buried elsewhere. _____, a discovery of bones in a Russian forest led to the mystery being solved. DNA tests confirmed that they were indeed the bones of Prince Alexei.

(a) Similarly
(b) Therefore
(c) In the end
(d) As a result

16. The way music is composed and played is often influenced by dramatic historical, political and cultural events. Composers often respond with music that is also dramatic or is of a radically new form. A classic example is Beethoven, whose music was influenced by the French Revolution and later the rise and fall of Napoleon. _____, changes in musical theory and practice can foreshadow political changes, at least according to Plato. In *The Republic* he wrote, *"When modes of music change, the fundamental laws of the state always change with them."*

(a) Thus
(b) Instead
(c) Regardless
(d) Conversely

Part II **Questions 17—37**

Read the passage and the question. Then choose the option that best answers the question.

17. Bread has been a cornerstone of the human diet from the earliest times. As a result, it has become a part of cultural traditions. It has long been a part of religious practices, such as the Jewish custom of blessing and breaking bread at meal times. The word bread is also used in the traditional expressions of many languages. The expression "our daily bread" from the Lord's Prayer refers to our necessities in life, and in colloquial English, the term "breadwinner" refers to the main wage earner of a household.

Q: What is the main topic of the passage?
(a) The origins of bread eating
(b) The reasons why bread is popular
(c) The uses of bread in different religions
(d) The influence of bread in human culture

18. A style of sculpture and painting called "academic art" emerged out of European art universities and academies. It was associated most notably with the conservative artistic standards set by the French Academy in the 19th century. Academic art embraced classicism, so it tended to be realistic in style and often featured moments from history or biblical or mythological subjects. Among the most famous exponents of academic art were the painters Jean-Leon Gerome and William Bouguereau.

Q: What is the main topic of the passage?
(a) A brief background to academic art
(b) A study of the appeal of academic art
(c) The artists best known for academic art
(d) The influence of France on academic art

19. It is common knowledge that the US and Europe will face a dramatic increase in their elderly populations over the next half century. However, the UN's annual "State of World Population" report points out a lesser known problem: the rest of the world will face a similar challenge later on. By 2050, nearly 20% of the population of Asia and Latin America will be over 65, and Africa will also see its percentage of pensioners double between now and then.

Q: What is the best title for the passage?
(a) The Burden of the Elderly
(b) The Aging Global Population
(c) The Oldest People in the World
(d) The World Population Explosion

20.

Dear Mr. Stone,

Thank you for subscribing to *Language Links*, the magazine dedicated to language-learning for business. Our magazine recognizes that globalization has created a business environment in which employers favor applicants who can speak more than one language. You'll appreciate the many tips and tricks we feature every week to help you quickly learn the language you need. Welcome to *Language Links*!

Sincerely,
D. Z. Thompson,
Managing Editor

Q: What is the email mainly saying about *Language Links*?
(a) It features useful articles on linguistics.
(b) It helps readers understand the business world.
(c) It keeps up with the latest news on globalization.
(d) It focuses on second-language acquisition for business.

21. Coaching can be an exciting and rewarding career. And there are all kinds of coaching positions out there that have nothing to do with sports. Coaches are needed to guide anything from debate teams to musical groups to a wide variety of team-oriented programs for kids and adults. Do you have leadership and people skills? Are you multitalented? Then, Apex Coaching will find the right coaching position for you. Suitable applicants will receive extra training. Contact Apex now at 555-8675 for more information.

Q: What is the main idea of the advertisement?
(a) Apex offers varied coaching opportunities.
(b) More people are required as sports coaches.
(c) Apex conducts many kinds of coaching courses.
(d) Coaching in many fields can help children develop.

22. A new study suggests that if breast cancer patients were to avoid gaining weight, they could have a better chance of surviving the disease. Researchers examined the history of more than 4,000 women diagnosed with breast cancer from the years 1989 to 2002. They found that for every 11 pounds of weight patients gained after they had been diagnosed with breast cancer, their risk of dying went up 14%. The finding points to a strong relationship between weight gain and the risk of dying from breast cancer, but further research is necessary.

Q: What is the passage mainly about?
(a) Diet and exercise can help fight cancer.
(b) Being overweight could cause breast cancer.
(c) Breast cancer diagnoses have been on the decline.
(d) Weight gain may increase breast cancer fatality rates.

23. The Arizona Trail is a diverse and scenic trail from Mexico to Utah measuring over 800 miles and stretching across Arizona. Designed for hiking, horseback riding, mountain biking, and cross country skiing, it spans the varied mountain ranges and ecosystems of Arizona. Most people start and stop at certain points along the trail, although there are rare individuals who choose to travel its full length. Trail difficulty ranges from easy to strenuous, and elevations span from 1,700 feet at the Gila River to 9,600 feet at the San Francisco Peaks.

Q: Which of the following is correct according to the passage?
(a) The trail begins in Arizona.
(b) People travel the trail by car.
(c) Few travel the entire trail course.
(d) The difficulty of the trail is average.

24. Want to advertise your company? Forget newspapers, radio, television, or the Internet. Why not show off your company's innovativeness in the sky? With our Cloud-Ad machine, your company's logo can be seen hundreds of feet above the crowds. Guaranteed to attract attention, a Cloud-Ad machine emits eco-friendly white foam "clouds" into the sky as big as four feet across. They can be shaped any way you like. Imagine—with a half-dozen machines, we can fill the sky with hundreds of your corporate logos. Call a Cloud-Ad representative now for a quote at 476-9988.

Q: Which of the following is correct about the Cloud-Ad?
(a) It has many different types of colors.
(b) It is shown four feet above ground.
(c) It does not harm the environment.
(d) It is limited in shape.

25. Charles Goodyear's obsession with making a durable rubber began in 1834, but he suffered many failures over the years. His businesses collapsed, he was briefly imprisoned for debt, and his family endured constant poverty. Then one day, in 1839, while experimenting in his kitchen, he made a breakthrough. He was boiling rubber gum mixed with sulfur on his stove and accidentally dropped some of it on a hotplate. It suddenly solidified into a solid rubber material, and with that, Goodyear had discovered the secret to producing a durable rubber.

Q: Which of the following is correct about Goodyear according to the passage?
(a) His early attempts at making durable rubber were very profitable.
(b) His family suffered while he attempted to make a lasting rubber.
(c) He made his discovery in a laboratory behind his house.
(d) He succeeded after dropping a hotplate in his kitchen.

26. The quiet life of the country has never appealed to me. City born and bred, I have always seen the country as something you look at through a train window or visit on a rare occasion. Unlike me, my friends sometimes talk of their hopes of living in the country, expressing a desire for a peaceful and healthy life. In fact, one of my friends actually tried living in the country. He went to live and work in a small country town, but he left after only six months. It turned out country living bored him. It was just too quiet and peaceful.

Q: Which of the following is correct about the writer?
(a) He thinks country life would be ideal.
(b) He travels to the country infrequently.
(c) He expresses a desire for country life.
(d) He has a friend who lives in the country.

27. A 175,000-year-old jawbone of an adult Neanderthal found last year in France has revealed ancient roots of caregiving for the injured or infirm. Hollow pockets in the lower part of the jawbone showed that severe abscesses had eaten into it. The adult individual had also been missing teeth for some time before death. These conditions would have been very painful and would have made chewing almost impossible. That means someone probably helped to feed him or her. Evidence of Neanderthal caregiving has been found before, but this jawbone provides the oldest example of it by about 120,000 years.

Q: Which of the following is correct about the jawbone according to the passage?
(a) It indicates how human teeth have evolved.
(b) It reveals the dental care of the Neanderthals.
(c) It shows evidence of a wound to the upper jaw.
(d) It is the oldest proof of Neanderthal caregiving.

28.

Dear Mr. Malloy,

This letter is a formal notice to inform you that you are in default of your obligation to repay the sum of $5,000 loaned to you by The Money Store. This amount is now one year overdue, and you have continually ignored requests to repay it. Unless the amount is repaid in full within ten days of the date of this letter, we will have no alternative but to exercise our rights by law to enforce such payment.

Sincerely,
Chuck Martel
Account Manager
The Money Store

Q: Which of the following is correct according to the letter?
(a) Mr. Malloy sent a letter to the Money Store.
(b) Mr. Malloy's debt is a few months overdue.
(c) The Money Store expects payment in one week.
(d) The Money Store is prepared to take legal action.

29. Jose Delgado was a Spanish professor of physiology who studied the electrical stimulation of the brain using radio transmissions. In 1963, he conducted a famous brain stimulation experiment on a bull in Spain. Delgado attached a tiny receiver with electrodes to the bull's head, which he controlled with a remote control. When the bull charged at him, Delgado pressed a button that electronically stimulated the bull's brain and caused it to stop. According to Delgado, the electrical stimulus had caused the bull to lose its aggressive instinct, but skeptics claimed it was the electrical shock that made the bull stop.

Q: Which of the following is correct about Delgado according to the passage?
(a) He conducted the experiment in Spain in the late 60s.
(b) He studied ways the brain produces radio transmissions.
(c) He electronically stimulated a bull's brain with electrodes.
(d) He convinced skeptics that he could change a bull's instincts.

30. The Food and Drug Administration (FDA) announced Wednesday the launch of a program to monitor the use of protein concentrates made from rice and wheat in food production. The program is in response to the contamination of pet foods with the protein concentrates. An FDA official said that there was no evidence of human foods being contaminated with rice or wheat proteins and that the program is simply a cautionary measure. However, monitoring should ensure that all manufacturers are aware of the possibility of contamination, and enable them to take extra care when using protein additives.

Q: Which of the following is correct according to the passage?
(a) The FDA has banned the use of all protein concentrates.
(b) The FDA's program began because of contaminated pet food.
(c) Manufacturers found some proof of contamination in human food.
(d) Manufacturers were never warned that protein additives could be tainted.

31. Scientists are constantly searching for ways to produce fuel cheaply. One method being researched is based on the way that microscopic organisms help turn a corn mixture into sugars and then into fuel. That is how ethanol is produced, a fuel that can be used in place of gas. But making ethanol involves the natural process of bacterial fermentation, and to produce hydrocarbon fuels in such a way would have to involve synthetic biology to engineer a new kind of bacteria. To that end, scientists are experimenting with adding genes to bacteria to alter their behavior.

Q: Which of the following is correct according to the passage?
(a) Scientists can now make a cheaper fuel.
(b) Ethanol may be replaced by sugar as a fuel.
(c) Ethanol is manufactured through fermentation.
(d) Scientists warn against altering bacterial behavior.

32. In Peru, researchers excavating an ancient Inca site at the ruins of a stone fortress called Sacsayhuaman have uncovered a unique temple. The researchers believe the temple as well as the fortress was built by the Killke people, a pre-Incan culture, around 1100 AD. They also think it once contained mummies and various religious idols, which is proof that the Sacsayhuaman fortress was not just a military installation. It was obviously used for spiritual ceremonies as well. The temple had 11 rooms and covered an area of some 250 square meters.

Q: Which of the following is correct according to the passage?
(a) The Killke were responsible for building Sacsayhuaman fortress.
(b) The Inca culture flourished in the region before the Killke culture.
(c) The Sacsayhuaman fortress was solely used for spiritual ceremonies.
(d) Researchers are unsure about the structural composition of the temple.

33. When you are preparing to sell your home, some simple improvements can make for a quick sale. First, make your house look roomy. Moving furniture out and tidying up clutter will make the available space seem bigger. Second, make sure everything is neat, and clean the house thoroughly to make it fresh and odor-free. If need be, repaint the interior or replace carpets or flooring. Outside, do some landscaping: add flowers, trim bushes, and mow your lawn. The key is to think of your house as a product you want to sell.

Q: What can be inferred about homebuyers from the passage?
(a) They are more critical of homes nowadays.
(b) They will not bargain if a house looks good.
(c) They care more about price than appearance.
(d) They care about the house's appearance in and out.

34. At 90 years old, John Whitemore is an athletic champion. He holds several world records in the shot put, discus, and javelin—all sports he took up at 70 years old when a bad knee confined him to stationary field events. Before that he was a prizewinning swimmer and tennis player. He says what he likes best about competing is winning. John is currently the only track-and-field participant in his age group in the United States, so he wins every time.

Q: What can be inferred about Whitemore from the passage?
(a) He is not likely to break any more records.
(b) He was not interested in sports as a young man.
(c) He injured his knee while in a javelin competition.
(d) He would still be a winner even if he performed badly.

35. Among societies emerging from traditionally low average incomes, it is common to see what is called conspicuous consumption. This refers to the way people spend lavishly on goods to show off their prosperity. In other words, they purchase luxury goods to display social status, or a desired status, rather than for the actual utility of those goods. Conspicuous consumption partly explains why emerging economies like Russia and China are such hot markets for luxury items today.

Q: What can be inferred from the passage?
(a) Most people dislike showing off newly acquired wealth.
(b) People in emerging economies tend to be frugal spenders.
(c) Some people base their self-worth on their spending power.
(d) People in developed countries are very careless with money.

36. The Ministry of Health announced today that it is set to launch a new program under which British schoolchildren from low-income families will receive free fruit each day. With the program the ministry hopes to ensure that these children, who commonly have poor diets, have regular access to healthy foods. Hundreds of children in 35 schools in London and Leicester will be the first to receive the free fruit from this week. Studies suggest that the initiative could lead to a 20% reduction in deaths from heart disease, stroke and cancer in adulthood.

Q: What can be inferred from the passage?
(a) London and Leicester have Britain's highest child mortality rates.
(b) Children from low-income families do not have balanced diets.
(c) People in low-income areas deliberately ignore good nutrition.
(d) Children these days generally have healthy eating habits.

37. Whether creationism has a place in science classrooms was the subject of intense debate at a recent Texas State Board of Education meeting. The board was reviewing new curriculum guidelines for science courses in Texas schools that include the mentioning of creationist ideas. Though a decision has not been reached, critics say that teaching creationism in the classroom paves the way for alternative explanations to replace more scientific, evolution-based ones. Further, they claim that the guidelines amount to an unnecessary modification of the science curriculum and a backward step in education.

Q: What can be inferred from the article?
(a) The Board members are all free from religious bias.
(b) Critics' opinions on the new curriculum will prevail.
(c) The Board is sure to adopt the new science guidelines.
(d) Critics believe the new curriculum guidelines denigrate science.

Part III **Questions 38—40**

Read the passage. Then identify the option that does NOT belong.

38. The electric-powered Segway is a unique personal transporter that runs on two wheels paired side-by-side. (a) Designer Dean Kamen once described it as the world's first self-balancing human transporter. (b) Computers and motors in the base of the device keep the machine upright when in use. (c) It runs at about 20 kilometers an hour and offers an alternative form of travel. (d) When moving, motors driving the wheels adjust automatically to keep the machine in perfect balance.

39. Ernest Hemingway was a prolific writer who wrote nine novels, over 100 short stories, and non-fiction. (a) He became famous after the publication of the semi-autobiographical *The Sun Also Rises* in 1926, now considered a modernist masterpiece. (b) More novels, also based on his personal experiences, followed up until 1940 and similarly met with critical acclaim. (c) Throughout his life, Hemingway had been a heavy drinker and succumbed to physical ailments and alcoholism in his later years. (d) His literary output declined in later years, but he nonetheless received a Pulitzer Prize and won the Nobel Prize in Literature in 1954.

40. Swiss philosopher Jean Jacques Rousseau's ideas about the sexes tend to make some of today's readers somewhat uncomfortable. (a) He claims that equality of the sexes is a foolish idea because there are clear differences between men and women. (b) Women, he argues, have the sole purpose of being dutiful wives and nurturing mothers. (c) Rousseau goes on to attack a series of notions about education and culture prevalent in his day. (d) Many today would label such views as chauvinistic, but, in fact, Rousseau was only voicing commonly held beliefs of his time.

This is the end of the Reading Comprehension section. Please remain seated until the proctor has instructed otherwise. You are NOT allowed to turn to any other section of the test.

서울대 최신기출 4

Listening Comprehension

Grammar

Vocabulary

Reading Comprehension

TEPS

LISTENING COMPREHENSION

Part I   Questions 1—15

You will now hear fifteen conversation fragments, each made up of a single spoken statement followed by four spoken responses. Choose the most appropriate response to the statement.

Part II   Questions 16—30

You will now hear fifteen conversation fragments, each made up of three spoken statements followed by four spoken responses. Choose the most appropriate response to complete the conversation.

Part III **Questions 31—45**

You will now hear fifteen complete conversations. For each item, you will hear a conversation and its corresponding question, both of which will be read twice. Then you will hear four options which will be read only once. Choose the option that best answers the question.

Part IV **Questions 46—60**

You will now hear fifteen spoken monologues. For each item, you will hear a monologue and its corresponding question, both of which will be read twice. Then you will hear four options which will be read only once. Choose the option that best answers the question.

TEPS

GRAMMAR

DIRECTIONS

This part of the exam tests your grammar skills. You will have 25 minutes to complete the 50 questions. Be sure to follow the directions given by the proctor.

Part I   **Questions 1—20**

Choose the best answer for the blank.

1. A: Come and watch this movie on TV with me.
   B: No, _____ that movie already.

   (a) I see
   (b) I've seen
   (c) I was seeing
   (d) I'll be seeing

2. A: What's your team's opinion about the coach?
   B: All of us _____ that he should be fired.

   (a) think
   (b) thinks
   (c) has thought
   (d) was thinking

3. A: Did you get the message I left for you?
   B: Of course I _____.

   (a) got
   (b) did
   (c) did it
   (d) did get

4. A: Why are you late again?
   B: Sorry. _____ the bus.

   (a) I miss
   (b) I missed
   (c) I had missed
   (d) I was missing

5. A: As your doctor, I urge you _____.
   B: I know I should, but it isn't easy.

   (a) exercise regular
   (b) regular exercising
   (c) exercising regularly
   (d) to exercise regularly

6. A: Was your hotel close to the ocean?
   B: Yes, it was _____ on the beach.

   (a) so
   (b) very
   (c) right
   (d) much

7. A: What happened to the _____ a laptop?
   B: He got impatient and left.

   (a) customer wants to buy
   (b) wanting customer of buying
   (c) customer who wanted to buy
   (d) buying customer who wanted

8. A: I can't decide whether to buy the red or blue dress.
   B: _____ one you buy, it'll suit you well.

   (a) That
   (b) What
   (c) However
   (d) Whichever

9. A: Why did you order so much food?

 B: I haven't eaten _____ since early this morning.

 (a) it
 (b) none
 (c) nothing
 (d) anything

10. A: What did you do this afternoon?

 B: I took _____ along the beach.

 (a) walk
 (b) a walk
 (c) the walk
 (d) some walk

11. A: _____ here?

 B: I'm not sure yet. Maybe 9 pm.

 (a) Will you be staying until what time
 (b) Until what time you will be staying
 (c) Staying you will be until what time
 (d) Until what time will you be staying

12. A: How did you get a bruise on your forehead?

 B: I tripped, _____ my head on a table.

 (a) bumped
 (b) to bump
 (c) bumping
 (d) have bumped

13. A: What did you say when Andrea complained about her schedule?

 B: I suggested she _____ to the boss about it.

 (a) talk
 (b) talks
 (c) talked
 (d) to talk

14. A: Which of these pictures do you like best?

 B: I like the one _____.

 (a) from a bridge fishes a man
 (b) of a man fishes on a bridge
 (c) from a bridge a man fishing
 (d) of a man fishing from a bridge

15. A: I'll never understand why Alice likes Pete.

 B: I agree. She _____ do a lot better.

 (a) will
 (b) may
 (c) could
 (d) would

16. A: How do you like living in Seoul?

 B: It's a great city _____!

 (a) of a night life amazing
 (b) with a night life amazing
 (c) with an amazing night life
 (d) and amazing is a night life

17. A: Last night's work party was rowdy.

 B: Yeah, people drank _____ too much.

 (a) way
 (b) such
 (c) quite
 (d) pretty

18. A: Please have your team finish the job as soon as possible.

 B: I'll make sure they complete it _____.

 (a) in the first of the morning tomorrow
 (b) first thing tomorrow in morning
 (c) as first thing of the morning
 (d) first thing in the morning

19. A: I can't believe what you've done with this apartment.

    B: _____ could be, I had to spruce it up.

    (a) As drab as
    (b) Being as drab as
    (c) It was as drab as
    (d) It being as drab as

20. A: The bill for my flowers should be $32, but it says $42.

    B: That's because the bill includes _____.

    (a) a delivery ten dollars extra
    (b) ten more dollars of delivery
    (c) an extra ten dollars for delivery
    (d) delivery of them extra ten dollars

Part II **Questions 21—40**

Choose the best answer for the blank.

---

21. Helen's computer skills were poor, _____ she was not considered for the job.

    (a) while
    (b) since
    (c) but
    (d) so

22. To avoid infection, tooth loss and other complications, people who have a history of cavities _____ get a dental x-ray taken every year.

    (a) should
    (b) would
    (c) might
    (d) could

23. As technological advances continue around the world, a developing nation has no choice but _____.

    (a) globalize
    (b) globalizes
    (c) globalizing
    (d) to globalize

24. The movie's large cast and fast-moving action may be _____ for some viewers.

    (a) confuse
    (b) confused
    (c) confusing
    (d) to confuse

25. The supersonic Concorde used to cross the Atlantic Ocean in much less time than _____ passenger airplanes.

    (a) another
    (b) every
    (c) other
    (d) few

26. The chronic shortage of engineers _____ in Germany, and many companies may begin recruiting from India.

    (a) has worsened
    (b) was worsening
    (c) have worsened
    (d) were worsening

27. People who live in Miami are
_____ Spanish as English.

(a) as likely as speaking
(b) likely as speaking
(c) as likely to speak
(d) to speak as likely

28. Glaciers are changing the shape of the
earth and _____ doing so for
millions of years.

(a) are
(b) were
(c) had been
(d) have been

29. In most history books, the rise of
humanism _____ as a significant
part of the transition from the Middle
Ages to the Renaissance.

(a) had been cited
(b) is citing
(c) is cited
(d) cites

30. Blood delivers the food and oxygen
_____ the body's cells use to
produce energy.

(a) that
(b) what
(c) whom
(d) whose

31. Everyone in the debate insisted that
their arguments were based on solid
facts, leaving listeners struggling
_____.

(a) whose evidence decide to believe
(b) decide to believe in whose evidence
(c) to decide to believe whose evidence
(d) to decide whose evidence to believe

32. The Aztecs built a great city in
_____ is now Mexico.

(a) where
(b) which
(c) what
(d) who

33. _____ lose our money but also
our credit cards and driver's licenses.

(a) Did we not only
(b) We not only did
(c) Not only did we
(d) Not that we did only

34. Death rates from cancer have been
dropping _____ an average of
2.1% a year in the United States.

(a) in
(b) by
(c) for
(d) with

35. The study of fossils has made it possible
_____.

(a) to know to rocks relative ages
(b) relative ages of rocks to know
(c) for relative ages of rocks to know
(d) to know the relative ages of rocks

36. Since there _____ no
improvement in the economy from
January to the present, investors are
becoming worried.

(a) is
(b) will be
(c) has been
(d) had been

G

RAMMAR

37. _____ is a huge challenge, as every webmaster knows.

(a) Up-to-date keeping a website
(b) A website keeping up-to-date
(c) Keeping a website up-to-date
(d) Keeping of up-to-date website

38. The lesson was on syllogisms, _____ logic is used to persuade others to agree with a certain argument.

(a) since
(b) though
(c) whereby
(d) therefore

39. Farms should separate _____ from other animals to control influenza.

(a) poultry
(b) poultries
(c) a poultry
(d) the poultries

40. Plants that have been sprayed with DDT, a powerful pesticide, _____ not safe to eat.

(a) is
(b) are
(c) is being
(d) are being

Identify the option that contains an awkward expression or an error in grammar.

41. (a) A: I wish I can come to your birthday party on Friday.
    (b) B: Me too. It's a shame you won't be able to make it.
    (c) A: Everyone's told me I'll be missing out on a good time.
    (d) B: That's right. I've got a lot of fun things planned.

42. (a) A: Friday's finally here! Let's have a drink tonight.
    (b) B: Thank you, but I've decided not to drink anymore.
    (c) A: Really? I'm surprised you've given it up completely.
    (d) B: It's for my health. I'm going to quit smoke, too.

43. (a) A: You're so good at making cookies. These taste great!
    (b) B: I'm glad you like them. I made them this morning.
    (c) A: Maybe you could give to me the recipe sometime.
    (d) B: Sure, I'd be happy to. They're not hard to make.

44. (a) A: Do you know Jenny's phone number?
    (b) B: No, sorry. I can't remember it right now.
    (c) A: Oh, no. I have to call her right away. It's urgent.
    (d) B: Then just look her up on the phone book.

45. (a) A: How do you like my new coat?
    (b) B: I love it! The style and cut are very flattering.
    (c) A: But what do you think of the color?
    (d) B: That shade of blue looks really nicely on you.

Part IV Questions 46—50

Identify the option that contains an awkward expression or an error in grammar.

46. (a) Upon receipt of your booking, we will send you an invoice and reserve you a seat. (b) Make sure you check your invoice, confirmed that the dates and other information are correct. (c) If all is in order, you must then send your payment within 10 working days to keep your seat. (d) Halo Bus Company will notify you once your payment is received and forward you all seating details.

47. (a) The leaves of many trees are actually different shades of orange, red, or yellow all year long. (b) But we could not see these colors because leaves contain chlorophyll for most of the year. (c) Chlorophyll is the green pigment within leaves that converts sun energy into food for plants. (d) In fall, when the chlorophyll disappears, the hidden colors in leaves are revealed.

48. (a) In 15th-century Portugal, the first great voyages of what is called the "Age of Exploration" began. (b) That was when Prince Henry of Portugal was giving command of the port of Ceuta and its ships. (c) It was he who was behind using Portuguese ships for various expeditions to the west coast of Africa. (d) After his death, expeditions were undertaken that extended around Africa and all the way to India.

49. (a) There are a number of immunizations normally recommending for travelers, though they vary by destination. (b) You should consult your doctor to decide which vaccinations are appropriate for you. (c) Make sure you get this information early enough to get the vaccines you need. (d) It is advisable to get your vaccines six to eight weeks before your trip to allow them to take effect.

50. (a) Many investors put their money into familiar companies like Microsoft, General Electric and Coca-Cola. (b) However, experts recommend putting half of your investment money into stocks of the small companies. (c) They say that if half of your money is invested in this way, you can expect a slightly higher annual return. (d) The catch is that you need to take a long term view, as these kinds of returns do not happen overnight.

This is the end of the Grammar section. Do NOT move on to the next section until instructed to do so. You are NOT allowed to turn to any other section of the test.

TEPS

VOCABULARY

VOCABULARY

Part I **Questions 1—25**

Choose the best answer for the blank.

1. A: I hope we can meet up again soon.
   B: Sure. Let's _____ in touch.

   (a) keep
   (b) hold
   (c) make
   (d) follow

2. A: I'm so sorry I forgot about your birthday.
   B: I guess I can _____ you this time.

   (a) challenge
   (b) forgive
   (c) accept
   (d) allow

3. A: That movie I chose for us to watch was terrible.
   B: I told you to let me _____ one.

   (a) fix
   (b) pick
   (c) grade
   (d) prefer

4. A: Excuse me, do you know if there's a restroom nearby?
   B: I'm afraid I have no _____.

   (a) hint
   (b) idea
   (c) guess
   (d) thought

5. A: The board wants to know how your project is going.
   B: Tell them I'm preparing a _____ on it.

   (a) list
   (b) detail
   (c) report
   (d) present

6. A: Is there any cake left?
   B: Yes, please _____ yourself.

   (a) satisfy
   (b) take
   (c) help
   (d) mix

7. A: I just bought a skirt online, but now I've changed my mind.
   B: Well, _____ the order, then.

   (a) exit
   (b) resist
   (c) cancel
   (d) affirm

8. A: It's late. Are you still working on your paper?
   B: Yeah, I have to _____ tomorrow.

   (a) turn it in
   (b) take it out
   (c) make it up
   (d) show it off

9. A: Hello, it's Stacy calling. Is Janice home?

   B: No, I don't _____ her until later.

   (a) tell
   (b) greet
   (c) expect
   (d) review

10. A: You won't forget to pick up the dry cleaning, will you?

    B: Maybe. You'd better call and _____ me.

    (a) remind
    (b) provide
    (c) warrant
    (d) memorize

11. A: Why don't we eat out tonight?

    B: OK. But this time it's my _____.

    (a) treat
    (b) offer
    (c) trade
    (d) favor

12. A: This soup really could've done with more mushrooms.

    B: Just eat it and stop _____.

    (a) abusing
    (b) rejecting
    (c) expressing
    (d) complaining

13. A: Your fingernails are getting long.

    B: Yes, I know. But I can't find the nail _____.

    (a) clippers
    (b) mowers
    (c) slicers
    (d) rulers

14. A: I'm worried about the vase we put in our check-in luggage.

    B: Me too. I hope the handlers aren't too _____.

    (a) bold
    (b) rough
    (c) naughty
    (d) insensitive

15. A: Why are you going to the Bahamas?

    B: I just need to _____ for a while.

    (a) move up
    (b) close off
    (c) get away
    (d) back down

16. A: I faxed those documents for you.

    B: Thank you so much. I _____ you one.

    (a) raise
    (b) give
    (c) lean
    (d) owe

17. A: Did you call Dr. Jackson's office and make an appointment?

    B: I called, but the _____ told me that she's all booked up.

    (a) operator
    (b) manager
    (c) accountant
    (d) receptionist

18. A: I can't believe I made such a big mistake in front of the class.

    B: Try not to _____ on it.

    (a) attach
    (b) dwell
    (c) hang
    (d) live

19. A: I'm going to win this chess game.

    B: I doubt it. You've never _____ me.

    (a) won
    (b) beaten
    (c) gained
    (d) conquered

20. A: Did you know John's in a coma?

    B: Yeah, he's been _____ for three whole days now.

    (a) unfeeling
    (b) incapable
    (c) inadvisable
    (d) unconscious

21. A: You slept through the best part of the movie!

    B: Oh. I must have _____.

    (a) struck out
    (b) woken up
    (c) dozed off
    (d) slept in

22. A: Once you've had chickenpox, you can't catch it again.

    B: I know. You become _____ to it.

    (a) potent
    (b) immune
    (c) defensive
    (d) infectious

23. A: What happens when tenants don't pay their rent?

    B: Usually, they're _____.

    (a) evicted
    (b) convicted
    (c) evacuated
    (d) discharged

24. A: We loved staying here. This hotel has such a welcoming feel to it.

    B: Thank you, sir. We strive to create a hospitable _____.

    (a) gratuity
    (b) ambience
    (c) camouflage
    (d) spuriousness

25. A: I hate it when people use insults during arguments.

    B: Yeah, _____ are never appropriate.

    (a) putdowns
    (b) breakups
    (c) shortcuts
    (d) blowouts

26. At Showboat Dinner Theater, you will be _____ by singing waiters.

(a) led
(b) sent
(c) served
(d) passed

27. There are many theories, but experts are still not _____ how the ancient Egyptians built the pyramids.

(a) certain
(b) secure
(c) exact
(d) true

28. Investigators found that the director did not earn enough to _____ such a luxurious apartment.

(a) fulfill
(b) invest
(c) afford
(d) enable

29. At our rooftop bar, guests have an excellent _____ of the sun as it sets on the water.

(a) look
(b) view
(c) sight
(d) vision

30. California is an easygoing and tolerant state that _____ every imaginable type of religion, lifestyle and fashion.

(a) prohibits
(b) embraces
(c) overcomes
(d) encounters

31. Brixton High needs a(n) _____ school uniform that students can be proud of.

(a) decent
(b) plentiful
(c) excessive
(d) mediocre

32. The soft, _____ sound of the ocean helped the man fall asleep quickly.

(a) roaring
(b) soothing
(c) tempting
(d) maturing

33. If inflammation of the skin occurs after _____ this lotion, discontinue use and see a doctor.

(a) issuing
(b) pressing
(c) applying
(d) contacting

34. Although _____ for writing the first historical novel should go to Madame de Lafayette, it was Walter Scott who popularized the form.

(a) merit
(b) credit
(c) statue
(d) award

35. When writing an operating manual for laypeople, technical writers must be as direct and _____ as possible.

(a) dull
(b) clear
(c) pure
(d) vague

36. A vacation extension of two weeks will be _____ to all employees in the new year.

(a) granted
(b) expanded
(c) transferred
(d) pronounced

37. The director's job is to _____ a handful of research assistants.

(a) operate
(b) oversee
(c) undermine
(d) underscore

38. Most dictators clamp down on any form of _____, from street protests to criticism in local newspapers.

(a) dissent
(b) friction
(c) anxiety
(d) exertion

39. Millions of children are being _____ into a lifetime of nicotine addiction by cigarette makers' clever advertising.

(a) lured
(b) stalked
(c) thwarted
(d) dissuaded

40. Many cultures have traditional stories about beings with _____ powers, such as the ability to change shape or fly.

(a) deliberate
(b) tyrannical
(c) impractical
(d) supernatural

41. Today's bioengineers can make crops that are better able to _____ diseases.

(a) withstand
(b) prolong
(c) dispute
(d) banish

42. James was _____ to the emergency room with stomach pains.

(a) admitted
(b) prepared
(c) processed
(d) accommodated

43. The greatness of this new novel has much to do with the author's keen _____ into the nature of 19th-century British society.

(a) tallies
(b) aspects
(c) insights
(d) contents

44. As sunshine _____ the thick fog, the view of the surrounding countryside was finally revealed.

(a) filtered
(b) obscured
(c) sprawled
(d) dispersed

45. Starting in March, the company will _____ $200 annually towards each employee's health insurance package.

(a) release
(b) transmit
(c) substitute
(d) contribute

46. Designing a stadium, where thousands of people must be able to _____ safely, presents special challenges for architects.

(a) conglomerate
(b) confederate
(c) consolidate
(d) congregate

47. Some experts argue that economic _____ are an effective way to penalize nations for undesirable behavior.

(a) sanctions
(b) appraisals
(c) fluctuations
(d) convolutions

48. The company's _____ reputation has affected its stock price, which plunged to a new low today.

(a) soaring
(b) faltering
(c) sobering
(d) burgeoning

49. The government is _____ a service tax on all transactions, but it is hard to see what service the government is actually providing.

(a) deflecting
(b) instituting
(c) extenuating
(d) brandishing

50. The reporter's journalism prize was _____ after an investigation revealed that he had fabricated some of his stories.

(a) repudiated
(b) rescinded
(c) recanted
(d) reverted

This is the end of the Vocabulary section. Do NOT move on to the Reading Comprehension section until instructed to do so. You are NOT allowed to turn to any other section of the test.

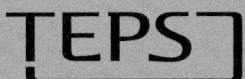

READING
COMPREHENSION

Part I Questions 1—16

Read the passage. Then choose the option that best completes the passage.

1. Become more mobile with the latest in laptops, the Sprint C6. The Sprint C6 offers flawless wireless technology and an extended battery life, allowing you to take care of business all day long. It also has a built-in camera for video conferencing. A perfect traveling companion, the Sprint C6 weighs just 1.7 kilograms and features a compact design with an innovative 14-inch widescreen display. Buy one now and

   _____.

   (a) watch the latest DVD releases
   (b) see why it is the best game console
   (c) do business anytime and anywhere
   (d) enjoy the best in desktop computers

2. Much research has gone into _____. As expected, surveys show that a minimum amount of material wealth is necessary. However, that is not the whole story. Wealthy people are no happier than middle-class people, so happiness cannot depend solely on money. According to the research, self-image, outlook on life and interactions with others are also crucial to happiness.

   (a) why some people are so wealthy
   (b) how money affects emotions
   (c) which genes cause sadness
   (d) what makes people happy

3. Unlike at a job interview, it is not always the first impression that matters at a job fair. If you visit a job fair and apply for jobs at recruiting booths, make sure you return to those booths before you leave. At each booth, thank the recruiters again for their time and let them know that you will be in touch. This will demonstrate how keen you are and help the recruiters remember your name and face. It may also encourage them to have a closer look at your application and résumé. So, basically, try to

   _____.

   (a) make a good impression before you leave
   (b) give recruiters an idea of your background
   (c) make your résumé as interesting as possible
   (d) give good answers to the recruiters' questions

4. The Old Stone Age was brought to an end by The Neolithic Revolution, which involved major changes in the life of humans through agriculture. It began in the Near East, around 8,000 BC, and took place over several thousands of years. Its two crucial developments were the domestication of animals and the planting of crops for food. Before these advances, humans had led unsettled lives as hunter-gatherers, living at the mercy of the environment. They lacked the knowledge necessary for

_____.

(a) regulating their food supply
(b) fighting diseases in the Stone Age
(c) diversifying their farming methods
(d) shaping stones for tools and weapons

5.

Dear Readers,

I received many replies to my commentary on the _____.
Some people emailed and accused me of criticizing America. But my complaint was with the use of the American date format in publishing, not with the country. One person emailed and pointed out that Americans say dates in a month-day order and that the way they write dates simply reflects this spoken order. That's fine, but my contention was that when you publish internationally, you should use internationally accepted date formats. I thought I had made that point quite clear.

John Tudor,
Senior Editor

(a) improper use of US date formats
(b) problems with US foreign policy
(c) changes to international date standards
(d) need to adopt the American date format

6. In 1996 just 6% of the planet's inhabitants spoke English as a first language, while 96% of all e-commerce websites were written primarily in English. However, companies soon realized that to target foreign markets, they needed to create sites with local languages and content. It was the only way they could truly maximize global revenues. This meant that local web designers were _____.

    (a) encouraged to learn English
    (b) increasingly in high demand
    (c) restricted to a few specialties
    (d) subject to greater competition

7. Sufferers of chronic fatigue syndrome (CFS) experience severe and prolonged tiredness or weariness. According to some researchers, it could be caused by a virus, perhaps what is called herpes virus-6. Others think the immune response or autoimmune process is to blame for CFS through causing inflammations of nervous system pathways. All we can safely say is that _____.

    (a) the cases of CFS have not increased
    (b) CFS continues to be regarded as rare
    (c) the exact cause of CFS remains unknown
    (d) CFS research still suffers from poor funding

8. At Vets Plus we have embarked on a strategy to diversify our products and enhance our mission of providing the best possible medical care for animals. To this end, we have partnered with several companies. Our valued partners now include the National Animal Hospital Association, Network of Professional Veterinarians, and Animal Friends Market Researchers. Vets Plus is proud that such fine organizations have joined us in sharing a passion for high-quality animal care. If you are interested in doing the same, please contact our Marketing Department. We are always keen to

    _____.

    (a) provide the best veterinary service to customers
    (b) form partnerships with like-minded organizations
    (c) stock new products that customers will appreciate
    (d) partner with veterinarians who meet our standards

9. A long-standing distinction in the art world exists between "fine art" and "folk art." The distinction is based on the idea that fine art is the kind of art made for aesthetic appreciation, produced by trained artists for its beauty rather than for something more practical. This implies that all other art is more appropriately called "folk" or "ethnic" art. Such art _____. Traditionally it has been practiced by unschooled artists for the purpose of adorning domestic items, such as pottery, as well as artifacts used for cultural rituals and in warfare.

    (a) tends to be created for its own sake
    (b) fulfills a decorative or utilitarian purpose
    (c) relies on the rejection of formal traditions
    (d) competes with pieces of fine art on the market

10. People's moods affect _____. For example, when people are angry, their attention is narrowly focused on the person or thing that is upsetting them and they probably have little room for input from another source. Thus, it is a good idea not to approach a co-worker with an important topic when he or she is irritated or down because you will not get the attention you deserve. Likewise, when feeling cheerful, people are typically much more receptive to input.

    (a) the sharpness of the criticism they offer
    (b) their feelings about those around them
    (c) the manner in which they convey ideas
    (d) their ability to absorb information

11. Often novel technologies _____. They start out as obscure laboratory findings reported in scientific journals that excite only a small number of researchers and academic professionals. Research on them can be long and laborious. But with successes in the lab, they become the subject of patents, perhaps massive research investment, and before long the public gets the end result, oblivious to what led up to it. Not long after that, the new technologies become routine, as with MRI for brain scans or the latest generation of pain relievers.

    (a) reflect the needs and wants of society
    (b) are developed in top-secret laboratories
    (c) are not successful without huge capital investment
    (d) have origins that seem to lack potential for application

12. The academic world I encountered in the tumultuous 1960s was surprisingly one of apolitical scholarship and intellectual inquiry. Ideologically, most of my history professors leaned to the left, but you couldn't infer their personal political affiliations from their teachings or syllabi. In my graduate classes, we assessed major historical debates based on logic and sound critical argument, as opposed to any political conviction. Similarly, when applying for academic jobs, I was asked only about my research and ideas on teaching. Personal political views were

_____.

(a) rarely touched upon for fear of more protests
(b) of no interest unless they were highly orthodox
(c) simply not deemed a relevant topic for discussion
(d) kept quiet in case they spoiled my career prospects

13. _____ seems an unlikely ambition for a young law graduate, but Russell Brewer is no ordinary graduate. He abandoned a promising legal career to open Leaders High School in a down-and-out area of Los Angeles, a school that takes in kids who never counted on getting into college. By demanding high standards, Brewer's school has been turning 95% of these kids into successful graduates that go on to attend college. On the back of his success, Brewer has opened up several other schools with the same aims, including one in the crime-ridden city of Richmond.

(a) Providing poor kids with a cheap college education
(b) Teaching high school math rather than points of law
(c) Giving leadership classes to underprivileged teenagers
(d) Helping high school students graduate and go on to college

14. Educators and policy-makers have long bemoaned the gulf of mutual incomprehension that divides the sciences and humanities. However, something is now being done about it by scholars who believe that the cultural chasm can be bridged with exercises in "fusion thinking." Among the most ambitious programs in this vein is the New Humanities Initiative at Binghamton University. Its coordinators take a crossover approach, demanding the capacity to think simultaneously in narrative and abstract as well as quantitative and qualitative terms. Program participants _____. Artistic processes, for example, are examined in the light of biological forces.

(a) select humanities as an elective for their science major
(b) come to appreciate the limitations of a scientific mindset
(c) study evolutionary biology and its importance in education
(d) extend scientific routines and parlance to humanities fields

15. Nelson Mandela first achieved world fame through his struggle against apartheid in South Africa. From the 1940s onward, he led campaigns against South Africa's racist policy of apartheid. Mandela was eventually arrested for his activities and imprisoned for 27 years. In 1991, he was released and went on to win the Nobel Peace Prize in 1993 along with F.W. de Klerk. _____, in 1994, he was elected as the first black President of South Africa.

(a) Likewise
(b) However
(c) Nevertheless
(d) Subsequently

16. A common stylistic element of detective fiction that can jar a reader in the first encounter is the occasional dropping of conjunctions. An example from an Erle Stanley Gardner novel reads: "He entered the room, turned on the light, surveyed the scene. The place was empty." The purpose of this technique is twofold: it generates a rapid flow of action and it conveys an increased sense of urgency or expectancy to the reader. _____, this stylistic convention increases the tension inherent in the plot.

(a) Otherwise
(b) In contrast
(c) Accordingly
(d) In spite of that

Read the passage and the question. Then choose the option that best answers the question.

17. As a non-profit institution, the Ravinia Festival depends almost entirely on the support of the public. Donations help keep Ravinia up and running and keep ticket prices low. They also fund music education in under-served schools and expert training for the next generation of classical musicians. With ticket sales accounting for only 30% of our operating budget, donations are vital to Ravinia's present and future success. Please give generously in support of Ravinia now.

Q: What is the main point of the advertisement?
(a) Ravinia will be running its festival soon.
(b) Ravinia needs to receive more donations.
(c) Ravinia is striving to keep ticket prices low.
(d) Ravinia should have another successful year.

18. Creating and posting class rules is a good way for new teachers to ensure that students are fully aware of what is and is not acceptable behavior. However, new teachers commonly make the mistake of posting rules that are too general. For example, a rule such as "Respect yourself and others" is so general that students might interpret it in different ways. As a new teacher, you should post clear and detailed rules, such as "Do not fight with or hit other students." Remember, it is better to provide too much guidance than too little.

Q: What is the writer's main advice for new teachers?
(a) Teach students the value of rules.
(b) Learn from other teachers' mistakes.
(c) Enforce rules consistently and fairly.
(d) Try to make specific classroom rules.

19. At Charles & Dunn, we can take the headache out of house hunting. All you have to do is let us know what your needs are, and then sit back and let us locate that special property on your behalf. Often, we can introduce buyers to Scottsdale properties before they are even advertised to the public, so why not let us do the searching for you? Call us now at 201-555-7189. Your dream home might be waiting for you.

Q: What is mainly being advertised?
(a) A bank that offers real-estate loans
(b) A property management company
(c) A real estate agency in Scottsdale
(d) A construction firm in Scottsdale

20. The expression "nuclear winter" refers to the conditions expected after a nuclear war. It is predicted that a nuclear war will spread smoke, soot and dust around the globe, thickening the atmosphere and blocking out the Sun. Without the Sun's radiation reaching the earth's surface, temperatures would begin to fall and the global climate would become colder, possibly causing extinctions. The same thing would happen if a large asteroid or comet hit the earth, although that would be described as an "impact winter."

Q: What is the main topic of the passage?
(a) The way nuclear and impact winters are similar
(b) The possibility of a nuclear winter after a war
(c) An explanation of what a nuclear winter is
(d) A prediction about future climate change

21. I presume that the reason our government has decided to drastically reduce funding for teaching history in schools is because learning history adds nothing to the economy. But what will result from such a policy? Children will be deprived of a sense of connection with the past. They will lose touch with our heritage. The very foundations of our society will be lost to future generations. I do not think the price for economic growth should be the loss of cultural identity. This decision lacks foresight and sets a bad precedent for the future of education.

Q: What is the main idea of the passage?
(a) Government should focus more on economic growth.
(b) Historical knowledge contributes to the economy.
(c) History should be an essential part of education.
(d) Funding cuts lead to a loss of social identity.

22. A recent study has found that minority students often do not do their best in formal testing situations. Many minority students interviewed for the study revealed that they did not see any point in doing well. When asked why, students were of the opinion that, regardless of test results, their life prospects would still be restricted by prejudice and discrimination. The students also cited peer expectations and pressure against intellectual success as reasons they did not strive to do well. The study suggests that low academic and social self-perception contributes significantly to students' poor exam results.

Q: What is the passage mainly about?
(a) Minority students' negative attitudes towards society
(b) Testing procedures that discriminate against minorities
(c) Reasons why minorities have fewer post-secondary prospects
(d) Factors influencing minority students' motivation when taking tests

23. As the British public's faith in Christianity weakened throughout the 19th century, the cult of the English gentleman gradually increased its hold, reaching its apotheosis in the early 20th century. It became the main moral force holding the English nation together, determining the manner in which individuals and classes treated one another. A true gentleman was loyal, honorable, and believed in duty and self-sacrifice. He would often be rich but not ostentatious, patriotic but not chauvinistic, and well-groomed but not vain.

Q: Which of the following is correct about the cult of the English gentleman according to the passage?
(a) It was a movement against Christianity.
(b) It declined at the beginning of the 20th century.
(c) It valued self-sacrifice in an individual's conduct.
(d) It was usually accompanied by displays of wealth.

24. The population of Australia's koalas has recently declined to just around 30,000 to 80,000 koalas. The main reason for this is the destruction of parts of their habitat on Australia's East Coast because of agriculture, logging, and urban development. These human activities have not only reduced their natural habitat, but also introduced other dangers. Roads built through the koalas' habitat have resulted in their getting run over and encroaching urban areas have led to more attacks on them by pet dogs.

Q: Which of the following is correct about koalas according to the passage?
(a) Their population has recently grown to reach 80,000.
(b) Their habitat is being destroyed by climate change.
(c) Pet dogs contribute to the decline in their numbers.
(d) Logging has increased the size of their habitat.

25. A social trend that I have recently noticed is that there are more and more people working part time. I have a neighbor, Lucille Taylor, who makes the minimum wage of $7.60 an hour working part time in the back room of a thrift store. Her paycheck is around $520 every two weeks, or about $15,000 a year. It is not nearly enough, and she is only just surviving. Something else I have noticed, besides the larger number of part-time employees, is the growing number of working people in poverty. It is clear to me that there is a link between the two.

Q: Which of the following is correct about the writer of the passage?
(a) He noticed a shortage of part-time workers.
(b) His neighbor is working in a store's back room.
(c) He believes that unemployment has led to poverty.
(d) He feels part-time work should not be so well paid.

26. The Cancun Club resort is located in Punta Cancun. Surrounded by gardens and the Nichupte Lagoon, our resort features luxury suites, three swimming pools, tennis courts, two gyms, convenience stores, and around-the-clock security guards. Just ten minutes walk away are several restaurants, nightclubs, beaches, and the Centro Convention Center. We also work in conjunction with a travel agency to easily arrange sailing, fishing, scuba-diving, or golf outings for you, plus bus tours to the ancient city of Coba and the marvelous ruins of Tulum.

Q: Which of the following is correct about the Cancun Club?
(a) It has a wide range of evening entertainment.
(b) Its grounds include the Cancun Convention Center.
(c) It cooperates with a local travel agency to offer tours.
(d) Its travel agency organizes hiking trips to Tulum and Coba.

27.

Dear Parents,

Our field trip to Angel Island is scheduled for Tuesday, September 16. We will take the Tiburon Ferry, which leaves at 11:00 am and reaches the island at approximately 11:20. In order to check in at the ferry dock by 10:45 am, students and drivers must be at North Davis School by 8:10 am. The ferry from Angel Island returns to Tiburon at 3:30 pm, so your children will arrive at North Davis for pickup between 5:30 and 6:00 pm.

Sincerely,
The Teaching Staff
North Davis School

Q: Which of the following is correct according to the letter?
(a) The field trip to Angel Island will take place on a Thursday.
(b) The Tiburon Ferry leaves for Angel Island around 11:20.
(c) Students must arrive at North Davis School by 10:45.
(d) Students will be back no later than 6:00 pm.

28. Blue Marble, a leading South African IT company, is seeking Java developers and programmers to provide software solutions for its clients. Vacancies range from Programmer to Senior Programmer, with all positions requiring comprehensive knowledge of software development and maintenance. Additional duties include software support for clients and the documentation of software developments and changes. Salaries are negotiable based on experience and education. Please contact us if you think a career at Blue Marble is right for you.

Q: Which of the following is correct according to the advertisement?
(a) Blue Marble is seeking recruits for IT companies.
(b) All applicants need to know how to develop software.
(c) Each position focuses mainly on software maintenance.
(d) Successful applicants will perform hardware support duties.

29. For centuries ancient texts were written on papyrus, which was a thick paper-like material made from the papyrus plant. The use of papyrus began in ancient Egypt and then spread throughout the known world. By 300 AD, however, another writing medium called "vellum" had gained prominence. It was parchment made from the dried skins of animals. The advantage of vellum was that it was more durable than papyrus, making it the parchment of choice for the next several hundred years. Vellum in turn fell out of use in favor of paper.

Q: Which of the following is correct according to the passage?
(a) Papyrus was used for writing solely in Egypt.
(b) Vellum was replaced by papyrus after 300 AD.
(c) Vellum had mostly fallen out of use by 300 AD.
(d) Papyrus did not possess the durability of vellum.

30. Over the past few decades there has been a battle over apple consumption in Britain, with domestic varieties losing ground to imports. Although British varieties are grown in an ideal climate and have flavors considered second-to-none, British shoppers are being lured by the low prices and cosmetic appeal of foreign apples. In particular, the bland-tasting Golden Delicious, championed by its French growers, is now outselling its British counterparts. With such shifts in consumer demand, things look bleak for the once beloved British apple.

Q: Which of the following is correct according to the passage?
(a) Changes in the climate are affecting British apples.
(b) The foreign apples sold in Britain are superior in taste.
(c) The attractive appearance of foreign apples aids their sales.
(d) British apple growers promote the Golden Delicious variety.

31. In the late 90s, funding for dot-coms and other high-tech start-ups began to dry up. The days of over-inflated stock valuations and easily available venture capital were over, and the so-called dot-com bubble was about to burst. When it did in 2000, many dot-coms faced total ruin, some having never turned a profit. Everyone from executives to small-time investors found their wealth slashed almost overnight when stocks plummeted.

Q: Which of the following is correct about the year 2000 according to the passage?
(a) Many dot-com companies were established then.
(b) Most dot-com firms had made huge profits by then.
(c) Most dot-com stock values started to recover that year.
(d) Entrepreneurial enthusiasm for dot-coms dissipated that year.

32. Low ridership and the withdrawal of federal financial backing have forced the operators of the Providence-Pawtucket ferry to sell its two vessels. These vessels were the backbone of service for the route. However, frequent delays caused by ferry breakdowns made travelers reluctant to use the service. In the fifteen months the service ran, ridership peaked at 3,800 passengers daily, approximately 1,200 below what was needed to break even. In January of last year, the boats carried fewer than fifteen people a day.

Q: Which of the following is correct according to the article?
(a) The government increased subsidies on the ferry.
(b) The vessels rarely experienced mechanical difficulties.
(c) The service's schedule delays drove passengers away.
(d) The ferry made only modest profits when ridership was highest.

33.

To Whom It May Concern:

I'm starting to despair at the lack of traffic enforcement in our busy city. Every day I am subjected to intimidation because I honor traffic laws. I refuse to jeopardize myself and my passengers by speeding, and yet I am constantly being tailgated or cut off. Because I do not run yellow lights, other drivers honk at me and accuse me of holding up traffic. They are the bad guys, not me, and yet I am treated like one. Something needs to be done about this soon.

Sincerely,
Sally Ryan

Q: What can be inferred from the passage?
(a) Some traffic laws are just not realistic.
(b) Bad driving is caused by a lack of attention.
(c) Drivers who are not cautious hold up traffic.
(d) Many drivers break the rules and get away with it.

34. The second half of the 19th century has been called the positivist age. It was an age of faith in all knowledge derived from science, and this had a major effect on the visual arts. Positivist thinking manifested itself in a widespread rejection of Romantic subjectivism and imagination in favor of so-called objective depictions of the ordinary, observable world. Painters began to set as a goal the accurate depiction of scenes from nature and modern life, rather than the imitation of works by past masters.

Q: What is the writer most likely to discuss next?
(a) Typical subjects of late 19th-century paintings
(b) Major scientific achievements of the 19th century
(c) The influence of subjectivism on contemporary art
(d) The most influential Romantic artists and their works

35. On September 22, the City Transit Authority (CTA) will be forced to increase fares, reduce services, and lay off more than 600 employees. This is because every year for the past decade, the CTA has faced funding shortfalls, and this year its budget deficit is a record $110 million. Simply put, the CTA has not received funding from the government to match inflation. The government must act to remedy this situation, or else the CTA will face a larger deficit next year, leading to further fare increases and service cutbacks.

Q: What is the writer most likely to agree with?
(a) The CTA should be managed by a private enterprise.
(b) The government must allocate more funding to the CTA.
(c) Fighting inflation has to be the government's top priority.
(d) Raising fares is the best way to make up for budget shortfalls.

36. An examination of desert soils can soon dispel the idea that all deserts are barren environments. Desert soils often contain a collection of seeds. For example, in the American Southwest, the soil of the Sonoran Desert has seed densities of anywhere from 5,000 to 10,000 seeds per square meter. Such high numbers are testament to the reproductive success of desert flora. Desert plants have mutually beneficial relationships with desert fauna, such as insects, birds, reptiles and mammals, which help fertilize plants and spread seeds around.

    Q: What does the passage imply about desert flora and fauna?
    (a) They are most plentiful in the American Southwest.
    (b) They include diverse species not yet discovered.
    (c) They are endangered by invading plant species.
    (d) They depend upon each other for survival.

37. One chronic problem with foreign aid is that it funds corrupt governments. In fact, a sad correlation has been observed between the aid a country gets and its lack of democracy. That is, the more aid a country receives, the less likely it is to promote democracy. It is not hard to find examples to support this situation: Paul Biya, Cameroon's dictator, receives two-fifths of his revenue from foreign aid. What motivation does he have to improve the lives of his country's people when their poverty and suffering are precisely what provide him with more aid revenue?

    Q: What would the writer most likely agree with?
    (a) Foreign aid should be denied to the people of Cameroon.
    (b) Foreign donors have questionable motives for giving aid.
    (c) Economic growth is positively correlated with foreign aid.
    (d) Recipients of foreign aid should be accountable for its use.

Part III **Questions 38—40**

Read the passage. Then identify the option that does NOT belong.

38. There is a good reason why J.K. Rowling has had phenomenal success with her fantasy books. (a) She is adept at using fantasy to address social issues that her many readers, young and old, can relate to. (b) Rowling's books imaginatively explore ideas on youth and maturity, gender equality, class, race and many other issues. (c) In particular, the self-serving nature of politicians has always been a favorite theme of satiric literature. (d) Her attention to such universal themes is part of the reason for the huge popularity of the Harry Potter series.

39. European exploration along the coast of Africa began with the Portuguese, who were looking for a safe route to India. (a) Most people do not realize that Christopher Columbus, who discovered the Americas, was actually Italian, not Spanish or Portuguese. (b) Bartholomeu Dias set out from Portugal and rounded the Cape of Good Hope at the southern tip of Africa in 1488. (c) Another Portuguese explorer, Vasco da Gama, visited the eastern coast of Africa and reached India in 1498. (d) Soon afterward, the Portuguese established settlements along Africa's coast and began trading in gold, spices, ivory and slaves.

40. You can become a more supportive parent by suggesting healthy coping skills to your adolescent son or daughter. (a) Indeed, many adolescents suffer immensely from a lack of self-esteem because they are not content with their looks. (b) Give examples of how to cope with stress, like setting realistic goals and learning to manage time effectively. (c) Encourage your child to get enough sleep and to engage in enjoyable physical activities, like sports or hiking. (d) Finally, help your child build the confidence to stand up to negative peer pressure.

This is the end of the Reading Comprehension section. Please remain seated until the proctor has instructed otherwise. You are NOT allowed to turn to any other section of the test.

서울대 최신기출 5

Listening Comprehension

Grammar

Vocabulary

Reading Comprehension

TEPS

LISTENING COMPREHENSION

Part I Questions 1—15

You will now hear fifteen conversation fragments, each made up of a single spoken statement followed by four spoken responses. Choose the most appropriate response to the statement.

Part II Questions 16—30

You will now hear fifteen conversation fragments, each made up of three spoken statements followed by four spoken responses. Choose the most appropriate response to complete the conversation.

Part III Questions 31—45

You will now hear fifteen complete conversations. For each item, you will hear a conversation and its corresponding question, both of which will be read twice. Then you will hear four options which will be read only once. Choose the option that best answers the question.

Part IV Questions 46—60

You will now hear fifteen spoken monologues. For each item, you will hear a monologue and its corresponding question, both of which will be read twice. Then you will hear four options which will be read only once. Choose the option that best answers the question.

GRAMMAR

GRAMMAR

Part I **Questions 1—20**

Choose the best answer for the blank.

1. A: You look great today, Jane.
   B: Thanks, _____.

   (a) you do so
   (b) so do you
   (c) do you so
   (d) you so do

2. A: I don't have anything to wear to the party.
   B: You _____ borrow something from me, if you want.

   (a) can
   (b) will
   (c) must
   (d) would

3. A: Did you hear that we're getting a bonus on payday?
   B: No, but that's _____ news.

   (a) excite
   (b) excited
   (c) exciting
   (d) to excite

4. A: What will you do if your house doesn't sell soon?
   B: I'll be forced _____ it at a lower price.

   (a) sell
   (b) to sell
   (c) selling
   (d) to have sold

5. A: I hope I'm not disturbing you.
   B: Not really, I _____ a book.

   (a) just read
   (b) had just read
   (c) was just reading
   (d) will just have read

6. A: Which of these cakes would you like?
   B: I don't know. Each of them _____ nice.

   (a) look
   (b) looks
   (c) has looked
   (d) have looked

7. A: I booked our flight, but it leaves at 6 am tomorrow.
   B: Oh, I didn't expect to leave _____ early.

   (a) so
   (b) ever
   (c) such
   (d) much

8. A: How come you only play with James at school?
   B: He's the only boy in my class _____ I get along with.

   (a) that
   (b) what
   (c) where
   (d) which

9. A: Have you been following the election?

    B: No, I'm not interested in _____.

    (a) a thing that type
    (b) that type of thing
    (c) a type of that thing
    (d) the type of the thing

10. A: Why are you rubbing your shoulder?

    B: I pulled _____ while working out.

    (a) muscle
    (b) a muscle
    (c) the muscle
    (d) any muscle

11. A: Haven't you finished that book yet?

    B: No. It's long, _____ it's taking forever to read.

    (a) as
    (b) for
    (c) yet
    (d) and

12. A: _____ on your next holiday?

    B: Spend as much time as possible at the beach.

    (a) What suppose you'll do
    (b) Do you suppose you'll do what
    (c) Do you suppose what you'll do
    (d) What do you suppose you'll do

13. A: You could try yoga for your back pain.

    B: I don't _____. It doesn't appeal to me.

    (a) want
    (b) want it
    (c) want to
    (d) want to do

14. A: My vacuum cleaner isn't working.

    B: You should _____.

    (a) take to the repair center
    (b) take it to the repair center
    (c) to the repair center take it
    (d) to the center take to repair

15. A: What does the recipe say to do next?

    B: Add one teaspoon of vanilla extract _____ the mixture.

    (a) to
    (b) at
    (c) inside
    (d) among

16. A: Will my dress be ready next week?

    B: Yes, I'm certain _____ it by then.

    (a) I finished
    (b) I've finished
    (c) I'll have finished
    (d) I'll have been finishing

17. A: Rob is planning to find a job after graduation.

    B: But I think it's important he _____ looking now.

    (a) start
    (b) started
    (c) will start
    (d) had started

18. A: You should've taken the class I recommended.

    B: Don't pressure me _____.

    (a) do things I have no interest
    (b) to do things my interest isn't
    (c) to do things I have no interest in
    (d) doing things of no interest I have

19. A: How will the school board spend its budget surplus this year?

    B: They're buying a lot of _____ for the science lab.

    (a) the equipments
    (b) an equipment
    (c) equipments
    (d) equipment

20. A: You played a great game today.

    B: Thank you, but I _____.

    (a) owe it to my coach all
    (b) owe it all to my coach
    (c) owe to my coach it all
    (d) all to my coach owe it

Part II **Questions 21—40**

Choose the best answer for the blank.

---

21. The retired ship captain enjoyed _____ whenever the weather was warm.

    (a) fished
    (b) to fish
    (c) fishing
    (d) having fished

22. Except during World War II, the World Cup has been held _____ four years since 1930.

    (a) all
    (b) the
    (c) each
    (d) every

23. Among the issues discussed at last week's meeting _____ the need for increased communication.

    (a) is
    (b) are
    (c) was
    (d) were

24. The battle _____ at Soares Creek was one of the most significant in the American Civil War.

    (a) fought
    (b) fighting
    (c) was fought
    (d) had been fought

25. Due to a lack of time, it _____ that the board should meet again for a breakfast meeting on May 22.

    (a) decides
    (b) decided
    (c) is decided
    (d) was decided

26. The growth rate of a lawn determines how much it _____.

    (a) to mow it needs
    (b) mowed is needing
    (c) be needing to mow
    (d) needs to be mowed

27. The police patrols in the city, _____ started declining 3 years ago, are now at an all-time low.

(a) that
(b) who
(c) what
(d) which

28. _____ at the prospect of the dentist working on her teeth, the little girl refused to sit in the dentist's chair.

(a) Terrified
(b) Her terrifying
(c) She was terrified
(d) Having been terrifying

29. Jack came late to the meeting and found that everyone _____ for some time.

(a) quarrels
(b) is quarreling
(c) was quarreling
(d) had been quarreling

30. A domestic child labor ban is impacting Indian society, _____ many businesses and even households without cheap labor.

(a) left
(b) it left
(c) leaving
(d) to leave

31. Journalism these days is as much about opinion and social commentary as it is about _____.

(a) reporting relevant facts simple
(b) relevant simple facts reporting
(c) reporting facts relevant simply
(d) simply reporting relevant facts

32. All lectures and computing sessions are to be held from 6 pm to 9 pm _____ indicated otherwise.

(a) while
(b) unless
(c) because
(d) whenever

33. What works for one person in terms of setting and reaching goals may not work for _____.

(a) each
(b) other
(c) those
(d) another

34. Red blood cells of an abnormal shape have difficulty _____ through the bloodstream.

(a) moves
(b) moving
(c) to move
(d) having moved

35. The husband put _____ the right birthday present for his wife.

(a) a lot of thought choosing
(b) thought a lot to choosing
(c) choosing a lot of thought into
(d) a lot of thought into choosing

36. One of the companies involved in the business venture told the press that on no account _____.

(a) the contract broken would be
(b) the contract would be broken
(c) would the contract be broken
(d) would be broken the contract

37. Students should seriously consider taking a course in English composition because it _____ in other academic areas.

    (a) will undoubtedly be helping
    (b) has undoubtedly helped
    (c) is undoubtedly helping
    (d) undoubtedly helps

38. Leonardo da Vinci was highly intelligent and _____.

    (a) observed nature astute
    (b) an astute observer of nature
    (c) observing nature was astute
    (d) was astute to observing nature

39. Mary was advised to consult a psychologist, but she _____ not hear of it.

    (a) must
    (b) could
    (c) would
    (d) should

40. The young student was thankful she could travel and have the opportunity to meet people _____.

    (a) from over all the world
    (b) all from over the world
    (c) over from the world
    (d) from the world over

Part III   Questions 41—45

Identify the option that contains an awkward expression or an error in grammar.

41. (a) A: When was it that you last visited London?
  (b) B: I was here back in 2002 on a business trip.
  (c) A: Really? I didn't know it was that longer ago.
  (d) B: Yeah, but it seems like I was here only recently.

42. (a) A: I've got something to tell you, but you might be shocked.
  (b) B: I'm sure whichever you have to say won't be that bad.
  (c) A: Well, I'm thinking of quitting my job sometime next month.
  (d) B: Really? That's a surprise! I thought you were happy with it.

43. (a) A: I've never ordered clothes online. How about you?
  (b) B: I had recently ordered two sweaters of the same size.
  (c) A: Really? Did you have any problems with your order?
  (d) B: Yes. One sweater was too big and the other too small.

44. (a) A: It's ridiculous how it's taking long to get tickets to the show.
  (b) B: Yeah, this line hasn't moved in at least 15 minutes.
  (c) A: There must be some kind of problem at the ticket office.
  (d) B: Well, if it isn't sorted out soon, we'll miss the start of the show.

45. (a) A: You don't seem nervous about today's interview.
  (b) B: I'm not. I think I'm exactly the person they're looking for.
  (c) A: Well, it seems that you're quite certain of outcome.
  (d) B: Yes, I'm pretty confident that the job will be mine.

Part IV Questions 46—50

Identify the option that contains an awkward expression or an error in grammar.

46. (a) Sea turtles are generally solitary creatures that spend most of their time submerged of the sea. (b) They rarely interact with one another outside of courtship and mating. (c) Sometimes they come together in large groups for nesting on land or feeding. (d) However, even when gathered in such large numbers, turtles tend to keep to themselves.

47. (a) A résumé is where a person records his or her achievements, work skills, and capabilities. (b) Ideally, it is a document that updates regularly throughout one's working life. (c) It is also wise to customize your résumé according to any job you might be applying for. (d) You can do this by highlighting the skills and qualifications relevant to each job.

48. (a) The Meridien is a luxury resort on the Mexican Caribbean offering a paradise of pools, gardens, and a magnificent white sandy beach. (b) The resort has four swimming pools, many restaurants, and very comfortable air-conditioned rooms. (c) All rooms are beautifully decorating with French windows that offer lovely views of the sea. (d) At the Meridien, an incredible variety of fun and entertainment awaits you night and day, all in five-star style.

49. (a) There has been heated controversy about the impact of negative advertising on American electoral politics. (b) Particularly prominent in the debate has been studies investigating the influence of negative advertising on voter turnout. (c) In an important study, Dr. Paul Graham concluded that negative advertising decreases voter turnout. (d) He also pointed out that political consultants use negative advertising precisely for such a purpose.

50. (a) Consumers snapping up the latest gadgets this month have lifted sales figures for electronics retailers. (b) A high demand for cell phones, flat-screen TVs, and digital cameras has been credited for a 13% jump in earnings. (c) Were it not for a decline in impulse buying, the increase has amounted to perhaps 20%. (d) Analysts suggest that impulse buying is down due to consumer concerns about a possible recession.

This is the end of the Grammar section. Do NOT move on to the next section until instructed to do so. You are NOT allowed to turn to any other section of the test.

TEPS

VOCABULARY

DIRECTIONS

This part of the exam tests your vocabulary skills. You will have
15 minutes to complete the 50 questions. Be sure to follow the
directions given by the proctor.

Part I **Questions 1—25**

Choose the best answer for the blank.

1. A: Hi, George. I missed you in biology class yesterday.
   B: Oh, hi Judy. I couldn't _____ because I had the flu.

   (a) go
   (b) meet
   (c) listen
   (d) arrive

2. A: Did you tell Mom you broke the vase?
   B: No. I'm too _____ to. I know how angry she'll be.

   (a) hard
   (b) silent
   (c) scared
   (d) difficult

3. A: Can you come to the workshop tomorrow?
   B: I can't. I have other _____.

   (a) sorts
   (b) plans
   (c) terms
   (d) means

4. A: Can I read that magazine next?
   B: Sure. I'm nearly _____ with it.

   (a) had
   (b) done
   (c) passed
   (d) completed

5. A: Hi, I'm calling to speak to the manager.
   B: I'll have to put you on _____. He's on another line.

   (a) call
   (b) hold
   (c) transfer
   (d) connection

6. A: Why did you leave your boyfriend?
   B: Well, he didn't _____ me very well.

   (a) deal
   (b) treat
   (c) intend
   (d) approach

7. A: Is there a parking lot nearby?
   B: Sure, _____ right at the next corner, and you'll see one there.

   (a) pull
   (b) give
   (c) turn
   (d) point

8. A: Mr. Smith pulled himself out of poverty and made a _____.
   B: Yeah, he's certainly a self-made man.

   (a) load
   (b) wealth
   (c) fortune
   (d) treasure

9. A: What made you decide to go into business for yourself?
   B: I've always wanted to be my own _____.

   (a) job
   (b) boss
   (c) worker
   (d) industry

10. A: You look great. What have you been doing differently?
    B: I recently _____ a vegetarian.

    (a) ate
    (b) made
    (c) became
    (d) changed

11. A: Look! There's a lizard on the path.
    B: Oh, no. I can't _____ reptiles.

    (a) preserve
    (b) surface
    (c) explain
    (d) stand

12. A: Did you remember to get milk?
    B: Sorry, it _____.

    (a) missed the mark
    (b) slipped my mind
    (c) left me in the cold
    (d) caught me red-handed

13. A: This mouthwash tastes good enough to drink.
    B: Yes, but you shouldn't. Just _____ it.

    (a) roll
    (b) rinse
    (c) slush
    (d) gargle

14. A: What was the verdict on the robber?
    B: He was _____ to two years in prison.

    (a) paroled
    (b) confined
    (c) penalized
    (d) sentenced

15. A: Did you hear that Tom's grandfather passed away?
    B: Yes, and I've already offered my _____.

    (a) sanctions
    (b) grievances
    (c) condolences
    (d) apprehensions

16. A: Do I have to state on this customs form that I'm bringing in $10,000?
    B: Yes, the law says you have to _____ large amounts of cash.

    (a) posit
    (b) declare
    (c) uphold
    (d) recognize

17. A: What type of car are you looking to rent, sir?
    B: I'd like something economical with good _____.

    (a) mileage
    (b) function
    (c) turnover
    (d) presence

18. A: What did you do last night?
    B: I just _____ some of my friends at the mall.

    (a) hung out with
    (b) came up with
    (c) got down to
    (d) stood up to

19. A: I've been offered a fantastic job!
    B: Great! You must be _____.

    (a) ecstatic
    (b) boastful
    (c) obsolete
    (d) tentative

20. A: Are you free to talk?
    B: Sure, you're not _____ anything.

    (a) cutting
    (b) undoing
    (c) preventing
    (d) interrupting

21. A: Did you see the doctor about the infection?
    B: Yes, and he _____ some antibiotics.

    (a) defused
    (b) diagnosed
    (c) prescribed
    (d) transmitted

22. A: Jenny likes to keep to herself, doesn't she?
    B: Yes, she's really _____ around people.

    (a) aloof
    (b) fervid
    (c) tractable
    (d) malleable

23. A: Did you read my essay?
    B: Yes, but some parts sounded _____. They could've been more straightforward.

    (a) forged
    (b) coerced
    (c) fabricated
    (d) convoluted

24. A: Why did you go to the concert with Anthony?
    B: He _____ me into it by offering to pay for my ticket.

    (a) coaxed
    (b) induced
    (c) ushered
    (d) expelled

25. A: This kind of work is new to me.
    B: You'll _____ as you go along.

    (a) pick it up
    (b) hang onto it
    (c) take it down
    (d) pull it through

26. Do not miss this great _____ to win a spectacular designer bracelet!

(a) try
(b) hope
(c) chance
(d) attempt

27. Janet is _____ to work the night shift on Tuesdays and Thursdays.

(a) fitted
(b) toned
(c) claimed
(d) scheduled

28. The newspaper _____ an article on antioxidants that should be taken daily.

(a) spread
(b) featured
(c) enclosed
(d) centered

29. The Lunar New Year, _____ in most Asian countries, falls on a different calendar day every year.

(a) obtained
(b) delivered
(c) borrowed
(d) celebrated

30. Even though debate continues over the causes of the warming trend, there is no _____ that global temperatures have risen since 1880.

(a) doubt
(b) mission
(c) statement
(d) assumption

31. The new public service project is expected to _____ 89,000 new jobs.

(a) create
(b) employ
(c) operate
(d) nourish

32. The old woman would sit on the porch and _____ for hours at the children playing.

(a) gaze
(b) gape
(c) gleam
(d) glance

33. For better posture, _____ the height of the chair so your thighs are horizontal and your feet are flat on the floor.

(a) adjust
(b) convert
(c) construct
(d) straighten

34. The exhibit is on _____ from 10 am to 5 pm Monday through Friday.

(a) public
(b) season
(c) display
(d) exposure

35. Visiting seaside resorts and gambling at casinos were among the new pastimes _____ by the prosperous middle classes during the 19th century.

(a) evoked
(b) adopted
(c) imposed
(d) mandated

36. Hakuba, where the 1998 Nagano Winter Olympics were _____, is one of the most famous skiing areas in Japan.

(a) held
(b) taken
(c) stood
(d) occurred

37. Research has found that elderly people are healthier and happier if they have a _____ to share their time with.

(a) recipient
(b) substitute
(c) participant
(d) companion

38. The novel is a thriller about a man who _____ his family background in order to conceal his humble origins.

(a) falsifies
(b) protracts
(c) invalidates
(d) abominates

39. The building in Paris called the Place des Vosges is the _____ of Henry IV, who had it built from 1605 to 1612.

(a) legacy
(b) memoir
(c) revenue
(d) tradition

40. Journalists covering the speech must present their press _____ to security personnel at the door.

(a) franchises
(b) credentials
(c) engagements
(d) deliberations

41. One of the best ways to _____ facial puffiness is to massage your face regularly, thereby improving blood flow and reducing water retention.

(a) upset
(b) erode
(c) counter
(d) obstruct

42. The convenience store robbery took place at 2:30 pm in _____ daylight.

(a) sharp
(b) broad
(c) whole
(d) exposed

43. Some plant seeds are lifted and blown to other locations by the wind, while others are _____ by birds in their droppings.

(a) swayed
(b) littered
(c) obtained
(d) dispersed

44. The need for equipment that can survive the harsh conditions of space travel has led to the development of extremely _____ materials.

(a) durable
(b) anterior
(c) stubborn
(d) vivacious

45. Usually, it is difficult to pin the blame on a single _____ for the spread of a contagious disease.

(a) task
(b) unit
(c) base
(d) source

46. At the last meeting, Thomas Stiller, council member, _____ that council minutes always be submitted for correction.

(a) elevated
(b) allowed
(c) moved
(d) stirred

47. When the Persian Emperor Darius died, his son Xerxes _____ him and soon launched an invasion into northern Greece.

(a) overtook
(b) inherited
(c) succeeded
(d) enthroned

48. The problems within the nation's education system are so _____ that short-term measures will not suffice.

(a) juvenile
(b) requisite
(c) pervasive
(d) miniscule

49. Babies are born with about 300-350 bones, but many of these _____ together as a person grows, leaving a total of 206 bones in adulthood.

(a) fuse
(b) blend
(c) weave
(d) mingle

50. Many authors have _____ the novel *Deep South*, but very few have praised it as much as Darwin Porter.

(a) eulogized
(b) unraveled
(c) disparaged
(d) consecrated

This is the end of the Vocabulary section. Do NOT move on to the Reading Comprehension section until instructed to do so. You are NOT allowed to turn to any other section of the test.

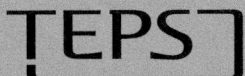

READING
COMPREHENSION

Part I **Questions 1—16**

Read the passage. Then choose the option that best completes the passage.

1. With the city of Los Angeles seeking to reduce smog, telecommuting, or working from home, could be part of the solution. A report released today states that if 15,000 employees telecommuted from home one and a half days a week, the city would meet its pollution reduction goals. Even though telecommuting is not practical for many people now, it is sure to become more widespread in the future. Experts say it is the best way to

   _____.

   (a) deal with the city's air pollution
   (b) save people from getting injured
   (c) block smog from entering your vehicle
   (d) prevent unemployment from rising further

2. Wouldn't it be great if you could make money by _____?
   Believe it or not, we are an online company that lets you do exactly that. There are many different ads to choose from. Just click on the advertisement banners on our site, and we will credit money to your account. While the pay may not seem like much, remember you are getting money for doing something you would be doing anyway—surfing the Net.

   (a) giving us your opinions
   (b) thinking of creative ideas
   (c) playing PC games all day
   (d) looking at advertisements

3. The way water evaporates from the earth's oceans, falls onto land, and then eventually flows back into the sea is called the water cycle. The sun's heat evaporates ocean water, which rises into the atmosphere as water vapor. The vaporized water gradually cools and condenses into clouds. These clouds sometimes rain water straight back into the ocean or else deposit it as rain or snow on land. Water that falls on land ends up in rivers that flow into the oceans. Thus, _____.

   (a) it helps water evaporation
   (b) it causes temperatures to rise
   (c) the world's water is circulated
   (d) the chance of flooding increases

4. The legendary American actor John Wayne was able to make his own rules on the sets of his movies. He once told the director Andrew McLaglen that he would not do a scene in which he eavesdropped on a young couple, and the director changed it. Wayne did not want to do anything that would make him seem petty or small. It was as if he had an acting rulebook of his own, which directors had to follow. He also got to say his lines the way he wanted to. In many ways, _____.

(a) he tried to be a hero
(b) he tended to be a loner
(c) he was his own director
(d) he was a mediocre actor

5. Teachers may have themselves to blame if their students are not doing their homework assignments. If a teacher waits until the end of class to assign homework, he or she has picked a time when students are least attentive. At the end of class, students are mentally preparing to leave, rather than paying attention to homework instructions. A better strategy is to give assignments before the end of class. In this way, students _____.

(a) can ask any questions about the lesson
(b) can review their lesson more efficiently
(c) will know what their final grades will be
(d) will be more focused on homework instructions

6. One of the first cooking shows on TV was aired in the US in 1963. The show was called *The French Chef* and was hosted by Julia Child. It lacked the precision and professionalism of the cooking shows we see now, but it was so popular that it screened nationally for ten years. People loved Child's enthusiasm and even her cooking blunders. Mistakes were what she called "teachable moments," and so they were not edited out. *The French Chef* truly was _____.

(a) one of Julia Child's major blunders
(b) different from today's slick productions
(c) an episode that caused a lot of embarrassment
(d) one of the most influential comedy shows of the 60s

7. It is a misconception that having money can ease the pain in times of crisis. Research shows that what is most crucial is _____. This is the finding of Alex Suchey, a professor of social sciences at Gath University in Ontario, Canada. According to Suchey, human beings are social animals and are not built to handle things alone, especially not a debilitating illness, for example, or the loss of a loved one. Other people can help reduce emotional pain, while money can only ease financial burdens.

(a) diversifying your financial investments
(b) the determination to survive at any cost
(c) having enough money to cover your needs
(d) the existence of strong relationships with others

8.

Dear Ms. Macy,

I am writing in reply to your _____. If you feel that you have been defrauded by a company, contact your local consumer protection agency to report the company involved. You could also contact the National Fraud Information Center, which is a non-profit organization that operates a consumer complaint hotline. It forwards appropriate complaints to the Federal Trading Commission. If you need further assistance, please contact us again.

Yours sincerely,
Andrew McAllen
Department of Trade and Industry

(a) complaint about our food products
(b) charges of fraud against our company
(c) inquiry about reporting company fraud
(d) questions on our government department

9. As a leader in real-time communications, Globalwired makes it easier than ever to bring your employees together no matter where they are in the world. By using our Web and video conferencing and telecommunications software, you can hold secure online company meetings in real time. All of our products incorporate the highest level of security available. Contact a sales representative now who will show you

_____.

(a) why we can offer the lowest travel rates
(b) why we provide the best phone services
(c) how much securer we can make your data
(d) how easy and secure teleconferencing can be

10. Ever since *Robert Drury's Journal* was published in 1729, debate has raged about
_____. The journal records a terrific tale of the 1703
shipwreck of the *Degrave* off the coast of Madagascar, Drury's enslavement, and his
escape and return to England 15 years later. In 1991, archaeologist Mike Parker Pearson
of the University of Sheffield led a team to Madagascar to research the accuracy of
Drury's account. He concluded that it was real. His team found the places described in
the journal as well as wreckage that was possibly from the *Degrave*.

(a) whether the account was authentic or not
(b) whether Drury was the one who wrote it
(c) what clues it has about sunken treasure
(d) what Drury was doing in Madagascar

11. When students become a part of Springfield Community College, they are
_____. The pursuit of learning is the primary goal at
Springfield Community College, and all students are urged to conduct themselves in
a manner befitting this goal. The College's established policies and procedures on
proper deportment can be found in the student handbook. We ask all students to become
familiar with our behavior standards. Needless to say, violations of College policies may
result in suspension.

(a) given all the academic support they need
(b) expected to adhere to our codes of conduct
(c) free to express their views without censorship
(d) able to participate in a range of clubs and activities

12. Voltaire's *Candide* is a novella that _____. The target of its most overt criticism is Optimism, a philosophical system that assumes God created the best of all possible worlds. With reference to disastrous historical events, Voltaire points out that the best of all possible worlds would be a lot better than the one we have. In the course of his attack, Voltaire also ridicules human stupidity and a host of human foibles involving religion, governments and philosophers.

(a) has been ridiculed for its positive outlook
(b) criticizes people who strive for political ends
(c) ranges widely in its satire and disillusionment
(d) is unrelenting on its attack on atheistic thinking

13. Parents who sued MIT over the apparent suicide of their daughter, arguing that the university did not do enough to protect her, have finally won the case that has riveted college administrators nationwide. Worried administrators had closely followed the debate surrounding how far college counselors should go if a student is thought to be a suicide risk. Their fear was that a trial might result in an expansion of the legal responsibility of university counselors. At present, counselors need only encourage students to let their parents know about their problems. However, the case settlement will likely result in _____.

(a) a policy change in the near future
(b) debates about students' workloads
(c) a reduction in the college suicide rate
(d) the dismissal of a number of counselors

14. Intense exercise can damage body cells because it increases oxygen uptake and causes oxidative stress, producing byproducts such as peroxides and free radicals. Apart from tissue damage, these are implicated in degenerative diseases and increased aging. Mild exercise, however, is not bad for cells because it activates protective structural and biochemical changes that compensate for oxidative stress. These act as antioxidant defense mechanisms. Accordingly, this kind of exercise

_____.

(a) exacerbates oxidative stress in athletes
(b) protects tissues and slows down aging
(c) increases the potential for oxidative damage
(d) augments production of free radicals in cells

15. The health of today's youth is getting worse. According to statistics, health problems related to drug abuse and alcoholism are on the rise among people aged 15 to 25. _____, an increasing number of young people are risking future health problems through poor diet, inadequate exercise and cigarette smoking. Health professionals say that better education is the key to reversing these unhealthy trends.

(a) Rather
(b) Moreover
(c) Therefore
(d) Nevertheless

16. Copyright law is designed to protect the rights of copyright owners and allow them to profit from their creative work. It also exists to serve the interests of society by allowing others the "fair use" of this copyrighted work, as stated in the Copyright Act of 1976. This important law does not exactly specify what is permissible in terms of use and what counts as infringement. _____, users must employ their own discretion to determine what constitutes the fair use of copyright materials.

(a) In contrast
(b) Otherwise
(c) Even so
(d) Instead

Part II Questions 17—37

Read the passage and the question. Then choose the option that best answers the question.

---

17. Born in Germany in 1653, the composer George Muffat studied music in Paris. Afterwards, he served as an organist in the French towns of Molsheim and Selestat until 1674. In 1678, he advanced to the position of organist to the bishop of Salzburg in Austria. Then, from 1690 until his death, Muffat worked as the musical director for the bishop of Passau in Germany. Muffat wrote important suites for string orchestras and fathered another gifted composer, Gottlieb Muffat.

    Q: What is the best title for the passage?
    (a) George Muffat's Travels as a Youth
    (b) A Brief Biography of George Muffat
    (c) George Muffat's Fame as an Organist
    (d) The Religious Music of George Muffat

18. While tropical rainforests are disappearing fast, coral reefs are disappearing faster—at about twice the rate. An estimated 20% of the world's coral reefs have vanished since 1980, and that number could triple by the century's end depending on the severity of a number of key factors. The leading factor contributing to their demise at the moment is warming ocean temperatures. An increase of one degree Celsius is enough to kill off the coral in tropical regions, where much of the world's coral exists.

    Q: What is the passage mainly about?
    (a) The danger of falling ocean temperatures
    (b) The rapid decline of coral reefs worldwide
    (c) The unhealthy state of tropical rainforests
    (d) The difference between coral reefs and rainforests

19. When Alexander the Great became king, he used art as a propaganda tool to reaffirm his power and status. He instructed the best artists of his time to make likenesses of him that elevated him to a divine stature. Thus, the court sculptor named Lysippos represented him as Apollo throwing a spear, and the court painter named Apelles portrayed him as Zeus throwing a thunderbolt. Such depictions served to confer god-like status upon Alexander and to convey the extent of his political power.

Q: What is the passage mainly about?
(a) Alexander's use of art forms for political purposes
(b) Alexander's strong belief in his status as a living god
(c) Alexander's special relationship with his court artists
(d) Alexander's accomplishments in sculpture and painting

20. The deep ocean floor is made up of relatively young rocks, since it is constantly being reformed as mid-ocean ridges separate. Tectonic forces pull apart these ocean ridges, allowing magma to rise up through cracks and form a new ocean floor. As new rock forms and spreads, older rock is pushed farther away from the ridges. Where older rock meets the Earth's continental plates, it is forced downwards underneath the continent and eventually returns to a molten state. In this way, the ocean floor is continuously being destroyed and remade.

Q: What is the main topic of the passage?
(a) Rocks at the bottom of the ocean
(b) The regeneration of the ocean floor
(c) The movements of the Earth's crust
(d) Forces behind ocean floor destruction

21. One of Woody Allen's best-loved films, *Annie Hall*, was released in 1977 to wide commercial and critical success. In many ways, it is a document of its time, an artifact that records the nature of dating and love, together with the intellectual climate in New York City in the late 1970s. Most of its jokes rely on knowledge of news events and cultural stereotypes. To watch *Annie Hall* is to be immersed in the life of Manhattan in 1977.

Q: What is the main topic of the passage?
(a) The socio-historical context of *Annie Hall*
(b) The factors that contributed to *Annie Hall*'s release
(c) The cultural atmosphere of Manhattan in the 1970s
(d) The common characteristics of Woody Allen's films

22. Global warming has killed off at least 70 frog species by exacerbating outbreaks of a deadly fungal disease, providing the first scientific evidence that worldwide climate change decreases ecological diversity, according to a team of international scientists. "We are seeing species rapidly going extinct," says Lockstern University biologist Laurel Loman, a member of the team. "It's already happened, and it's continuing to happen." Loman reports that, in addition, animal populations are moving northward, plants are blooming earlier, and pests and parasites are increasing in number.

Q: What is the best title for the passage?
(a) Harmful Ecological Effects of Global Warming
(b) Preventing Animal Extinction due to Climate Change
(c) The Latest Conclusions on Reducing World Temperatures
(d) The Drop in Endangered Animal Species due to Global Warming

23. The Chinese began immigrating to Canada around 1858 when they heard of the British Columbia gold rush. Some years later, more Chinese went to Canada to work on the Canadian Pacific Railway. More than 15,000 Chinese arrived in Canada between 1881 and 1884, with about 6,500 employed to work on the railway. However, once the railway was finished in 1885, the Canadian government tried to restrict Chinese immigration. In that year, the Canadian government passed a law imposing a tax of $50 upon each Chinese person entering the country.

Q: When did the Canadian government impose a tax on Chinese immigrants?
(a) 1858
(b) 1881
(c) 1884
(d) 1885

24. The Humboldt International Film and Video Festival (HIFVF) is hosted at Humboldt State University. Founded in 1967, the festival is the oldest student-run festival in the US, and its screenings are in the oldest movie house in the nation—the University's Minor Theater. Each year the festival showcases independent films of any genre and of less than 60 minutes in duration. If you wish to enter your film for consideration, please submit it with a $30 entry fee to HIFVF, Theater Arts Department, Humboldt State University, California, no later than May 9.

Q: Which of the following is correct about the HIFVF?
(a) It is put on by an international film company.
(b) It runs movies that are over one hour long.
(c) It will start accepting films after May 9th.
(d) It is presented annually at an old theater.

25. The ancient Pueblo people lived in what is now the American Southwest. They are best known for the villages of sandstone dwellings they built along cliff walls. Made with sandstone walls and wooden roofs, and often protected by overhanging rock, the dwellings were cool in summer and warm in winter. They were built close to water, wood, and wildlife and offered excellent protection from invaders. Some Pueblo villages were only accessible by rope or through rock climbing.

Q: Which of the following is correct about the Pueblo people according to the passage?
(a) They lived high up on the tops of hills.
(b) Their houses were warm all year round.
(c) Their homes were partly made of wood.
(d) They found it difficult to obtain water and food.

26. Nothing beats a Best Bear trip! Each outing includes a 1-hour scenic flight from Homer to Katmai, a 3-hour guided tour for bear viewing with a naturalist guide, a sumptuous lunch at our Wilderness Camp in Katmai, and an afternoon of canoeing on Naknek Lake before a return flight from Katmai to Homer. We also cater to handicapped guests at no additional cost. Please consult our Best Bear brochure for details.

Q: Which of the following is correct according to the advertisement?
(a) It takes 3 hours to fly from Katmai to Homer.
(b) Bear viewing is an optional part of the trip.
(c) Three meals are provided during the trip.
(d) Disabled travelers incur no extra charges.

27. When repainting your home interior with a light-colored paint, take steps to avoid a visible undercoat or patchy discoloration because of an original dark color. Always put a white undercoat over existing dark paint. That will give you a blank canvas for a top coat. Also, since colors appear lighter over a large surface area, choose a paint a shade or two darker than your desired color. If the result is too bold, you can soften it by applying glaze with a sponge—a technique called color-washing.

Q: Which of the following is correct according to the instructions?
(a) Apply a dark undercoat for all paint jobs.
(b) Mix your paint with white before applying it.
(c) Choose a lighter color for larger surface areas.
(d) Try color-washing to make a color seem less bold.

28. Some children are musically gifted, with talents that should be nurtured and developed, but their parents might not be able to afford the costs involved. That's where the Youth Music Foundation comes in. Through our financial assistance, gifted young people nationwide can realize their musical potential. We provide awards and scholarships based on talent and financial need. Applications are open to all music students aged between 5 and 12. For more information, please call 1-800-577-YMFA.

Q: Which of the following is correct about the foundation according to the passage?
(a) It gives money to musicians of all ages.
(b) It introduces gifted young people to music.
(c) It provides awards to students around the world.
(d) It helps underprivileged children develop musical skills.

29. In the 1700s, John Bartram, a Pennsylvanian Quaker, became interested in botany after reading about it in a book. He began collecting local cuttings and seeds and sending them to another Quaker he knew in London. This led to more ambitious enterprises, including journeys into the wilderness that took him hundreds of miles from home. Though self-taught, Bartram had a knack for discovering unknown species, which he kept track of in a journal. During the colonial period in America, 800 plants were discovered, a quarter of them by Bartram.

Q: Which of the following is correct about John Bartram according to the passage?
(a) He received an extensive education in botany while young.
(b) He visited London with a collection of seeds and cuttings.
(c) He discovered close to 800 plants during his lifetime.
(d) He catalogued a large number of new plant species.

30.

Dear Sir:

We have received your refund request as well as your explanation regarding the problems you had with your desk ensemble. Your request for a refund falls outside of our 30-day time limit for returns, as per our return policy. However, we remain committed to our customers' satisfaction, and your difficulties with our product have made us aware of potential problems that others may encounter. Therefore, if you bring your purchase back to our store, we will give you a full refund. Please don't hesitate to contact me if you require any further information.

Yours sincerely,
Gerald Jenkins
Store Manager

Q: Which of the following is correct according to the letter?
(a) The customer requested a refund within 30 days.
(b) The customer is asked to pay for the damaged product.
(c) The writer will refund only part of the purchase amount.
(d) The writer of the letter offers reimbursement for a return.

31. Confirmation bias, a long-observed problematic aspect of human reasoning, refers to the way people seek or interpret evidence in ways that support existing beliefs or expectations. In other words, it is a kind of selective thinking. Recently, researchers used MRI brain scans to uncover how confirmation bias arises in the brain. What they found is that it is unconsciously driven by emotions as opposed to a reasoning process. It appears that emotions delude people into believing that their bias or selective thinking is critical for reasoned thinking, which makes them feel justified and right in their beliefs.

Q: Which of the following is correct according to the passage?
(a) Confirmation bias has little to do with people's emotions.
(b) People are unaware of how emotions affect their thinking.
(c) MRI scans solved the mystery of where emotions originate.
(d) Researchers have uncovered the nonexistence of confirmation bias.

32. A crucial period in the history of the English novel was from 1760 to 1780. During this time, a new element was added to the novel, primarily by author Lawrence Sterne, but also by writers considered to be his disciples. In their writing, what is commonly referred to as sentiment or emotional expression was employed more than had hitherto been the practice. As a consequence, the individuality and personality of these writers were impressed more unreservedly upon their fiction. Sterne, it need hardly be said, was ahead of his time and was the undisputed master of this style of writing during this period.

Q: Which of the following is correct about the English novel from 1760 to 1780?
(a) Sterne influenced novelists to write books based on their own lives.
(b) Authorial presence came to the fore through sentimental expression.
(c) Authors tried to prevent their personality from surfacing in their novels.
(d) Sterne explored the consequences of unchecked individualism in society.

33. These days, a lot of people are happier in workplaces with family-friendly policies even if their salaries are slightly lower. They enjoy the comfort of knowing that if they have to take days off because their kids are sick, they will not be penalized for it. Their allotted vacation days and valuable family time will stay the same. Companies that offer this kind of flexibility provide peace of mind and benefits that you really cannot put a dollars-and-cents value on.

Q: What can be inferred from the passage?
(a) It is more difficult now for people to find flexible workplaces.
(b) A career is not the number-one priority in many people's lives.
(c) Salary is what people think of most when considering a job offer.
(d) A person that works hard is more likely to be given more benefits.

34. A government advisory panel will look into whether scientific criticisms of antibacterial products warrant stricter product controls. Over the past decade, sales of soaps and other products with antibacterial properties skyrocketed as hospitals used them in an effort to prevent the spread of disease and consumers purchased them to make homes healthier. However, critics have argued that regular soaps are just as effective and that antibacterial products cause antibiotic resistance in bacteria, which is of major concern.

Q: What is most likely to be discussed next?
(a) How antibacterial soaps prevent disease
(b) Why consumers keep buying antibacterial products
(c) How important hand washing is for stopping germs
(d) Why the issue of antibiotic resistance is so important

35. Capella Inc. provided shareholders with a solid return on their investment in the last financial year. We also took significant steps to generate continued growth in the years ahead, ensuring future dividends through increased revenues and profitability. One project scheduled for completion next year is our Mobitone Theater complex, which will be a complete entertainment destination, boasting revolutionary theater concepts. This project represents only the beginning of our strategy to branch out into digital cinema and eventually digital film production.

Q: What can be inferred about Capella Inc. from the report?
(a) Its new theater features digital cinema capabilities.
(b) Its shareholders will get lower dividends this year.
(c) It has a good reputation for digital film technology.
(d) It will eventually focus entirely on digital film production.

36. In 1920, Indian leader Mahatma Gandhi called for a boycott of British textiles in favor of using traditional home-spun, home-woven textiles. He saw this as an integral part of India's road to self-sufficiency and independence. However, India has greatly changed since then, and Indians now zealously embrace international commerce, buying up international goods like never before. Although naysayers hark back to Gandhi's teachings, pointing out that such an appetite for imports threatens domestic producers and the nation's self-sufficiency, not many are listening.

Q: What can be inferred from the passage?
(a) India's cotton industry has fueled its rapid economic growth.
(b) Most Indians worry about India's reliance on imported goods.
(c) Indians have abandoned business ideals advocated by Gandhi.
(d) Gandhi's thinking prevails among a new generation of Indians.

37.

To the Editor,

I strongly disagree with George McQueen's ludicrous complaint about *University Magazine* ("Alumni Letters," Jan. 2008). Contrary to his opinion, I find that *University Magazine*'s articles still reflect the university I remember from over 30 years ago. I was most impressed with two pieces in the January issue: "Up and Coming," which profiled several current students, and "Heated Discussion," which looked at research on global warming. Both articles demonstrated the same institutional excellence and scholarship I remember.

Anne Sabel
South Hurstville, NSW

Q: What did Mr. McQueen most likely write about *University Magazine*?
(a) Its articles fall short of the standard of the university.
(b) It does not appeal to recent graduates of the university.
(c) Its positions on national and political events are biased.
(d) It focuses on humorous issues rather than on important ones.

Part III   **Questions 38—40**

Read the passage. Then identify the option that does NOT belong.

---

38. There are several reasons why countries seek to trade with each other. (a) First, even a technologically advanced nation cannot produce everything its people need, so it must import. (b) Next, some nations can become or remain very wealthy through exporting goods or natural resources. (c) Also, not too long ago, countries consumed goods predominately produced within their borders. (d) Finally, many nations cannot survive and will suffer economic collapse if they cannot trade with others.

39. I'll be ordering Keswick Theater tickets online from now on after trying it and seeing how convenient it was. (a) I got tickets that were issued on a "best-available" basis, just as you do at the box office, except that I could get them quicker. (b) This improved my chances at having good seats close to the front, which to me is the best thing about online ticketing. (c) Upon confirmation, my tickets were automatically mailed to me, and I got an email saying they were on the way. (d) The theater was happy to take membership details over the phone, if I wanted my orders processed sooner.

40. From May 12 through August 11, Philadelphia will host a one-of-a-kind exhibit of works by Impressionist artist Edgar Degas. (a) Visitors will be privileged to see some of Degas' most well-known paintings, accompanied by some of his famously candid, naturalistic sculptures. (b) Degas spent his life investigating "The Figure in Motion," and all of his subjects are represented at this exhibit. (c) The selected pieces are judiciously displayed so viewers can appreciate the full scope of Degas' skill for representation. (d) Degas wanted his depictions of people to seem as though their movements were captured in a private moment.

This is the end of the Reading Comprehension section. Please remain seated until the proctor has instructed otherwise. You are NOT allowed to turn to any other section of the test.

서울대 최신기출 6

Listening Comprehension

Grammar

Vocabulary

Reading Comprehension

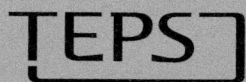

Listening
Comprehension

Scripts P 316 / 정답 P 331

Part I **Questions 1—15**

You will now hear fifteen conversation fragments, each made up of a single spoken statement followed by four spoken responses. Choose the most appropriate response to the statement.

Part II **Questions 16—30**

You will now hear fifteen conversation fragments, each made up of three spoken statements followed by four spoken responses. Choose the most appropriate response to complete the conversation.

Part III **Questions 31—45**

You will now hear fifteen complete conversations. For each item, you will hear a conversation and its corresponding question, both of which will be read twice. Then you will hear four options which will be read only once. Choose the option that best answers the question.

Part IV **Questions 46—60**

You will now hear fifteen spoken monologues. For each item, you will hear a monologue and its corresponding question, both of which will be read twice. Then you will hear four options which will be read only once. Choose the option that best answers the question.

TEPS

GRAMMAR

Part I **Questions 1—20**

Choose the best answer for the blank.

1. A: What was your childhood like?
    B: There _____ a lot of happy times and some sad times.

    (a) is
    (b) are
    (c) was
    (d) were

2. A: One of our Russian teachers just quit at the last minute.
    B: Luckily, I know someone _____ can teach basic Russian.

    (a) who
    (b) which
    (c) whom
    (d) whose

3. A: _____, Kirk?
    B: I got stuck in traffic.

    (a) Why you are late
    (b) Why are you late
    (c) Are you late
    (d) You are late

4. A: How is the weather over in Chicago?
    B: It _____ for two hours.

    (a) had been raining
    (b) has been raining
    (c) was raining
    (d) is raining

5. A: Why aren't you having any dessert?
    B: My doctor _____.

    (a) advised me not to
    (b) advised not to me
    (c) didn't to advise me
    (d) didn't to me advise

6. A: Will Peter get the promotion?
    B: I seriously doubt that, since the boss _____.

    (a) seems not like to him
    (b) seems to like not him
    (c) doesn't seem like him
    (d) doesn't seem to like him

7. A: I'm thinking of getting a puppy.
    B: Really? Well, make sure you get _____ that's already house-trained.

    (a) it
    (b) one
    (c) him
    (d) any

8. A: Do you know who'll be transferred to the London branch office?
    B: I'm not sure, but I can get _____ for you.

    (a) the informations
    (b) the information
    (c) an information
    (d) informations

9. A: Don't forget to bring your camera.
   B: Don't worry. I _____ .

   (a) won't
   (b) won't do
   (c) won't do to
   (d) won't forget to bring

10. A: Denise's baby is so cute, _____?
    B: Yeah, she's got such big eyes.

    (a) don't you think
    (b) you don't think
    (c) think don't you
    (d) think you don't

11. A: Did you watch the soccer game?
    B: A little, but then I went to bed, _____ that our team was losing.

    (a) was seeing
    (b) seeing
    (c) to see
    (d) see

12. A: I've never tried skiing on the expert slope before.
    B: _____ . It's too steep for me.

    (a) I have neither
    (b) I neither have
    (c) Neither I have
    (d) Neither have I

13. A: I'm sorry _____ .
    B: That's OK. I just arrived myself.

    (a) having you waited
    (b) keeping you to wait
    (c) to keep you to waiting
    (d) to have kept you waiting

14. A: The new machine is difficult to operate.
    B: That's OK. Not everything _____ to be easy at first try.

    (a) has been expected
    (b) can be expected
    (c) has expected
    (d) can expect

15. A: Tell me. Did you take the money?
    B: You can't make _____ .

    (a) me what I didn't do to confess
    (b) me confess to what I didn't do
    (c) confessing me of not doing that
    (d) what I'm not confessing that I did

16. A: Welcome to Day Spring Spa Center. Can I help you?
    B: Yes, I'd like to get _____ .

    (a) massage
    (b) massages
    (c) a massage
    (d) the massages

17. A: Thanks for inviting me. I had a good time.
    B: We _____ delighted to have you over.

    (a) are
    (b) were
    (c) will be
    (d) had been

18. A: I got up very late, and I barely got to the airport in time.
    B: Well, you _____ been relieved to have made it.

    (a) must've
    (b) could've
    (c) might've
    (d) would've

19. A: You seem very excited. What's up?

    B: I sure am. _____ around the mall today, I ran into a sports star!

    (a) I walked
    (b) I was walking
    (c) While walked
    (d) While walking

20. A: Shall I come over on Saturday?

    B: No, we're expecting _____ then.

    (a) company
    (b) companies
    (c) a company
    (d) the company

Part II   **Questions 21—40**

Choose the best answer for the blank.

---

21. Tina told her daughter _____ less time in the sun.

    (a) spend
    (b) to spend
    (c) spending
    (d) having spent

22. Blood vessels transport nutrients and _____ carry away waste products.

    (a) so
    (b) also
    (c) since
    (d) therefore

23. Nine out of ten people _____ the country say they will return in old age.

    (a) leaving
    (b) leaves
    (c) leave
    (d) left

24. As he knew that the rumors were false, the dean did not attach _____ significance to the allegations of corruption.

    (a) each
    (b) some
    (c) every
    (d) much

25. The residents hit by the storm said the wind _____ that hard before.

    (a) never blows
    (b) had never blown
    (c) is never blowing
    (d) was never blowing

26. Uncle Matt brought Bill a computer game to share with his brothers, _____ led to endless fighting.

    (a) as
    (b) that
    (c) who
    (d) which

27. At the end of this month, the Jacksons
_____ for 20 years.

(a) are married
(b) will be married
(c) have been married
(d) will have been married

28. _____ a number of arrests after a
fight in a city bar.

(a) Police are reported to make
(b) It is reported police to make
(c) Police reported to have made
(d) It is reported that police made

29. Given the magnitude of the political
mistake, the penalty for those who made
it was not _____ high.

(a) that
(b) only
(c) such
(d) rather

30. A schedule of activities for students on
_____ in Madison Hall.

(a) weeknight and weekend is posted
(b) weeknight and weekend are posted
(c) weeknights and weekends is posted
(d) weeknights and weekends are posted

31. There are three methods _____
the federal government refunds taxes to
state and local governments.

(a) in what
(b) whatever
(c) by which
(d) whichever

32. Researchers say public speaking can
cause blood pressure to increase
_____ 10 to 50%.

(a) by
(b) for
(c) with
(d) over

33. For _____, call 222-4444 or visit
freethewhales.com.

(a) further details
(b) a further detail
(c) the further details
(d) some further detail

34. If the ceasefire _____ be broken,
there would be another war.

(a) could
(b) might
(c) had to
(d) were to

35. _____ as high as $500, the
Internet has become invaluable for
students looking for inexpensive, used
textbooks.

(a) Book costs for a semester
(b) For a semester, book costs
(c) For book costs a semester with
(d) With book costs for a semester

36. Despite _____ the Palestinians'
right to return to their homes in Israel,
Israel did not allow it.

(a) a UN resolution recognizing
(b) a UN resolution to recognizing
(c) of a UN resolution recognizing
(d) that of a UN resolution recognized

37. The woman accused the man _____ inappropriate comments.

    (a) for making
    (b) of making
    (c) to making
    (d) to make

38. The tourists' map was of little help when they got lost _____ the tour.

    (a) to
    (b) in
    (c) on
    (d) for

39. It was during the reign of Isabella I and Ferdinand V _____ Spain began to build an empire.

    (a) that
    (b) until
    (c) since
    (d) because

40. Stocking up on all the family's necessities _____ the last thing Sara wants to do on the weekends.

    (a) is
    (b) are
    (c) is to be
    (d) are to be

Part III **Questions 41—45**

Identify the option that contains an awkward expression or an error in grammar.

41. (a) A: What should we do tomorrow?
    (b) B: How about going swimming?
    (c) A: Where? At the swimming pool?
    (d) B: Yes, or we can go the beach.

42. (a) A: Are you planning to tour Europe next year?
    (b) B: I'd like to, but I'm not sure if I would afford it.
    (c) A: It's not too expensive in the winter, you know.
    (d) B: Is that right? Well, maybe I'll look into it.

43. (a) A: John, are you OK? You've been looking really stressed late.
    (b) B: Yeah, I've been so busy with work that I haven't been sleeping well.
    (c) A: Why don't you take a holiday? We can cover for you.
    (d) B: That's not a bad idea. I think I'll ask the boss about it.

44. (a) A: I'm not going to that appliance store ever again!
    (b) B: But you always get your appliances there. What happened?
    (c) A: The owner shall not give me a refund for a toaster I've used only once.
    (d) B: Well, that's understandable. It's a store policy not to do that.

45. (a) A: Is it true that you were admitted to Rawlings University?
    (b) B: Yes, it is. I got a letter of acceptance yesterday.
    (c) A: That's great! Congratulations! You must be very excited.
    (d) B: Yes, I've really been looking forward to hear from them.

Identify the option that contains an awkward expression or an error in grammar.

46. (a) Our town is in desperate need of a new hospital. (b) The existing hospital was built over 50 years ago. (c) Besides to be too small, it was in need of many repairs. (d) In fact, the old hospital was itself a health hazard.

47. (a) Dinosaurs lived in New Mexico for about 154 million years. (b) They thrived in the area from the late Triassic period to the end of the Jurassic period. (c) A wide variety of dinosaur fossils and other remains from that age have found throughout New Mexico. (d) One of the most important of these remains is the group of footprints found at Clayton Lake.

48. (a) Buzzards have eyesight very keen and hunt by scanning the ground carefully for a target. (b) Their favorite prey is the rabbit, and when they spot one, they swoop down, catching the animal with their sharp, strong claws. (c) They then use their hooked, pointed beaks to rip the flesh from the body. (d) These birds prefer to live in wooded areas and frequently perch on trees to watch for their prey.

49. (a) For the first time since 1994, credit card debt has been reduced. (b) This has come as a welcome surprise to analysts and industry insiders. (c) After the credit boom, analysts expected the tumult of a debt-ridden society. (d) But instead, the economy has grown healthier, and consumers repaying their debts.

50. (a) The unsanitary conditions created by human feces on Mount McKinley can cause diarrhea among climbers. (b) This can lead to problems when combined with the physical stress of a mountain expedition. (c) Of 132 climbers interviewing, more than a quarter reported having trouble with diarrhea. (d) At high altitudes and in cold temperatures, such complications can be severe and potentially dangerous.

This is the end of the Grammar section. Do NOT move on to the next section until instructed to do so. You are NOT allowed to turn to any other section of the test.

VOCABULARY

Part I Questions 1—25

Choose the best answer for the blank.

1. A: You can trust me. I promise I won't tell anyone else.

    B: Well, as long as you can keep it a _____.

    (a) sign
    (b) habit
    (c) secret
    (d) notice

2. A: Hi. Can you connect me to the Customer Service department, please?

    B: I'll _____ you through right away.

    (a) put
    (b) take
    (c) hold
    (d) allow

3. A: Thanks for helping me with my research, Sarah.

    B: Oh, it was no _____ at all.

    (a) business
    (b) trouble
    (c) thanks
    (d) matter

4. A: We should try to save more money.

    B: But it's a lot harder than you _____.

    (a) get
    (b) pay
    (c) think
    (d) move

5. A: I hope you get over your illness soon.

    B: Thanks. I also hope to make a quick _____.

    (a) cure
    (b) health
    (c) recovery
    (d) treatment

6. A: How do I look?

    B: Great! I really like your _____.

    (a) type
    (b) outfit
    (c) fabric
    (d) brand

7. A: Where's the nearest drugstore?

    B: There's one about a _____ away down that road.

    (a) yard
    (b) walk
    (c) block
    (d) length

8. A: Jane was really embarrassed by her classmates' jokes.

    B: I know. They shouldn't have _____ her like that.

    (a) teased
    (b) played
    (c) assisted
    (d) regulated

9. A: Excuse me, do you have any messages for Suite 213?

    B: No, we haven't _____ any.

    (a) received
    (b) reached
    (c) given
    (d) sent

10. A: Our CEO quit yesterday.

    B: Is that right? Wow, that's quite a _____ to hear.

    (a) catch
    (b) shock
    (c) glory
    (d) wonder

11. A: How much are the items you purchased abroad worth, sir?

    B: The total _____? Around 300 dollars, I suppose.

    (a) fee
    (b) tax
    (c) value
    (d) degree

12. A: Phil, this is my wife, Melissa.

    B: Pleased to make your _____, Melissa.

    (a) meeting
    (b) friendship
    (c) association
    (d) acquaintance

13. A: Have you decided on what to order?

    B: Not yet. I need more time to _____ the menu.

    (a) address
    (b) choose
    (c) study
    (d) learn

14. A: Excuse me. I believe the bag you just took is mine.

    B: Is it? I'm terribly sorry, my _____.

    (a) mistake
    (b) mixture
    (c) reaction
    (d) confusion

15. A: What does this line say?

    B: I'm afraid I can't _____ what it says.

    (a) turn in
    (b) make out
    (c) push over
    (d) come across

16. A: Let's watch a movie tonight.

    B: Great idea! But are there any good ones _____?

    (a) filming
    (b) viewing
    (c) showing
    (d) reporting

17. A: How was the workshop you organized?

    B: Perfect. Everything _____ without a glitch.

    (a) dug in
    (b) went off
    (c) spun out
    (d) pulled up

18. A: Can I see Dr. Sullivan this Thursday?

    B: He has a(n) _____ in his schedule at 3 pm. Is that all right?

    (a) interval
    (b) opening
    (c) potential
    (d) transition

19. A: That actor is creating a lot of controversy.

    B: Yes. He has _____ considerable debate.

    (a) sparked
    (b) amassed
    (c) exploded
    (d) disturbed

20. A: It looks like we missed the last train.

    B: What do you _____ we do now?

    (a) suggest
    (b) present
    (c) imply
    (d) offer

21. A: There seem to be many European descendants in Australia.

    B: That's because immigrants from war-torn countries _____ there after World War II.

    (a) lulled
    (b) evaded
    (c) flocked
    (d) tramped

22. A: So, how do you like living in the countryside?

    B: Well, it's very peaceful compared with the _____ pace of New York.

    (a) remote
    (b) unruly
    (c) solitary
    (d) bustling

23. A: This apartment building is very dirty.

    B: I know. It's also _____ with cockroaches and mice.

    (a) infested
    (b) invested
    (c) inhibited
    (d) inhabited

24. A: On top of winning the tournament, none of our players suffered any injuries.

    B: Wow, that's the _____! Congratulations!

    (a) winner takes all
    (b) icing on the cake
    (c) cream of the crop
    (d) par for the course

25. A: Alison seems to have difficulty breathing sometimes.

    B: Yes. She has _____.

    (a) asthma
    (b) anemia
    (c) aphasia
    (d) arthritis

Choose the best answer for the blank.

26. The manager will give a(n) _____ on the effects of the recent increase in oil prices.

(a) dialogue
(b) expression
(c) presentation
(d) performance

27. In the 1430s, the Ottoman Empire was swept by a famine during which the bark of trees was _____ to make bread.

(a) used
(b) glued
(c) carved
(d) formed

28. The couple bought a better sofa so that they would be more _____ when watching TV.

(a) delicious
(b) advanced
(c) comfortable
(d) entertaining

29. The team failed to _____ a goal in the second half of the game.

(a) find
(b) carry
(c) score
(d) match

30. All passengers were _____ to check their belongings before they disembarked.

(a) limited
(b) specified
(c) reminded
(d) explained

31. Do not approach a dog if it _____ at you.

(a) bows
(b) pants
(c) yawns
(d) growls

32. Scientists try to _____ a logical conclusion based on their observations.

(a) draw
(b) stand
(c) move
(d) stretch

33. Every sick pet should be taken to a _____ for a thorough check-up.

(a) veterinarian
(b) psychiatrist
(c) anesthetist
(d) therapist

VOCABULARY

34. Some teachers think that grammar and spelling errors should be _____ at first, so that beginning students are not discouraged by too many corrections.

    (a) overlooked
    (b) evaluated
    (c) foreseen
    (d) checked

35. Please note that the workshop on bilingual education will be moved to Room 107 to _____ a larger audience.

    (a) collaborate
    (b) substantiate
    (c) differentiate
    (d) accommodate

36. Instead of addressing the country's domestic issues, the politicians focused _____ on foreign policy.

    (a) primarily
    (b) effectively
    (c) incidentally
    (d) superficially

37. The discovery of the HIV virus was _____ in 1984 by a French scientist named Luc Montagnier.

    (a) held
    (b) taken
    (c) made
    (d) found

38. It is _____ to expect schools to provide enough physical activity to prevent obesity.

    (a) scarce
    (b) unseen
    (c) shrewd
    (d) unrealistic

39. Technology has played a huge part in _____ the US economy in recent years.

    (a) forcing
    (b) driving
    (c) chasing
    (d) pressing

40. The _____ of many of *Aesop's fables* is that we should not be greedy.

    (a) creed
    (b) moral
    (c) feature
    (d) metaphor

41. The scientist worked for a long time before he came upon the _____ solution.

    (a) fuzzy
    (b) perfect
    (c) spacious
    (d) matching

42. A lit cigarette _____ 250 toxic compounds into the air.

    (a) emits
    (b) remits
    (c) admits
    (d) permits

43. Economic development has brought _____ to small business owners.

    (a) liability
    (b) diversity
    (c) solidarity
    (d) prosperity

246

44. All her life, Jenna tried to _____ the offensive attitude of others toward her because of her disability.

(a) restore
(b) contrive
(c) overcome
(d) substitute

45. Most investors, not wanting to sell stocks at current low prices, are waiting for signs of a market _____.

(a) price
(b) stance
(c) fixture
(d) upturn

46. Finding a solution for global warming is imperative; what is at _____ is the survival of our species.

(a) cost
(b) stake
(c) hinge
(d) balance

47. The financial status of the company has become _____ after several bad decisions by upper management.

(a) stalwart
(b) mutinous
(c) precarious
(d) plummeted

48. The truly innovative ideas in high technology do not come from the large companies in the industry but from those on the _____.

(a) peaks
(b) fringes
(c) summits
(d) surroundings

49. The inability to recall how to perform daily routines is an early warning sign of the _____ of Alzheimer's disease.

(a) gist
(b) core
(c) onset
(d) expiry

50. The popularity of sculpture is _____ because a lack of funding in the arts is not encouraging new talent.

(a) relieving
(b) surging
(c) waning
(d) chafing

This is the end of the Vocabulary section. Do NOT move on to the Reading Comprehension section until instructed to do so. You are NOT allowed to turn to any other section of the test.

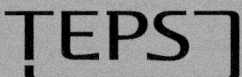

Reading
COMPREHENSION

Part I   Questions 1–16

Read the passage. Then choose the option that best completes the passage.

---

1. Scientists have observed that small animals tend to live shorter lives and _____. Larger animals, on the other hand, usually live longer than smaller ones and have fewer offspring. A female of a larger species that can live between 60 and 100 years, for example, might produce only two to three babies in her lifetime, while a female of a smaller species that lives for only ten years, such as the rabbit, might produce ten babies per litter.

   (a) live in warmer climates
   (b) have a lower intelligence
   (c) produce a lot of offspring
   (d) are hunted by many predators

2. Great art, like Mozart's, can _____. The superior quality of such art may even cause some people to feel depressed, as its greatness can induce tremendous anxiety in those who wish to create great art themselves. One such sufferer was the composer Gounod, whose ambitions were humbled when he compared his efforts with those of Mozart. He despaired that he simply could not match Mozart's genius.

   (a) affect one's attitude to music
   (b) leave many people mystified
   (c) cause discomfort rather than joy
   (d) inspire people to do great things

3. State Police Commissioner Thomas Brady announced plans today to _____. The goal, according to Commissioner Brady, is to cut the average time to complete an investigation from 20 months to 13 months. It is further hoped that the average time in bringing cases to trial will also be reduced. The announcement came after government criticism of police operations following a damning report into police affairs.

   (a) order a report into police affairs
   (b) increase the salary of police officers
   (c) appoint a new Deputy Commissioner
   (d) speed up police investigation processes

4. Most homes are full of items that can be dangerous to small children. Parents are usually aware of the obvious dangers, but there are other everyday items that may not be so obvious. Medicine, for instance, may not cause any harm to an adult, but can make a child seriously ill. This is also true of alcohol and cigarettes. Chemicals and soaps used for cleaning are often very poisonous, too. All these things should be

_____ .

(a) labeled correctly by producers
(b) kept out of the reach of children
(c) inspected by any worried parents
(d) carefully purchased by consumers

5. In the early years of printing, books were heavy and the cost of transporting paper was high, often severely affecting book prices. In order to reduce the weight and bulk of books, it was the habit to dispatch them "white," that is, without their binding. But this practice had disadvantages. Booksellers who received book consignments had to check that all pages were in the right order when readying the books to sell. Many mistakes were made, and booksellers' correspondences of the period were full of complaints about

_____ .

(a) the stains in the pages of the books
(b) the high charges for book deliveries
(c) having books that were not popular
(d) missing sheets and defective volumes

6. _____ not known for sure. Legend has it that about 100 years ago a candy store located near the New Jersey Shore was flooded during a great storm. Afterwards, the owner of the store discovered that saltwater had covered a half-prepared batch of taffy, but the candy-maker decided to finish preparing the taffy and to sell it anyway. To his surprise, customers loved his taffy! Word got around and soon other candy-makers along the shore started putting saltwater in their taffy, and thus a new tasty candy was born.

(a) The reason for saltwater taffy's success is
(b) The exact ingredients for saltwater taffy are
(c) The way saltwater taffy was first invented is
(d) The medicinal properties of saltwater taffy are

7. Richard Hickock and Perry Smith, the killers in Truman Capote's famous book *In Cold Blood*, were hanged in April 1965. They were buried at Kansas's Mount Muncie Cemetery, under tombstones paid for by Capote himself. In 1980, these tombstones were stolen but were quickly replaced by authorities. Twenty years later, the Kansas Bureau of Investigation _____. But no one knew what to do with them because they had already been replaced. Eventually, a museum in Topeka took them and has held them ever since.

(a) discovered who the killers were
(b) recovered the stolen tombstones
(c) questioned Capote about the crime
(d) dug up the replacement tombstones

8. While many people saw painter Frida Kahlo as someone who walked through life in good spirits and with a happy disposition, it was only the way she portrayed herself to the outside world. Most people were therefore _____. But this ongoing struggle was expressed in her paintings in such a way as to give them a tremendous emotional depth. In fact, her greatest works were painted while she was in a deep depression.

(a) convinced that she was an excellent artist
(b) oblivious to the problems in her paintings
(c) unaware of the inner turmoil she was experiencing
(d) surprised to find that she was always in a cheerful mood

9.

Dear Principal Swanson,

I was horrified to learn recently that the school is planning to set aside special rooms for students who want to smoke. As the parent of a high school student, I am appalled that such an illogical and harmful idea would even be considered by school officials. The twisted logic behind this new policy defies explanation. It will do nothing to prevent students from smoking; it will encourage them to start! Don't you realize that this will only increase the popularity of smoking? I hope this idea is

_____.

Sincerely,
Peggy Hanson

(a) abandoned before the health of more students is put at risk
(b) adopted so that students learn about the effects of smoking
(c) explored further in light of the space available at our school
(d) put on hold until our students' needs can be better understood

10. A new bill being debated in South Dakota is intended to help college students pay their student loans by allowing them to teach in areas where there is a shortage of teachers. The bill, which could become law sometime later this year, requires students to teach in a designated area for two years to cancel a loan for one year of school. Legislators believe the measure will do a lot to _____.

(a) alleviate the shortage of rural teachers
(b) reduce the number of loan repayments
(c) increase community college attendance
(d) boost enrollments at the state university

11. Major economic hardship could be in store for many older workers who will be forced to take mandatory retirement. If prevented from working, they will be unable to build up their retirement funds. This adverse economic impact will affect two groups of older workers in particular: women and recent immigrants. They often have irregular career histories, and consequently many of them will not benefit as much from public or employer pension plans and may lack sufficient retirement funds. The only solution is for society _____.

(a) to help workers to take early retirement
(b) not to force retirement on older employees
(c) to increase the minimum wage to help the poor
(d) not to discriminate against women and immigrants

12. For many centuries, religion and science have been in conflict, especially over Darwin's evolutionary theory. Evolution has been accepted by most scientists but rejected by religious groups because it undermines the idea of a creator or "God." In response to evolution, religious thinkers created pseudo-sciences, such as "creation science" and "intelligent design." These are still put forward today as alternatives to neo-Darwinian evolutionary science, even though evolution is widely accepted and taught in public schools. This, perhaps more than any other issue, has left

_____.

(a) a number of people doubting the existence of God
(b) the gulf between religion and science as wide as ever
(c) parents angry about changes to the public school system
(d) scientists divided as either Darwinists or neo-Darwinists

13. The publication of philosopher John Dewey's *How We Think* prompted people to reevaluate the nature of education. Dewey argued that education should not merely teach students a lot of dead facts, but rather place more emphasis on broadening the intellect and developing students' problem solving and critical thinking skills. That is to say, in place of memorization, Dewey proposed inductive reasoning. Not surprisingly, the pedagogical implications of his thought led to debate on the mission of education and

_____.

(a) a strong rejection of rote learning in the classroom
(b) a debate on the teaching of critical theory in schools
(c) a call for teachers to adopt a more dogmatic approach
(d) a reform of critical thinking skills currently being taught

14. Our lives are more interconnected than ever before. Modern communications technology lets us share information and experiences instantaneously around the globe. Major events, such as the toppling of the Twin Towers, become known to people throughout the world as they happen. The communications revolution is now so pervasive that it is easy to forget how much the world has changed in such a short time; people did not have television in the US until the late 1950s, and it was only 15 years ago that the Internet became public. As never before, _____.

(a) cultural understanding is possible among all nations
(b) people are subjected to intrusions by the mass media
(c) the world is a closer and better-informed community
(d) we are witnesses to catastrophes beyond our control

15. Modern researchers are now seriously investigating the common experiences and practices of traditional shamanism. Shamanism has been largely ignored in the past, but it is receiving more attention now that the nature and history of consciousness is emerging as a new and exciting field in psychology. _____, ancient shamanic techniques, such as those for entering into altered states of consciousness, have attracted the interest of a growing number of scholars.

(a) Instead
(b) By contrast
(c) For instance
(d) Nonetheless

16. Visit Oahu's most popular tourist attraction! Come and see traditional Hawaiian dance. Watch Hawaiians make jewelry from leaves, clothing out of bark, and homes without nails. And you'll be amazed at the many uses of coconuts. _____, at the 40-acre Hawaiian Cultural Center, the culture, lifestyle, crafts, and hospitality of seven pacific cultures come alive. Don't miss out—purchase tickets at the Royal Shopping Center or phone 293-3434.

(a) Indeed
(b) Likewise
(c) Meanwhile
(d) Specifically

17. The color of the ocean is created by the absorption and reflection of sunlight. In water, the blue wavelengths of sunlight are reflected, and the red wavelengths are absorbed. That is why the ocean looks blue most of the time. Sometimes the ocean is an aqua, green, yellow, or brown color. This is most likely caused by various impurities in the water. The Yellow Sea, for example, looks yellow because of the great amounts of yellow mud carried into it by rivers.

Q: What is the main topic of the passage?
(a) The mystery of the Yellow Sea
(b) Why the ocean reflects sunlight
(c) Why oceans have different colors
(d) The differences in the wavelengths of light

18. Skinline is now proud to offer a new anti-aging skin supplement called DermaCare. DermaCare is a special blend of vitamins and minerals that dramatically improves skin softness and smoothness, and reduces fine lines and wrinkles. Take one Skinline DermaCare capsule a day, and you will see visible results after just two months. And after four months, it will have reduced lines by 44% and increased skin elasticity by 19.6%. Achieve these amazing results at the low price of just $30 per bottle!

Q: What does the passage advertise?
(a) A pill to improve the skin
(b) A new anti-aging lotion
(c) A skin cleansing cream
(d) A way to treat pimples

19. Wallpapering can be quite simple if you follow the right steps. First, remove any previous layers of wallpaper. Second, smooth out the wall surface. Thick paper will cover minor unevenness, but it is best to fill holes with plaster and sand before papering. Third, apply the wallpaper by first placing the top edge of the wallpaper sheet to where the wall meets the ceiling. Smooth the paper to prevent air pockets and make sure that it sticks. Then fold the paper where it meets the floor and cut along the fold with wallpaper scissors.

Q: What is the passage mainly about?
(a) Ways to make your walls look better
(b) Steps to take in removing wall stains
(c) Problems that occur in plastering walls
(d) Things to do when putting up wallpaper

20. Riding a bike in urban areas is fraught with dangers. Cyclists share the urban jungle with many other, much larger vehicles—buses, trucks, vans and cars. Bicycles are more exposed and vulnerable than any other vehicles on the road. Because there are so many dangers, cities should provide safer pathways where cyclists can ride without fear of harm, just as they do for pedestrians.

Q: What is the main point of the passage?
(a) City streets should be made safer for road users.
(b) Cities should build bike paths to protect cyclists.
(c) Cyclists should not use roads meant for pedestrians.
(d) Cyclists are exposed to a multitude of threats in a city.

21. Until the 15th century, seas were sailed in square-rigged ships, which mainly carried one mast with one sail. But the early 15th century saw the development of a better, two-masted ship. This led to the sailing ship of the mid-16th century, which had more masts, improved hull design, greater cargo capacity, better rigging and superior mobility—all needed for trade, exploration and warfare. It was in ships such as these that Vasco da Gama and Columbus made their revolutionary journeys. In the 1700s, larger full-rigged ships came into use, featuring at least three masts, and all of them rigged with at least three square sails.

Q: What is the passage mainly about?
(a) The 15th-century origins of the sailing ship
(b) The history of the development of sailing ships
(c) The background to Columbus' and da Gama's ships
(d) The superiority of full-rigged ships over other ships

22. A team of engineers has developed a new way of using light to herd and separate microscopic particles suspended in liquid. The particles in the liquid were first sandwiched between a piece of glass and a piece of light-sensitive silicon. Light from a laser was then shone through the glass onto the silicon to generate electrical fields. The engineers found that the particles caught on the silicon either gathered at the area of laser light or skittered away from it, depending on their electrical properties. Using this technique, the engineers could shuffle up to 10,000 particles at a time.

Q: What is the passage mainly about?
(a) The effects of laser light on light-sensitive silicon
(b) The shuffling of silicon particles suspended in liquid
(c) A technique of generating electrical fields with lasers
(d) A method of manipulating particles using light-sensitive silicon

23. *Oregon Trail*, a popular computer game widely played in elementary schools, gives school children the opportunity to practice the skills necessary for leadership. The object of the game is to get your wagon train from St. Louis to Oregon. To be successful, you must plan your trip well; for example, you have to decide what supplies you will need and how much of them to take. Then you have to solve numerous problems along the way, from storms to wary natives to sickness and accidents. The goal is to choose wisely and make sure that as many people as possible on your wagon train make it all the way to Oregon.

Q: Which of the following is correct about *Oregon Trail*?
(a) It is a computer game made in Oregon.
(b) It is used in military training programs.
(c) It helps teachers to teach American history.
(d) It helps children improve their leadership skills.

24.

Dear Josh,

How is everything? I just got back from my grandparents' farm where I had been staying for the last two weeks. I had thought it would be really boring, but actually it was great. My grandmother is a fantastic cook. We had delicious ravioli and roast chicken dinners, and she even baked apple pies. Most of the time, I helped out on the farm by doing things like feeding the animals and driving a tractor around. It was a lot of fun. I also went out hunting ducks with my grandfather.
You'll have to come along with me next year.

See you soon,
Jeremy

Q: Which of the following is correct about the writer?
(a) He found very little to do on the farm.
(b) He enjoyed his grandmother's cooking.
(c) He did not like to go out hunting ducks.
(d) He liked chicken dinners more than ravioli.

25. In 1950, during the Cold War, Pablo Picasso created a quandary for US State Department and FBI officials by applying for a visa. He intended to lead 12 members of a Communist group called the World Congress of Peace Partisans to Washington, where they hoped to persuade President Truman to ban the atomic bomb. Picasso himself was regarded by authorities as a leading member of the French Communist Party and had been monitored by the FBI since 1944. Such affiliations were perceived as a threat and prompted officials to deny Picasso and his entire delegation their visas.

Q: Why did the American government deny Picasso a visa?
(a) He had been found guilty of a conspiracy in 1944.
(b) His political allegiances were considered a threat.
(c) His advocacy of the atomic bomb was not welcome.
(d) He used his fame to criticize American foreign policy.

26. Life can be unfair, but people can do little things to create a sense of fair play. For
instance, yesterday I was waiting in a long checkout line at the supermarket when they
opened the empty checkout lane next to me. Then, straightaway, the person behind me
pushed his cart past mine and made a mad dash to the newly opened checkout. But the
checkout clerk politely asked that pushy customer to allow those who were in front of
him to go first. Everyone there approved of what the checkout clerk did, and the pushy
customer had to wait—that's what I mean by fair play.

Q: Which of the following is correct according to the passage?
(a) A pushy customer got upset and shouted at a clerk.
(b) A clerk did not let a pushy customer get served first.
(c) One of the writer's friends works as a checkout clerk.
(d) The writer got into an argument with another customer.

27. In the past, people used to think of animals as machine-like, without genuine emotions or
feelings. However, science, moral philosophy, and a more civilized society have led us
to understand that animals are sentient and can suffer from bad treatment just as we can.
We now know that animals are like us in all kinds of ways, and science has even shown
that almost 99% of our genes are similar to those of the chimpanzee. We now recognize
that it is morally reprehensible to inflict suffering upon animals and that as sentient
beings they deserve our protection and consideration.

Q: Which of the following is correct according to the passage?
(a) Animals do not feel pleasure and happiness.
(b) Bad treatment of animals is justified by philosophy.
(c) Humans were once ignorant that animals have emotions.
(d) Human genes have nothing in common with those of chimpanzees.

28.
> Dear Ms. Hammond,
>
> Recently, we have experienced a series of problems in obtaining full payment from
> you for products we have delivered, and this issue still remains unresolved. Because
> you have not yet paid for your previous order in full, we cannot deliver any more
> goods to you. I regret that you leave us no alternative other than to withhold all
> further deliveries. We urge your prompt attention to this matter.
>
> Sincerely,
> Emily Brown
> Collections Manager

Q: According to the letter, what will happen if Ms. Hammond does not pay for her delivery?
(a) She will need to return the goods.
(b) Her account will have to be closed.
(c) Her previous order will be cancelled.
(d) She will not receive any more deliveries.

29. From the evidence available on the clothing worn in ancient Incan society, we know that the Incas were very good weavers. They used wool, which they dyed with coloring made from various plants. And a professional weaver usually had the task of weaving the wool, sometimes using differently colored wools and creating fabrics with complicated patterns. These fabrics were then used to make clothing.

Q: According to the passage, which of the following is correct about ancient Incan society?
(a) Plant dyes were used to color wool.
(b) Colored clothing was hard to make.
(c) Weaving was usually done by servants.
(d) Complicated patterns were rare for Incans.

30. While people have sought the mysterious lost island of Atlantis for thousands of years, it seems likely that the island never existed. It was first mentioned by Plato, who depicted its destruction by violent earthquakes and coastal flooding. However, historians believe that Plato's narration is fictional, an account inspired by myth or other catastrophes in the ancient world. Most think it originated from legends of the massive volcanic eruption on the island of Thera in the Mediterranean Sea, dated around 1500 BC. The eruption caused a massive tsunami that, experts hypothesize, devastated the Minoan civilization on the nearby island of Crete.

Q: Which of the following is correct about the island of Atlantis according to the passage?
(a) Plato considered it to be a mythological place.
(b) None of its inhabitants survived a massive tsunami.
(c) Historians believe it was destroyed by an earthquake.
(d) Plato's account of it could be based on Thera's eruption.

31. Lakeside University wishes to thank Ron Fisher of the Theater Department for his efforts in establishing a partnership with the Royal Shakespeare Company (RSC). When the RSC was conducting its first four-week residency on campus four years ago, Ron attended all educational and social events scheduled. Inspired by what he saw, he wrote to the RSC and to Lakeside faculty to propose that if actors from the RSC were coming here to perform, perhaps we should also send Lakeside students to Stratford, England, to learn. That led to us sending two students to Stratford each summer as part of the partnership. Well done, Ron!

Q: Which of the following is correct according to the announcement?
(a) Ron Fisher has acted with the RSC for the last four years.
(b) The RSC performs at Lakeside University every four years.
(c) Ron Fisher instigated RSC residencies at Lakeside University.
(d) The Lakeside program in Stratford was Ron Fisher's initiative.

32. New Humanism was a school of literary criticism that was popular in America from 1910 to 1930. It emerged as a reaction against naturalism and its materialistic emphasis on biological determinism and human nature's animal qualities. New Humanism sought to reassert the importance of human reason and free will and emphasize the moral qualities of literature. New humanists also placed science and religion at odds, stressing that enlightened human reason could "check" base instincts and serve in place of religious principles.

Q: Which of the following is correct about New Humanism?
(a) It saw man as hopelessly subject to animal desires.
(b) It opposed the deterministic world view of naturalism.
(c) It questioned the validity of human reasoning in all matters.
(d) It insisted that science and religion were mutually harmonious.

33. In order to demonstrate the safety advantages of using winter tires, the Transportation Safety Committee conducted a test by driving two vehicles around obstacles set up on an icy road. The vehicles were identical, except that one was equipped with all-season tires and the other with winter tires. Measurements of traction and stopping distances of both vehicles were made. Not surprisingly, a marked difference was found between the handling ability of each vehicle, with the vehicle that had winter tires performing better in all areas.

Q: What can be inferred from the report?
(a) Winter tires are not safe for summer driving.
(b) All-season tires are unsafe and should not be used.
(c) Winter tires are more expensive than all-season tires.
(d) Certain tires make driving on icy roads less dangerous.

34. IndoAid, an aid organization in Indonesia, recently came up with a creative solution to help the poor in Indonesia at very little cost. It provided a loan of five chickens to a local family. When these chickens began laying eggs, the family could eat fresh eggs every day. They were also able to sell some eggs and raise egg-laying chickens of their own. Eventually, they had enough to give back five chickens to IndoAid, and these chickens were then given as a loan to another family in need. Other aid agencies are closely monitoring the program to see if any long-term benefits will make it a worthwhile alternative to traditional aid efforts.

Q: What is the writer most likely to agree with?
(a) Donating money may not be the most effective way in helping the poor.
(b) Indonesian families are very generous in helping their neighbors.
(c) The poverty problem in Indonesia will get worse over time.
(d) Indonesian families will get sick of eating eggs every day.

35. A teenage girl's body image is psychological in nature. It is not what she actually looks like in the mirror, but how she sees herself in her mind's eye. If negative thoughts are introduced, they can affect a girl's body image and can damage her self-esteem. As a positive self-image is a building block for success in life, it is important for parents to supply constructive images to help their daughter develop a healthy view of her body.

Q: What can be inferred from the passage?
(a) Positive body image will guarantee success in life.
(b) A positive body image can lead to high self-esteem.
(c) Teens with good looks do not have negative self-esteem.
(d) Some parents feel that too much emphasis is placed on looks.

36. Emanating a quiet charm right in the middle of the action, Vacation Inn in Darling Harbour has the best that Sydney has to offer on its doorstep. Situated in the southern end of the Central Business District (CBD), Vacation Inn is within walking distance of Sydney's best restaurants, theaters and shopping complexes. Take a leisurely stroll to the harbour, enjoy the vibrant Chinatown right behind the hotel or spend an evening at the Sydney Entertainment Centre right across the road. Vacation Inn helps you make the most of your visit to Sydney.

Q: What can be inferred from the advertisement?
(a) All Vacation Inn rooms have views of Darling Harbour.
(b) Darling Harbour hotels are the most expensive in Sydney.
(c) People from many different cultures live in Sydney's CBD.
(d) Sydney's southern CBD attracts a large number of visitors.

37. A few inches behind the bridge of the nose is a region of the brain that may explain why some people are prone to a negative outlook on life. This became evident in a recent study attempting to examine the neurological roots of the so-called "the negative effect," which is a trait that predisposes people to unpleasant moods such as anxiety and anger. Researchers used powerful brain imaging technology to locate areas of the brain thought to be responsible for various emotions. Test showed that negative emotions were registered in an area of the brain behind the nose.

Q: What can be inferred from the study?
(a) The shape of a person's nose can indicate personality traits.
(b) Psychological therapy is the key to stopping "the negative effect."
(c) A predisposition to negativity might be corrected with brain surgery.
(d) Negative emotions may not be caused solely by a person's upbringing.

Read the passage. Then identify the option that does NOT belong.

---

38. If women smoke during pregnancy, they increase the risk of their child being born with a disability. (a) While some children grow up to develop mental disorders, nicotine has not been proven as a factor. (b) The fact is that the fetus is exposed to high concentrations of nicotine by expectant mothers who smoke. (c) Receptors for dopamine, which is an essential biological chemical for brain development, are then altered as a result. (d) The effect is to harm fetal development and cause anomalies, such as deficits in learning and behavior, and even death.

39. Joseph Heller's most famous novel was based on his wartime experiences with the US Air Force. (a) After graduating from Abraham Lincoln High School in 1941, Heller served as a bombardier in the Second World War. (b) But it was after he had left the military and was working in advertising that he began to write his anti-war novel. (c) There are often paradoxes evident in the decisions of leaders during times of war. (d) The paradox of a no-win situation, or a so-called Catch-22, was the basis for his novel, which Heller aptly titled *Catch-22*.

40. Loss of heat in an area of a building is usually indicative of an inadequate or malfunctioning heating system. (a) In such a situation, maintenance staff should first check the heating system for faults and correct any malfunctions immediately. (b) If the system is functioning properly, then they need to examine wall and ceiling structures to locate the source of heat loss. (c) Staff might alternatively install mobile heaters to poorly heated areas. (d) Once the problem has been identified, a permanent fix should be implemented in an efficient and timely manner.

This is the end of the Reading Comprehension section. Please remain seated until the proctor has instructed otherwise. You are NOT allowed to turn to any other section of the test.

서울대 최신기출 **1**

Listening Comprehension **Scripts**

1

M Guess what? I got into London University!

W _____

(a) You'll be accepted.
(b) I appreciate the offer.
(c) That's great! Well done.
(d) I haven't been given one.

2

W How come your flight arrived late?

M _____

(a) It landed smoothly.
(b) I'm not sure how late.
(c) I confirmed it in advance.
(d) It was delayed by bad weather.

3

M When is your uncle supposed to get here?

W _____

(a) He's taking a bus.
(b) He'll arrive around 7.
(c) I don't know what he'll say.
(d) I spoke to him earlier today.

4

W I hope it'll rain and cool things down a bit.

M _____

(a) Yeah, it's awfully hot today.
(b) Yes, things will settle down.
(c) The weather's quite cool indeed.
(d) We're going to have showers instead.

5

M When did you last have a day off?

W _____

(a) It isn't on my schedule.
(b) Tomorrow is a holiday.
(c) We can set a date for it.
(d) It was sometime in May.

6

W It's a lovely party, but I must go now.

M _____

(a) Don't wait up for me.
(b) I'll go to the party, too.
(c) Sure. I'll clean up in time for it.
(d) OK, then. I'm glad you came.

7

M John must be happy with his promotion.

W _____

(a) Yes, and he deserves it.
(b) He seemed happier then.
(c) He'll do better next time.
(d) Right, you should tell him.

8

W I ran as hard as I could but only came fifth in the race.

M _____

(a) The fourth one looks better.
(b) Maybe the others weren't ready.
(c) Well, you had tough competition.
(d) Right. Life is full of pleasant surprises.

9

M This suit isn't worth the money I spent on it.

W _____

(a) What a bargain it was!
(b) It does look great on you.
(c) Yes, I'd say it was overpriced.
(d) Yes. You can pay with your credit card.

10

W Hey, Peter, should we take a shopping cart?

M _____

(a) Of course. We have a lot to get.
(b) We can go shopping anytime.
(c) I don't think it's being used.
(d) OK. Take over the wheel.

11

M Did you manage to patch things up with Mark?

W _____

(a) No, he and I stayed home.
(b) Sure, he'll get better soon.
(c) Things are still a bit awkward.
(d) I've enjoyed working here, though.

12

W Hi, Craig. Jessica speaking. Are you free to talk?

M _____

(a) That's the best thing to do.
(b) OK, let's go into the other room.
(c) I'm too busy to write a reply now.
(d) Well, you caught me at a bad time.

13

M Honey, aren't you ready to go out yet?

W _____

(a) Not quite. I'll finish by this week.
(b) I've just got to put on my jacket.
(c) But I'm not sure what to order.
(d) I'm tired. Let's go home.

14

W I'll be back as soon as I can.

M _____

(a) You weren't that late.
(b) There's no need to hurry.
(c) Thanks for answering so fast.
(d) I didn't know you'd come back soon.

15

M I thought Jason was too argumentative last night.

W _____

(a) He was definitely way out of line.
(b) Jason couldn't make it last night.
(c) You're right. I'll apologize to him.
(d) That's at the center of my argument.

16

M Hi. You must be our new accountant.

W Yes. I'm Claudia Jennings.

M I'm George. Welcome to the company.

W _____

(a) I'm in the accounting department.
(b) Thanks. It's good to be here.
(c) You've been a great help.
(d) I've also worked there.

17

W You look worried. What's wrong?

M I've got to speak to James, but I can't find him.

W Why do you want to speak to him?

M _____

(a) Call him at home.
(b) He has a book I need.
(c) He might be at work.
(d) It wasn't that long ago.

18

M Will you be busy tomorrow night?

W No, not really. Why?

M I need some help with my math.

W _____

(a) I've been busy teaching.
(b) I'd be glad to help out.
(c) The math is all wrong.
(d) I've nearly finished it.

19

W Steve, how are you doing with the sales report?

M It should be ready later this afternoon.

W But wasn't it due by noon?

M _____

(a) It was, but I've had problems with it.

(b) Well, I'm never late for anything.

(c) The meeting is still at noon.

(d) That's the report I meant.

20

M I'll take this chocolate bar, please.

W That'll be three dollars, sir.

M Three? But it said two dollars on the shelf.

W _____

(a) That's for the smaller ones.

(b) Oh, what a pleasant change!

(c) No, we don't take returns.

(d) Maybe you dropped it.

21

W You look great in that suit, Peter.

M Thanks! But don't you think it's too tight?

W No! It makes you look younger.

M _____

(a) Well, I think it fits perfectly.

(b) That's nice of you to say.

(c) Thank you, but I'm fine.

(d) Let me try it on first.

22

M Does the bus for the national library stop here?

W Yes, but it only comes every half hour.

M I see. Is there a quicker way?

W _____

(a) No, it's best to go by bus.

(b) You could try the bookstore.

(c) Yes, that's the shortest route.

(d) It depends where you want to go.

23

W The Omega Hotel. May I help you?

M Yes, I'd like to reserve a single room, please.

W For how long, sir?

M _____

(a) Something with a view.

(b) Make it enough for three.

(c) Two nights, July 11 and 12.

(d) The beginning of next week.

24

M We should buy that car in the showroom.

W I'd love a car like that, but we can't afford it.

M I think we could make the payments.

W _____

(a) We'll probably get a new one.

(b) But the insurance would be high.

(c) Sure, that one is in our price range.

(d) Yes, but it just doesn't appeal to me.

25

W My family is going camping this weekend.

M That's great! It's lovely outdoors this time of year.

W Are you interested in joining us?

M _____

(a) I've got a wedding to go to.

(b) You'll have a great weekend.

(c) Sure. Stay as long as you want.

(d) I didn't think your family would.

26

M Jenny, you're home early. I thought you'd be late.

W The meeting I was supposed to go to got cancelled.

M Why? What happened?

W _____

(a) It's because I didn't attend.

(b) It started later than I thought.

(c) I left when the meeting ended.

(d) A key member couldn't make it.

27

W Hi, this is Matt Anderson's wife calling.
M Oh hi, Mrs. Anderson. How may I help you?
W I need to reach Matt, but his cell phone is off.
M _____

(a) You should've called 911.
(b) OK, let me leave a message with you.
(c) He usually leaves home around seven.
(d) Oh, he's giving a seminar presentation.

28

M What great weather! I'm going for a bike ride.
W Really? They said it might rain later.
M I doubt it. It's not that cloudy.
W _____

(a) I don't mind it when it's cloudy.
(b) Then, we'll go somewhere else.
(c) Let's cycle over there and have a look.
(d) But I can see dark clouds on the horizon.

29

W Did you see the apartment complex brochure?
M I did, but the apartments are out of our range.
W I thought the prices were good.
M _____

(a) I can give you a discount.
(b) I'm resolved to push it forward.
(c) It's good, but we still have to move.
(d) The down payments are too high, though.

30

M How many courses are you taking this semester?
W Five, but I might change one.
M When does the course change period end?
W _____

(a) You have to sign up for the course.
(b) Today is the last day of class.
(c) I have to decide by tomorrow.
(d) I don't want to drop a course.

31

W Could you help me rearrange my office furniture?
M Sure. What do you need me to do?
W Just help me move the desk to the window.
M OK. Which end should I take?
W You take that end, and I'll take this one.
M All right, I've got it. Let's go.

Q: What is the woman mainly doing in the conversation?
(a) Moving into a new office.
(b) Buying a new office desk.
(c) Getting help moving a desk.
(d) Changing offices with the man.

32

M Would you be able to babysit James this Saturday?
W Do you mean in the afternoon or evening?
M In the afternoon.
W Sure. What time do you need me?
M Could you come over around 3?
W OK. I'll see you then.

Q: What is the man mainly doing in the conversation?
(a) Making plans for Saturday evening.
(b) Getting permission to see James.
(c) Arranging for a babysitter.
(d) Asking the woman out on a date.

33

W What do you think? Should I buy these shoes?
M The toes look a bit too pointed.
W OK. What about those brown ones?
M They're better, but I prefer the blue ones we saw before.
W Those were expensive, though.
M I know, but they were the best.

Q: What are the man and woman mainly doing in the conversation?
(a) Shopping for shoes.
(b) Deciding what to wear.
(c) Discussing shoe prices.
(d) Preparing to go for a walk.

34

M How are your studies going?

W Well, I'm enjoying everything except my psychology course.

M Why? What's wrong with it?

W It just involves statistics and not much else.

M Really? That's not what I would've expected.

W Me neither. And it doesn't interest me.

Q: What is the main topic of the conversation?

(a) The woman's failure in psychology class.

(b) The difficulties the woman has in studying.

(c) The statistics used in the woman's courses.

(d) The woman's dislike of her psychology course.

35

M Which laptop should I get out of these two?

W I'm not sure. I don't know much about laptops.

M Well, which one do you think looks better?

W I guess the one with the white case.

M Yeah, me too. It's much lighter, as well.

W Then, I'd go for that one.

Q: What are the man and woman mainly doing in the conversation?

(a) Looking at functions on a laptop.

(b) Judging the latest in laptop designs.

(c) Determining which laptop to purchase.

(d) Discussing the merits of using a laptop.

36

W Welcome to the Seafood Café.

M Hi, we'd like a table for two, please.

W OK, there's about a half-hour wait. Is that all right?

M I guess so. Can we go for a stroll and come back?

W Certainly. I'll add your name to the waiting list.

M It's Brandon. We'll be back in about 20 minutes.

Q: What is the man mainly doing in the conversation?

(a) Getting a café table for two people.

(b) Deciding whether to go out for a walk.

(c) Inquiring about the menu at a restaurant.

(d) Asking for directions to a café.

37

M Wendy, do you spend a lot of time on the Internet?

W Sure, about two hours every day.

M What on earth do you do in all that time?

W Email, or sometimes I chat or do some shopping.

M Online shopping? Aren't you worried about the risk?

W No. I do most of my shopping online these days.

Q: What is the conversation mainly about?

(a) The reasons people like online shopping.

(b) The security risks of shopping online.

(c) The woman's usage of the Internet.

(d) The pros and cons of the Internet.

38

M Are you all ready for your trip, Rebecca?

W Almost. The Chinese Embassy said they'd call me.

M About your visa?

W Yes, I haven't received it yet.

M But today's Wednesday, and your flight's on Friday!

W I'm not worried. They said it would be done by tomorrow.

Q: Which is correct about the woman according to the conversation?

(a) She is at the Chinese Embassy.

(b) She is still waiting for her visa.

(c) She was asked to call the embassy.

(d) She plans to leave on Wednesday.

39

M I might have to look for a new job.

W Why? Don't you like where you work?

M I do, but my company is downsizing.

W Oh, and you think you will be let go?

M Possibly. They have to cut staff by half.

W That's drastic. I hope your job will be safe.

Q: Which is correct according to the conversation?
(a) The man has found a new job.
(b) The man's company is hiring staff.
(c) The man dislikes his current work.
(d) The man thinks he may lose his job.

40

W I heard you're going mountain climbing tomorrow.
M Yes. A friend and I are going to Mount Bradley.
W Well, be careful. It's dangerous there.
M Don't worry. We're prepared for it.
W So was I when I went there, but I still found it treacherous.
M OK, thanks for the tip. I'll take extra care.

Q: Which is correct according to the conversation?
(a) The man is set to go climbing with two friends.
(b) The woman felt safe climbing Mount Bradley.
(c) The man ignores the woman's advice.
(d) The woman has been to Mount Bradley.

41

W Do you do anything interesting after work?
M Starting this month, I'm going to.
W Oh, yeah? What do you have in mind?
M Well, I'm going to take up some new hobbies.
W What kinds of things do you mean?
M I'll get into astronomy and photography.

Q: Which is correct about the man according to the conversation?
(a) He has begun his photography hobby.
(b) He wants to spend less time on hobbies.
(c) He plans to start astronomy as a hobby.
(d) He has made no definite plans for hobbies.

42

M I just can't seem to save money these days.
W Are you making an effort to spend less?
M No, I've never been very good at that.
W Well, you can start by keeping track of your spending.
M But I wouldn't know where to start.
W Do what I do. Whenever you spend money, just note it down.

Q: Which is correct according to the conversation?
(a) The man has began cutting back on spending.
(b) The man monitors his spending carefully.
(c) The woman writes down what she spends.
(d) The woman asks for tips on how to save money.

43

M Did you finish yesterday's homework, Alice?
W Sorry, Mr. Stuart, I didn't.
M What happened? You're usually prepared.
W My computer crashed at 11 o'clock last night.
M That's too bad. I hope you can get it fixed.
W Oh, yes. My brother said he'd look at it today.

Q: What can be inferred about the woman from the conversation?
(a) She did not get any sleep last night.
(b) She will probably buy a new computer.
(c) She uses her computer to do homework.
(d) She forgot about yesterday's homework.

44

M Ellen, how have your stocks been doing?

W Not great. The market's down at the moment.

M Then, this might be a good time to buy, right?

W Well, if you do, I'd recommend a mutual fund.

M Really? I had some stocks in mind.

W But mutual funds are a lot safer.

Q: What can be inferred from the conversation?

(a) The man wants to become a stockbroker.

(b) The man is keen to make an investment.

(c) The woman has lost a lot of money.

(d) The woman is the man's boss.

45

W Did you hear about the President's alleged tax cut?

M Yeah, but why do you say "alleged?"

W Well, for most of us it won't mean much.

M But even a small tax cut is better than nothing.

W Well, I think it's just a political ploy to gain popularity.

M Maybe. But at least taxes didn't go up.

Q: What can be inferred from the conversation?

(a) The woman wants the tax plan to be reversed.

(b) The man wishes he were more politically minded.

(c) The man is unlikely to be a tax-cut beneficiary.

(d) The woman is critical of the President's tax-cut plan.

46

The Brain Map is a book that can train your mind to make the most of your studies. It will help you improve your grades, take more effective notes, write better essays, and develop a better memory. It's not just for students; it's for anyone who wants to improve their brainpower and enhance their memory. Get *The Brain Map* now at all major bookstores.

Q: What is mainly being advertised about *The Brain Map*?

(a) Its use for writing college essays.

(b) That it improves mental skills.

(c) Its focus on being a good student.

(d) That it promotes positive thinking.

47

According to a study done by our faculty, the idea that women are much more talkative than men is a myth. We outfitted 396 college students with devices that recorded their conversations throughout a typical day. From the recordings, we found that on average, women speak a little more than 16,000 words a day, while men speak slightly under 16,000 words.

Q: What is the lecture mainly about?

(a) A study on the talkativeness of men and women.

(b) The number of words an average person knows.

(c) The conversational habits of college students.

(d) A speech contest between men and women.

48

Harry Landen has the expertise you need to give your film and video projects a professional look. Harry has been in the industry for over 25 years and is the author of *Professional Home Video*, a standard reference for independent filmmakers. Harry also founded videopro.com, one of the best sites for information on digital video production. For all your film production needs, contact Harry Landen at 555-5919.

Q: What is the main purpose of the advertisement?

(a) To sell Harry Landen's book.

(b) To inform people about videopro.com.

(c) To explain Harry Landen's film projects.

(d) To promote the services of Harry Landen.

49

Most students here today probably believe that as people get older, their mental faculties decline. The truth is that people have the ability to sharpen mental skills at any time. The brain can be thought of as a muscle; to keep it in top condition, it must be exercised regularly. Thus, anyone who wants to improve their mental functions should regularly apply their minds to mentally challenging activities.

Q: What is the main idea of the talk?
(a) Older people think less clearly.
(b) Regular exercise can slow down aging.
(c) Young people are more mentally active.
(d) People can improve their mental faculties with effort.

50

Monthly budgets should now be prepared according to the revised Aiken method, which I described in detail at our last managers' meeting. Managers will be required to provide the accounting department with progress updates on changing their current accounting practices and adopting the new system. It is expected that all departments will have adopted this new accounting method prior to the next quarter.

Q: What is the main idea of the talk?
(a) Each department has to phase out the Aiken method.
(b) Departments must all adopt the new accounting method.
(c) All budgets should be finalized before managers' meetings.
(d) Managers' budgets must be approved at the managers' meeting.

51

Introducing the Entourage X5: the sports car you only need to refuel once a year. It's a hybrid like no other, with emission-free driving for the first 50 miles after every recharge. The greenest car ever to hit the road, the Entourage X5 is powered by a small gasoline engine and a lithium ion battery pack, which work in harmony using technology developed for US military reconnaissance vehicles. Drive for a cleaner future. Drive the Entourage X5—debuting now at showrooms nationwide.

Q: What is mainly being advertised about the Entourage X5?
(a) It saves on gas because it rarely needs to be refueled.
(b) It has gained a good reputation as a high-tech green car.
(c) It incorporates hybrid technology used by the US military.
(d) It provides an environmentally friendly driving experience.

52

Ladies and gentlemen, unfortunately for developing countries, the institutions with the greatest power over the global economic system are not motivated by altruism. The World Bank, the International Monetary Fund, and the World Trade Organization dominate global social and economic policy, but they represent the interests of the rich while excluding the voices of the poor. We need reforms that can counteract this imbalance, such as a global development tax.

Q: What is the speaker's main point?
(a) Developing countries need to reform their economic and social policies.
(b) Global tax systems need to be altered to facilitate development.
(c) The economic gap within developing countries is widening.
(d) Changes are needed to counter the dominance of global institutions.

53

According to the Energy Information Agency, since 2000, the amount of electricity generated by wind farms across the United States has more than quadrupled. Nevertheless, wind farms account for only one percent of the nation's electricity. That figure should rise when more wind farms are completed, including ongoing offshore wind farm projects in Texas, Massachusetts, and New York. Currently, Texas creates the most wind energy of any state, followed by California, Iowa, and Minnesota.

Q: Which is correct according to the news report?
(a) Energy from US wind farms has increased over the years.
(b) Texas has no wind farm operational at the moment.
(c) New York State creates the most wind energy in the US.
(d) Wind farms generate four percent of America's electricity.

54

I'd like to tell you a few key facts about milk production. First of all, milk intended for commercial use is heated, known as pasteurization, in order to kill any disease-carrying microorganisms. Only once it is pasteurized can milk be processed and sold in various forms. Thirty percent is sold in liquid form, which, as you should know, is almost 90 percent water. Another 25 percent goes to making ice cream, butter, yogurt, and sour cream. The remainder becomes cheese.

Q: Which is correct according to the talk?
(a) Milk is pasteurized prior to processing.
(b) Over half of milk is sold in liquid form.
(c) Liquid milk contains a maximum of 30 percent water.
(d) Ice cream makes up 25 percent of milk products.

55

Thank you for calling Global Airways. To access automated flight information, please stay on the line and have your ticket number and personal identification ready. Press one if you are calling regarding domestic flights. For international flights, please press two now. To speak to a customer service associate, please call back during our regular business hours.

Q: Which is correct according to the instructions?
(a) Callers should hold to speak with a representative.
(b) Callers are asked to enter their flight number to get information.
(c) People traveling within the country should press one.
(d) Customer service associates can be reached 24 hours a day.

56

Scottish technology could bring the end of traditional DJs. At the University of Edinburgh, programmers are developing software that simulates DJ talk and reflects the listener's interests. The idea was inspired by Internet radio broadcasts that allow listeners to choose musical preferences. With the new software, when a user selects music, a web station not only plays the selection but offers digitized DJ chatter about it as well, along with suggestions for further listening.

Q: Which is correct about the new software according to the news report?
(a) It was developed by aspiring DJs.
(b) It was a natural development from traditional radio.
(c) It does not include any verbal component.
(d) It makes musical recommendations to users.

57

The next American novelist I want to discuss is Richard Yates, a writer whose thematic obsession was the inescapability of the past. Yates's characters are arrested by their personal histories, mired in memory. Their pasts dictate the crushed hopes and disappointments in their lives. Thus, their defeats are of their own doing. Yates's vision is bleak and unsparing. In fact, few can surpass him at portraying how the high hopes of the 1940s and '50s ended in bitter disillusionment.

Q: Which is correct about Yates according to the lecture?
(a) He believed that the past was irrelevant to the present.
(b) He wrote about characters defeated by their own pasts.
(c) He explored how people remember the past incorrectly.
(d) He sought to offer hope to readers in the 1940s and '50s.

58

You have reached Professor Gibson's voicemail. Effective until next semester, I am out of the office on sabbatical. If you need to contact me about an urgent matter, you may leave word with the department secretary and she will make sure I receive your message and contact information. Alternately, you may send an email to gibson@usfca.edu. I will respond as soon as possible.

Q: What can be inferred about Professor Gibson from the phone message?
(a) He does not want people to call him directly.
(b) He is not expecting to receive many messages.
(c) He would prefer not to be emailed while abroad.
(d) He is worried about his long absence from work.

59

Improving education among immigrants is a pressing issue. In the past twelve years alone, nearly eight million immigrants have come to the United States, half of whom are considered illegal immigrants. Now, today's legal immigrants are surely better off education-wise than those who arrived in this country a decade ago. But the same is not true for illegal immigrants. And since this issue of education bears on matters of policy, it warrants closer scrutiny.

Q: What is the speaker most likely to do next?
(a) Explain how to raise the standard of US education.
(b) Discuss ways to prevent illegal immigration.
(c) Talk about the immigrant populations of various states.
(d) Go into detail about the education level of illegal immigrants.

60

Before talking about the English Civil War in more detail, I'll give you some background. The war began in 1642 out of a conflict between King Charles I and the English Parliament over who would govern religious and civil affairs. The central issue was Charles's belief in the divine right of kings, meaning that he saw himself as an absolute ruler chosen by God. After Parliament repudiated this assertion, England descended into civil war.

Q: What can be inferred from the lecture?
(a) Charles was not interested in governing civil affairs.
(b) Parliament wished to place limits on the king's power.
(c) Religious authorities rejected the king's divine prerogative.
(d) Some Parliamentarians were victims of religious persecution.

1

M I'd put on a warm jacket, if I were you.

W _____

(a) Good idea. I'll go get one.
(b) Yes, it's warm outside.
(c) I like that jacket, too.
(d) It's very expensive.

2

W Jeffery, can you keep a secret?

M _____

(a) That's not what I heard, though.
(b) You probably could've asked.
(c) Of course. You can trust me.
(d) Possibly. Bring it here.

3

M I can't wait to see the Eiffel Tower.

W _____

(a) I'm looking forward to it, too.
(b) It's an interesting event.
(c) You could've gone later.
(d) Well, go home, then.

4

W Hello, is Pam Kane there?

M _____

(a) I'll definitely ask her.
(b) Hi, Pam. Glad you called.
(c) Yes, I'll leave a message.
(d) Sorry, she's unavailable now.

5

M This movie is just terrible.

W _____

(a) You made some bad decisions.
(b) Let's hurry or we'll miss it.
(c) In that case, take it down.
(d) Frankly, I've seen worse.

6

W Would you like to join me for a bite to eat?

M _____

(a) I can't. It's my lunch hour.
(b) Thanks, you helped me a lot.
(c) Sure, just let me finish this email.
(d) No, I'll choose something else later.

7

M Are we out of all our new game consoles already?

W _____

(a) I bought myself one yesterday.
(b) They're supposed to be popular.
(c) No, but they'll be sold out in no time.
(d) Yes, people are asking for better quality.

8

W What a strong argument you presented at the meeting today!

M _____

(a) That panned out differently.
(b) But some points were valid.
(c) You look like you're in good shape.
(d) Well, I've been pondering it for a while.

9

M I'm so worried. I have an exam this afternoon.

W _____

(a) Knowing you, I'm sure you'll do fine.
(b) Really? Please pass on my regards.
(c) Best of luck with the big move.
(d) That's OK. I don't have one.

10

W Do you know anything about the next convention?

M _____

(a) Just that it'll be in August.
(b) No theory has been established.
(c) It certainly ended on a high note.
(d) It'll be available in the near future.

11

M I'm afraid we hired the wrong person.

W _____

(a) Just work hard and you'll improve.
(b) There are lots of good candidates.
(c) You're not in the right position.
(d) It's a little premature to judge.

12

W Why do you always put me on the spot in class?

M _____

(a) I apologize. I didn't know you were there.
(b) Sorry if I made you feel uncomfortable.
(c) Well, I came early to get that spot.
(d) I didn't think to check first.

13

M This physics problem has really got me stumped.

W _____

(a) It's as black and white as you said.
(b) I'm sure that assumption's erroneous.
(c) That's what first grabbed my attention.
(d) Maybe look at it from a different angle.

14

W I heard you're a fitness fanatic. What's your workout regimen?

M _____

(a) I'm going to exercise that option soon.
(b) I don't know. You should've asked sooner.
(c) I concentrate on distance running training.
(d) Well, I'm stuck working every day of the week.

15

M I'm not sure if I should apply for this position.

W _____

(a) Judging by its many perks, I would.
(b) It applies regardless of the outcome.
(c) Break it down to manageable portions.
(d) I guess you'll work it out another way.

16

W Make sure you don't get sunburned today.
M Don't worry. I have a hat.
W I think you'll need more than that.
M _____

(a) I'll put on sunscreen.
(b) It's very sunny today.
(c) I just got this new hat.
(d) I'll think of something nice.

17

M Don't you have a television?
W No, and I don't want one.
M So, what do you do instead?
W _____

(a) You may be right.
(b) I watch a lot of TV.
(c) I really like to read.
(d) You can do it yourself.

18

W Hi, I'm Alice. Welcome to the company. How's everything?
M Great. Much better than my old job.
W Really? Where were you working before?
M _____

(a) In a few months.
(b) Thanks. I'm doing fine.
(c) I have a really good job here.
(d) At a small company downtown.

19

M You look like you work here. Can you help me?

W Sure. What do you need?

M Where can I find the outdoor house paints?

W _____

(a) I recommend a different brand.

(b) On that house across the street.

(c) Aisle 5. Follow me, I'll show you.

(d) That store has changed locations.

20

W What did you do over the break?

M I finally finished that novel I've been writing.

W Wow. You must be happy.

M _____

(a) Sure. I can't wait to read it.

(b) Not true. Read it over again.

(c) Well, that's not what I wrote.

(d) Yes, but now I need a publisher.

21

M How do you like your new job?

W It's great, except for one thing.

M What's that, too much work?

W _____

(a) Right. I can't keep up.

(b) I definitely got the job.

(c) Not really. I'm so busy.

(d) I think your idea is better.

22

W Hello, sir. How can I help you today?

M I need to get reimbursed for my travel expenses.

W OK, you just need to fill out this reimbursement form.

M _____

(a) You need to send me the form.

(b) Certainly. I'll do that right away.

(c) Sure, you can tell me about it later.

(d) You should've told me where they are.

23

M Excuse me. Would you mind sharing your table with me?

W Not at all. This place is so packed at lunchtime.

M Thanks. Hey, aren't you in Dr. Yoon's history class?

W _____

(a) So that's where I've seen you before.

(b) I'm taking fewer classes this semester.

(c) We can just sit at that other table, then.

(d) I agree. His history class is really interesting.

24

W Excuse me. Where's the subway entrance?

M Just keep walking to the next intersection.

W Oh, you mean way up there?

M _____

(a) You can take the subway.

(b) Subways are efficient.

(c) We can't go that far.

(d) That's the one.

25

M Your division always has new faces.

W Yeah. People come and go all the time.

M Why the constant turnover?

W _____

(a) The company is reputable.

(b) People help each other out.

(c) The pay isn't exactly competitive.

(d) Job security is precious these days.

26

W Finally, all the tour members are through immigration.

M That took ages. What a pain to get through!

W Yeah, and now we've got to get our luggage.

M _____

(a) These ones are heavy to carry.

(b) Hopefully that won't take quite as long.

(c) If we've passed that, we must be close.

(d) There's enough to go around for everyone.

27

M Wow, you look stunning in that new dress.

W Thanks, I thought I'd wear it to the reception tonight.

M I think you'll attract some envious glances.

W _____

(a) That's why we'll need to meet at 6.

(b) Of course, I look forward to redoing it.

(c) I'm sure all the women will look just as good.

(d) That's true. It's going to be a luxurious wedding.

28

W Well, I've decided against doing my PhD.

M Why? It'd be a career boost.

W I don't think I can handle writing a dissertation.

M _____

(a) I think you're selling yourself short.

(b) Maybe writing isn't the ideal field for you.

(c) Being ambitious is nothing to be ashamed of.

(d) You'll find another PhD program that interests you.

29

M If anyone asked me, I'd say don't marry too early.

W Really? But for some people, it's the best thing.

M Maybe, but for most people it'd be better to think twice.

W _____

(a) Well, sometimes I take it personally.

(b) I think you're generalizing too much.

(c) That's a good enough reason to delay.

(d) In contrast, I regret it but others don't.

30

W Hey, you missed my birthday party.

M Sorry. An emergency came up at work.

W Too bad. We really missed you.

M _____

(a) I need to check my schedule.

(b) I can't imagine ever missing out.

(c) Not as much as I missed being there.

(d) I'll definitely come once I've finished.

31

M Can I help you, ma'am?

W Yes, I'd like to get my money back for this sandwich.

M OK. But what's the problem with it?

W I think it's gone bad.

M Are you sure? All our sandwiches are refrigerated.

W I don't know, but it definitely tastes strange.

Q: What is the woman mainly doing in the conversation?

(a) Complaining about the sandwich she bought.

(b) Asking about certain sandwich ingredients.

(c) Ordering a different kind of sandwich.

(d) Picking up the sandwich she ordered.

32

M I've had such a bad morning.

W Why, problems at the office?

M No, my wallet was stolen!

W Seriously? Where did that happen?

M On the subway, I think.

W Hmm. It seems nowhere is safe these days.

Q: What is the conversation mainly about?

(a) The dangers of the subway.

(b) The theft of the man's wallet.

(c) The bad morning at the office.

(d) The wallet the man just bought.

33

W   So, do you like sharing your office with James?

M   Sure. It's better than being by myself.

W   But doesn't it interrupt your work?

M   Not really. I can still concentrate.

W   Even when he's on the phone?

M   Well, that can be distracting.

Q: What is the main topic of the conversation?

(a) Sharing an office with a co-worker.

(b) Problems with having a small office.

(c) Daily work interruptions in an office.

(d) Ways to get along with a co-worker.

34

M   Want to see my college class photo?

W   Sure. Oh, who's that blond guy?

M   Tim Williams. We were pretty good friends in college.

W   What did he do after college?

M   I think he went to Harvard Business School. Why?

W   Somehow his face looks familiar.

Q: What are the man and woman mainly doing in the conversation?

(a) Discussing Harvard Business School.

(b) Taking photos at a college graduation.

(c) Deciding what they will do after college.

(d) Talking about a student in a photograph.

35

W   Honey, have you seen my silk blouse?

M   Um, about the blouse. I need to tell you something.

W   That doesn't sound good. What is it?

M   Well, I mistakenly washed it with the other laundry.

W   Don't tell me it's ruined!

M   It is. I'm so sorry. I'll buy you another one today.

Q: What is the main topic of the conversation?

(a) How the man misplaced the woman's blouse.

(b) The purchase of a silk blouse by the woman.

(c) The laundering method followed by the woman.

(d) How the man accidentally ruined the woman's blouse.

36

M   Hello, Goldmeyer residence.

W   Hello, Mr. Goldmeyer?

M   Yes, that's right.

W   Hi, this is June Bennet. Is my son Fred with your son?

M   In fact, he is. They're playing in the backyard as we speak.

W   That's a relief. Fred is late and I wasn't sure where he was.

M   Really? Fred told me he had called you. Here, let me go get him.

W   Thanks, I think he needs a good talking-to.

Q: What is the woman mainly doing in the conversation?

(a) Inquiring if her son will be late.

(b) Checking on her son's whereabouts.

(c) Criticizing the man for not calling her.

(d) Answering a phone call about her son.

37

M   I'm having second thoughts about quitting university.

W   I'm not surprised. Job prospects are zilch without a university diploma.

M   Unfortunately, that's becoming abundantly clear to me.

W   So, are you going to go back to school?

M   Part of me wants to, but the other part thinks it's too late.

W   Well, I think you should listen to the part that wants to.

Q: What is the conversation mainly about?

(a) The man's wide career prospects.

(b) The man's advice on returning to school.

(c) The man's uncertainty about his future course.

(d) The man's theoretical take on higher education.

38

W   Any idea where I can take my parents to dinner?

M   Why not try the Veni? It's an Italian restaurant.

W   Oh, I've never heard of it.

M It's good. I'm a regular there.

W Maybe we'll go there, then.

M Just be sure to make a reservation beforehand.

Q: Which is correct according to the conversation?

(a) The woman will cook for her parents.

(b) The woman has dined at the Veni before.

(c) The man has never visited the Veni before.

(d) The man recommends booking a table first.

39

W Would you like to go roller skating today?

M That's a great idea. Sure!

W Do you have skates?

M I know I have an old pair somewhere.

W You can always rent a pair if you can't find them.

M I might have to, since I haven't seen them in years.

Q: Which is correct about the man according to the conversation?

(a) He asked the woman to go roller skating.

(b) He agrees to go roller skating with the woman.

(c) He knows where to find his old roller skates.

(d) He used his old roller skates not too long ago.

40

W Can you take minutes at tomorrow's meeting?

M Again? I just did it last week.

W I know, and I really liked the job you did.

M But shouldn't Marcie or Bill take a stab at it?

W They'll be presenting some reports.

M Oh, OK, I guess I'll do it again, then.

Q: Which is correct according to the conversation?

(a) The man last took minutes over a month ago.

(b) The woman approved of how the man took minutes.

(c) The man feels that the same person must take minutes.

(d) The woman plans to take minutes at the meeting herself.

41

M Hello, Dr. Lee. I enjoyed your talk today.

W Thank you. It's Dr. Anderson, isn't it, from England?

M That's right. I'm flattered you remember.

W Sure I remember. By the way, are you giving a talk, too?

M Yes, in the next session.

W Great. I'll be sure to stick around for it.

Q: Which is correct according to the conversation?

(a) The man just gave an interesting talk to Dr. Lee.

(b) The woman remembered the man's country of origin.

(c) The man expected the woman to remember his name.

(d) The woman will be unable to attend the man's lecture.

42

W Hi, I need to extend my stay at the hotel a day. It's room 257.

M I'm afraid your room has been booked for the next three days.

W Uh-oh. Is there anything else available?

M Only a single. Does that work for you?

W My two children are accompanying me, so, not really.

M No problem. We'll put a couple of cots in the single for them, gratis.

Q: Which is correct according to the conversation?

(a) The woman needs to occupy her room for longer than planned.

(b) The man offers to replace the woman's single room with a double.

(c) The woman is staying in her room another day with her colleagues.

(d) The man is charging the woman an extra fee for additional furnishings.

43

W Excuse me, has a backpack been turned in here?

M Yes. Can you describe what it looks like?

W It's a grey backpack with two pockets.

M And could you tell me what was inside?

W Two books and a dictionary.

M OK, looks like the one turned in is yours. Here you go.

Q: What can be inferred from the conversation?
(a) The man stole the woman's backpack.
(b) The woman mislaid her backpack recently.
(c) The woman uses her backpack for shopping.
(d) The man gave the backpack to the lost-and-found.

44

M Excuse me, is this Fifth Avenue?

W No. Fifth is way back that way.

M Then, I'm completely turned around. I'm looking for the Regis Building.

W Oh. You might want to jump on a bus or grab a cab, then.

M Really? It's not within walking distance?

W Well, it'd take a good chunk of time to walk it.

Q: What can be inferred from the conversation?
(a) The man is late for an appointment.
(b) Bus routes are needlessly confusing.
(c) The Regis Building is rather far away.
(d) Fifth Avenue is congested with traffic.

45

M So, is this your first time visiting Costa Rica?

W No, I did some graduate research here years ago.

M Really? What were you researching?

W Primarily different kinds of insects.

M Well, we sure have many unusual insects here.

W Yes, I couldn't see them all last time, so I came back.

Q: What can be inferred from the conversation?
(a) The woman is a resident of Costa Rica.
(b) The man is on a package tour of Costa Rica.
(c) The man knows little about the local insects.
(d) The woman intends to continue her research.

46

The Halburg Investment Workshop is for beginning investors and those slightly more experienced who want to have greater control over their stock market investments. From the basics of stock market investing to reading financial data, we cover it all. By the end of the workshop, we guarantee that you'll be as good as the experts at identifying trends and making solid investment decisions. Sign up today as spaces are limited!

Q: What is mainly being advertised?
(a) A study on stocks showing the most potential.
(b) A gathering for learning about investing money.
(c) A plan for managing investments in retirement.
(d) A conference for people who got rich investing money.

47

Thanks, everyone, for your participation today. But before you leave, let me remind you that we will begin final presentations early next month, and I need all of you to choose a date that suits you. On this paper, I have set out a list of dates, and I'd like each of you to write your name down beside your preference. Only two presentations will be allowed per day, so if your first choice is full, please choose another date.

Q: What is the announcement mainly about?
(a) Changing presentation topics.
(b) Assessing peer presentations.
(c) Deciding dates for presentations.
(d) Establishing presentation partners.

48

I'd now like to touch on the three distinct stages people go through during culture shock. Typically, people start out excited about the new culture—everything is interesting. They then move to anxiety—when the newness becomes a source of stress. And finally, they achieve some balance and adjust. The entire process of culture shock takes several months to get over, after which life in the new country settles down considerably.

Q: What is the main topic of the talk?
(a) People's interest in new cultures.
(b) Predictable phases of culture shock.
(c) Coping mechanisms for culture shock.
(d) Cultural differences that are hard to overcome.

49

I mentioned earlier how ethanol to fuel vehicles is made from plants that absorb carbon dioxide when alive. It is for this reason that ethanol can result in lower net carbon emissions than gasoline. This is good news, except that most car engines are designed for gasoline and must be adapted to use ethanol, which can be very expensive. To solve this problem, researchers have developed a chemical process that turns plant products into a new form of regular gasoline usable in existing engines.

Q: What is the main topic of the lecture?
(a) Ethanol-friendly vehicles.
(b) Plant-based fuels for vehicles.
(c) Breakthroughs in ethanol research.
(d) Technological advances in car engines.

50

Now for business news. US retailers have been experiencing the most severe challenges to sales in years amid a prolonged recession. The biggest drop occurred during the traditional November-December holiday shopping period—a make-or-break period for retailers—when total sales plunged by up to 8 percent. And there's been no improvement in the months following, with sales continuing their downward slope despite retailers' slashing of prices to woo shoppers.

Q: What is the news report mainly about?
(a) The continuing sales downturn in the US.
(b) US strategies to overcome the recession.
(c) Ways US retailers triggered the sales plunge.
(d) The immunity of US retailers to the recession.

51

Today I'm going to talk about archaeological expeditions in the Middle East. These expeditions frequently confirm ancient narrative records. For example, one team of archaeologists recently discovered a huge network of 3,000-year-old copper mines in Jordan, and they say the mines could be the biblical mines of Edom controlled by King Solomon. Archaeologists have also found what appear to be the water shafts mentioned in biblical accounts of a battle for Jerusalem.

Q: What is the lecture mainly about?
(a) Evidence for and against certain biblical narratives.
(b) Archaeologists' methods for interpreting ancient records.
(c) Archaeological discoveries that corroborate historical accounts.
(d) The Middle East as the primary focus of archaeological research.

52

Hello. You have reached the office of Gabriella Seagram. I'll be out of the office and cannot offer regular consulting assistance until Monday, June 15th. If your call is urgent, it is possible to arrange teleconferencing, but some delay will be inevitable. If your call is very urgent and can't wait for such teleconferencing, please call the main office at 234-8877 during regular business hours to speak to another consultant. If your call is not urgent, please leave a message after the tone and I'll get back to you as soon as I can. Thank you.

Q: What is the main purpose of Gabriella Seagram's recorded message?
(a) To give instructions on arranging teleconferences.
(b) To clarify how callers with urgent business can contact her.
(c) To explain how inquiries will be handled during her absence.
(d) To inform callers she has suspended her counseling hours indefinitely.

53

The city will test its emergency warning system at 10 am on Tuesday, June 16th. The test will include sounding the 12 sirens placed throughout the city to warn residents of natural disasters. You will hear a verbal message followed by activation of the sirens in the wail mode for approximately two minutes. Residents are instructed to refrain from moving to another location for the duration of the test.

Q: Which is correct according to the announcement?
(a) The test of the warning system will be in the early evening.
(b) A verbal message will be heard before the sirens wail.
(c) The sirens are going to last for about five minutes.
(d) Moving around the city during the test is allowed.

54

Today's lecture will cover different countries' requirements for products to be labeled "organic." The US requires 95 percent minimum organic content and no synthetic preservatives. The UK is nearly the same, but allows certain synthetic preservatives. Germany has no organic content requirement, but bans the use of synthetic preservatives. And France allows products with 10 percent organic content to be labeled "organic."

Q: Which is correct according to the lecture?
(a) The US allows synthetic preservatives in organic foods.
(b) The UK's organic food regulations are vastly different from the US's.
(c) Germany is not strict about the amount of organic content.
(d) France enforces an extremely high minimum organic content rule.

55

And finally tonight, here's an interesting report about Yeti, apelike creatures that Himalayan Sherpas have long claimed roam the Himalayas. While no scientific evidence has proven these creatures exist, zoologists investigating Mt. Everest's Khumbu region recently uncovered some mysterious footprints. They are now analyzing these footprints to determine what species they originate from, findings which may end up confirming the Sherpas' claims.

Q: Which is correct according to the news report?
(a) Sherpas caught a Yeti in the Himalayas.
(b) Much evidence supports the existence of the Yeti.
(c) Zoologists have determined the origin of the footprints.
(d) Analysis results may prove Sherpa claims to be correct.

56

TV advertising directed at young consumers is under attack worldwide. First, the US and Britain launched campaigns to ban advertising to children under five, then Sweden proposed an EU-wide ban for under-12s. Frankly, I question these bans. If children are totally screened from advertisements, they could be defenseless when they are exposed to them, especially when considering all the advertising images they will face when they get older. The only way our children will become wise consumers later is for parents to teach them to be critical of advertising images early, and this demands exposure to advertising, not bans.

Q: What would the speaker most likely agree with?
(a) Advertising should only be banned to children under five.
(b) Overprotection ultimately does greater harm to children than good.
(c) Children should be exposed to more advertisements than they currently are.
(d) Schools should be in charge of teaching children to be critical of advertisements.

57

Our topic today is the New Historicists, literary theorists who believe that literature must be studied and interpreted within the historical context of the author and the critic. These theorists consider what influence the author's social sphere, psychological background and intellectual bent had on the work itself. They also lay out their own backgrounds and biases when analyzing a work. Basically, they believe all works of literature—and critics of those works—are heavily influenced by inner and outer forces, so they openly examine these forces in their criticism.

Q: Which is correct about New Historicists according to the lecture?
(a) They interpret texts with the author's and critic's historical context in mind.
(b) They avoid consideration of the author's psychological state in their criticism.
(c) They disregard their own backgrounds in their criticism.
(d) They believe texts are incorruptible by outside forces.

58

Today we'll focus on the caste system in India. Although the caste system is related to race, they are not the same and should not be confused. The caste system is a social class system based on heredity. In other words, an individual is born into a caste that defines his or her social position. Castes all have their own sets of rules and traditions, and these affect all areas of life including social class, occupation, marriage, and diet. Interestingly, caste restrictions vary in rigidity from region to region.

Q: Which is correct about the caste system according to the lecture?
(a) It is synonymous with the concept of race.
(b) It must be earned through personal merit.
(c) It affects a person's social and personal life.
(d) Its rigidity does not vary from region to region.

59

Hello everyone! I called this meeting to familiarize admin staff with our newest product—the Communicator Basic. This cell phone, to be launched next month, is like a mini-computer with many special functions. As you see it's quite unique and unlike any previous model. It'll retail for around $500, and an enhanced version will come out later with more features and, naturally, a higher price tag. In order for all of you to get to know this device, everyone will be given their own Communicator Basic to keep.

Q: What can be inferred about the Communicator Basic from the talk?
(a) It will have to be returned by employees later.
(b) Its retail price will decrease after the promotion.
(c) Its functions are wider in range than other cell phones.
(d) It will be marketed as an upgrade to an existing model.

60

First, let me say that my husband and I are both honored to have been invited to speak here at the Conference on Homeless Youth. The efforts of all of us here to tackle the homeless youth problem are vital to our society; after all, young people truly are the future. With this in mind, let's take this opportunity to put our heads together and come up with sustainable ideas to solve the problem. And let's make all-out efforts after this conference to immediately put these ideas into action.

Q: What can be inferred about the speaker?
(a) She thinks some excellent proposals have been made.
(b) She hopes ideas will be implemented in a timely manner.
(c) She holds homeless youth responsible for their situations.
(d) She feels sufficient work is being done for homeless youth.

1

W   Nice to meet you, Tom. Jill's told me a lot about you.

M   _____

(a) I didn't hear the news.
(b) Nothing bad, I hope.
(c) It's a good meeting.
(d) Fine, thank you.

2

M   Do you have anything for a headache?

W   _____

(a) I can't take that much.
(b) You always take care of me.
(c) I have aspirin somewhere.
(d) The doctor recommends it.

3

W   You really should exercise more.

M   _____

(a) But I just don't have time.
(b) It's better to be informed.
(c) The exercise isn't hard.
(d) I'll order some soon.

4

M   I hate having to work late.

W   _____

(a) I don't like it, either.
(b) I won't be late again.
(c) The work is on my desk.
(d) The boss agreed with me.

5

W   Hi Jim. I got your text message to call you.

M   _____

(a) Well, maybe I shouldn't call right now.
(b) Yes. I've been waiting to talk to you.
(c) Sure, that's what I said, too.
(d) OK, send a text message.

6

M   How long does it take to get downtown?

W   _____

(a) I'll soon find out how.
(b) It'll take a lot of work.
(c) It's about a 20-minute drive.
(d) We arrived 30 minutes early.

7

W   I'm tired. I'm going to turn in.

M   _____

(a) No, just go straight.
(b) OK, have a good night.
(c) Yes, that's the right way.
(d) Thanks, I'll see you inside.

8

M   What should I do about this leaky ceiling?

W   _____

(a) I have no idea when it'll stop.
(b) You'd better call a repairman.
(c) Put the hole somewhere else.
(d) Squeeze to make it tighter.

9

W   Alice's suggestion was good, wasn't it?

M   _____

(a) I wonder who said it.
(b) I'll do whatever you think.
(c) She didn't suggest that to me.
(d) It's definitely worth looking into.

10

M   Did you enjoy the video I made for you?

W   _____

(a) Maybe, if I have time for it.
(b) No, it was already released.
(c) Sure, we can get together again.
(d) Yeah, you're great with a camera.

11

W How did you find out about this restaurant?

M _____

(a) I don't see any sign.
(b) Surfing the Net yesterday.
(c) I tried it and it was also tasty.
(d) It has a big menu to choose from.

12

M I feel sleepy. I need to wake myself up.

W _____

(a) Sorry. I'd better let you rest.
(b) Me too. I feel much better.
(c) Then, let's go get a coffee.
(d) Sure, I can set the alarm.

13

W I'm impressed at how expertly you played that piano sonata.

M _____

(a) Well, the piano was out of tune.
(b) Sorry. I'm still just an apprentice.
(c) Thanks. It took a while to review.
(d) Yes. It was my best rendition yet.

14

M My sore back's showing no signs of improving.

W _____

(a) You've been taking that for granted.
(b) Get a background check done on it.
(c) There's always something to replace.
(d) Have it looked at before it gets worse.

15

W Did airport security take the cutlery in your bag?

M _____

(a) They made sure it was restrained.
(b) They were just as taken aback by it.
(c) That's right. I'll purchase a new one.
(d) Yeah, and they confiscated my sunscreen, too.

16

M How did you do on the test?

W Not bad. But I was hoping to do better.

M What was your final score?

W _____

(a) I managed to get 87 percent.
(b) I thought it was hard.
(c) I hope I did well.
(d) I'll try for 100 percent.

17

W I won't finish my essay on time.

M It isn't due for another week.

W Yes, but I haven't even started it.

M _____

(a) I believe you'll find it out.
(b) I heard you aren't too bad.
(c) I wasn't expecting it so soon.
(d) I'm sure you'll get it finished.

18

M Excuse me. Where is the bank?

W Which bank? There are several in this area.

M I'm looking for Commerce Bank.

W _____

(a) There is one there, too.
(b) That's one possible way.
(c) You can look around, then.
(d) It's farther along on your left.

19

W I'll have a slice of vegetarian pizza, please.

M OK. That comes to $3.50.

W Oh, and do you have tomato juice?

M _____

(a) Yes, you can change your order.
(b) Sure. That'll be another $1.55.
(c) I'd rather not have any juice.
(d) I hope you enjoy your pizza.

20

M Do you want to study French together?

W I'd like to, but I don't have the time.

M Are you sure? It'll be fun.

W _____

(a) It'll be a lot more fun.

(b) It really wasn't my idea.

(c) I'm very busy these days.

(d) I heard about that already.

21

W Is it possible to exchange this blouse?

M Yes. Do you have the receipt?

W Yes, just a moment. Oh, it's not in my bag.

M _____

(a) I'm afraid I'll need to see it.

(b) But we don't have any left.

(c) Then, the pink one is fine.

(d) We'll have to change that.

22

M Kate! I haven't seen you in ages!

W Well, I was in France for three weeks.

M What were you doing there?

W _____

(a) It was really interesting.

(b) I also saw the Eiffel Tower.

(c) I read about it in a magazine.

(d) I was just visiting a friend of mine.

23

W What do you think of laser treatment?

M Why? Do you want to have some done?

W Yeah, on the wrinkles around my eyes.

M _____

(a) I can't see any smears.

(b) I told you it would hurt.

(c) I knew it wouldn't work.

(d) I'd consider other options first.

24

M You look surprised. What happened?

W I just saw my midterm results.

M Oh, did you do well?

W _____

(a) Actually, I did better than I expected.

(b) You're right, I'm not feeling well.

(c) Yes, it's getting much easier.

(d) No, I didn't see my score.

25

W Does this hotel offer guided tours?

M Yes. We offer tours of the island.

W How about scuba diving trips?

M _____

(a) We hope you'll enjoy them, ma'am.

(b) Yes, most of those were our doing.

(c) Oh, don't worry. They're quite safe.

(d) No, but we can help you arrange one.

26

M I can't attend today's meeting, sorry.

W Should we postpone it?

M No, go ahead, but let me know what I miss.

W _____

(a) OK. I'll be sure to do that.

(b) That's fine. It's not postponed.

(c) Yes, the minutes are right here.

(d) I agree. A different day is better.

27

W I'm getting a lot of spam lately.

M It's so annoying, isn't it?

W Yeah, and it's happening with a new email account.

M _____

(a) I don't know the address yet.

(b) Talk to your mailman about it.

(c) Sorry, I didn't mean to send it.

(d) Check if your spam filter is on.

28

M That was an excellent presentation, Lisa.

W Thanks, I hope it was informative.

M It was, especially the handouts.

W _____

(a) I'll be glad if you attend.

(b) Sorry. I ran out of handouts.

(c) Good. A lot of effort went into those.

(d) You'll get the handouts after the break.

29

W Do you advertise your business?

M No. We can't afford to.

W Then, how come you get so many customers?

M _____

(a) It's mostly by word of mouth.

(b) I found out about it from a friend.

(c) People see our ads in the newspaper.

(d) Because it was enough to satisfy them.

30

M I finished the project a week early.

W I can't believe you were able to do that!

M Well, it was such interesting work.

W _____

(a) But it's hard to ascertain the extent.

(b) I'm sure you'll find that less taxing.

(c) OK, that's fair. I'll allow it through.

(d) Even so, that's a fast turnaround.

31

W Can I use this photocopier?

M Unfortunately, it's out of order.

W Well, that's annoying.

M Yes, but a repairman is on his way now.

W Is the copier on the next floor working?

M It was the last time I checked.

Q: What is the woman mainly doing in the conversation?

(a) Finding a copier to use.

(b) Fixing the man's copier.

(c) Trying to print a document.

(d) Talking about what she broke.

32

M Thanks for volunteering to help our cause.

W I'm glad to. Will there be any training?

M Yes, we'll have an orientation session tomorrow.

W What time will that be?

M At 3 pm. Is that OK?

W Sure, that sounds fine.

Q: What are the man and woman mainly discussing?

(a) The goal of volunteer work.

(b) The work there is left to do.

(c) The training for volunteer work.

(d) The cause they are volunteering for.

33

M Good morning. Bicton Health Clinic.

W This is Mrs. Wilson. I'm calling about my appointment today.

M Let's see—that's today at 3:30 with Dr. Fletcher.

W Yes, but I'm afraid I can't make it.

M Oh, would you like to reschedule?

W No thanks, I'll just cancel for now.

Q: What is the woman mainly doing in the conversation?

(a) Planning to go to a health clinic.

(b) Cancelling a doctor's appointment.

(c) Scheduling when to see Dr. Fletcher.

(d) Changing the date of an appointment.

34

W I was really annoyed with Sally yesterday.

M Why? What did she do?

W She joked about what I was wearing in front of Mike.

M You mean Mike James, the guy you just started dating?

W That's right. She was so rude.

M Yeah, that was pretty tactless of her.

Q: What is the main topic of the conversation?

(a) Sally's peculiar fashion sense.

(b) Sally's relationship with Mike.

(c) Why Sally is annoying to everyone.

(d) What Sally did to upset the woman.

35

W   Hello, Mayville Police Department. How may I help you?

M   Yes, I'd like to report a crime.

W   What happened and where did it occur?

M   My car was vandalized this morning on Lawrence Avenue.

W   OK. I'll need your name and phone number.

M   My name is Bill Sands and my number is 456-8765.

Q: What is the main topic of the conversation?
(a) A car the man had vandalized.
(b) Recent reports of illegal activity.
(c) A crime involving the man's vehicle.
(d) Crimes witnessed on Lawrence Avenue.

36

M   I've really had it with my job.

W   Was it another hectic day?

M   I'll say. And the boss was on my case.

W   Things really have to improve.

M   I know. It's so stressful these days.

W   Well, if you ever want to leave, I'll support the decision.

Q: What is the conversation mainly about?
(a) The man's work performance.
(b) Problems the man faces at his job.
(c) Work handed out by the man's boss.
(d) The man's desire not to work anymore.

37

W   I bought some awesome CDs last night.

M   Really? CDs are so expensive these days. I can't afford them.

W   Yeah, but I'm against free downloading.

M   Why? I do it all the time.

W   Well, I guess I think more from a musician's point of view.

M   I see. But since CDs are so pricey, I think I'll keep downloading.

Q: What is the main topic of the conversation?
(a) The unaffordability of music downloading.
(b) Purchasing CDs versus downloading music online.
(c) Musicians' openness to music downloading culture.
(d) The superior quality of CDs over music downloads.

38

W   I'm going running this Sunday. Do you want to go?

M   No, I think running is boring.

W   Well, what kinds of sports do you like?

M   I like tennis. I play a few nights a week.

W   OK, well, how about a game of tennis on Sunday?

M   Sure. Sounds like fun.

Q: Which is correct according to the conversation?
(a) The man enjoys running.
(b) The man does not exercise.
(c) The woman wants to play tennis.
(d) The woman is very busy on Sundays.

39

W   Do you think this dress is appropriate for the party?

M   It's a bit much. The party will be pretty casual.

W   Hmm.... I can't think of what to wear.

M   Jeans and a t-shirt should be fine.

W   What are you going to wear?

M   Just jeans and a t-shirt.

Q: Which is correct according to the conversation?
(a) The woman will attend a formal party.
(b) The woman is not sure what to wear.
(c) The man will not go to the party.
(d) The man plans on wearing a suit.

40

M We'd better get moving, or we'll miss our flight.

W Don't worry. We'll get to the airport on time.

M Have you ever missed a flight?

W No, never. That'd be terrible. How about you?

M Yes, once I missed one because I was stuck in traffic.

W Really? Well, that's not going to happen today.

Q: Which is correct according to the conversation?

(a) The man and woman have boarded their plane.

(b) The woman is meeting the man at the airport.

(c) The woman felt terrible after missing a flight.

(d) The man missed a flight on one occasion.

41

M Stacey, do you tip your hairdresser?

W No, I don't, and I don't see why I should.

M Oh good. I thought I was being too cheap.

W Not at all! Hairdressers charge too much, anyway.

M But I always feel pressure to tip. Don't you?

W Actually, it rarely crosses my mind.

Q: Which is correct according to the conversation?

(a) The woman tips her hairdresser.

(b) The man is worried he over-tipped.

(c) The woman believes hairdressers overcharge.

(d) The man thinks one should be pressured to tip.

42

M I noticed you drink a lot of bottled water.

W Yeah, I prefer the taste to tap water.

M But bottled water has become an environmental problem.

W I heard that. But I think it's an exaggeration.

M I don't. Producing that stuff uses up a lot of resources.

W Well, it's better for my body, so I'll keep drinking it.

Q: Which is correct about the woman according to the conversation?

(a) She avoids bottled water in favor of tap water.

(b) She dislikes the flavor of certain bottled water.

(c) She thinks some bottled water issues are overstated.

(d) She plans to start drinking tap water for better health.

43

M You seem tired. Did you have a late night?

W Not really. But my sleep was interrupted a lot.

M Why? Was your neighbor's dog barking like before?

W No. This time it was text messages on my cell phone at odd hours.

M You should turn the message alert off.

W Oh, I didn't realize I could. I'll do that tonight.

Q: What can be inferred about the woman from the conversation?

(a) Her sleep had been disturbed on previous nights.

(b) Her current cell phone keeps malfunctioning.

(c) She is slow to answer text messages.

(d) She likes to stay out late at night.

44

M Is it true you're going on sabbatical this year?

W That's right. I'm going to the University of Washington.

M Fantastic. I gave a lecture there a few years back.

W Is that right? What did you think of the university?

M Great. The faculty is excellent, and it has a well-stocked library.

W Yeah, those are some of the reasons why I chose it.

Q: What can be inferred about the speakers?

(a) They both work at universities.

(b) They do research in a similar area.

(c) They will each have a sabbatical this year.

(d) They graduated from the University of Washington.

45

M Who is speaking at the seminar this evening?

W I think Jim Hall will discuss controlling sea lanes.

M But is anyone talking about maritime legal matters?

W Oh yes, Kim Ellis will go over some current issues.

M Good. I need to keep abreast of the latest developments.

W Yes, then it should be right up your alley.

Q: What can be inferred from the conversation?

(a) The woman will give a presentation at the seminar.

(b) The woman is an expert in the field of shipping.

(c) The man and woman organized the seminar.

(d) The man is most eager to hear Kim Ellis.

46

Welcome, everyone, to our weightlifting course. First off, you should know that weightlifting only builds muscle if it's done slowly. Also, lifting weights correctly is far more important than the actual weight you lift. To lift correctly, breathe in when lowering weights and out when lifting them. This helps oxygen get to your muscles faster, giving you more energy for your workout and a quicker recovery time.

Q: What is the talk mainly about?

(a) Tips for proper weightlifting.

(b) Different kinds of weight training.

(c) Common mistakes in weightlifting.

(d) Breathing properly during workouts.

47

By analyzing the latest statistics on former graduates, researchers have found that future salary is indeed positively affected by education level. The statistics showed that employees with a master's degree earn an average of $50,000 a year compared to $43,500 for employees with a bachelor's degree. However, employees with bachelor's degrees enjoy salaries that are 27 percent higher than employees with two-year college degrees and 52 percent higher than employees with high school diplomas.

Q: What is the main idea of the news report?

(a) More education results in more pay.

(b) Educated people deserve more money.

(c) Master's degrees are essential these days.

(d) Education makes life easier for many people.

48

I spoke earlier about the impact of hero worship on how youngsters think, and of course, that extends to how they dress. In the 80s, you could hardly walk down the street without seeing Madonna lookalikes. And some years later, Britney Spears became an icon of fashion for young girls. Male rappers like Diddy and Nelly today have guys wearing sports jerseys and baggy pants.

Q: What is the speaker's main point about young people?

(a) They dress according to peer pressure.

(b) They copy the dress styles of those they admire.

(c) They are negatively influenced by celebrities.

(d) They use clothes to rebel against their parents.

49

Thank you all for attending tonight's union meeting. For years now, we have put up with low pay at this airline, not to mention poor working conditions. Meanwhile, it has been making huge profits, and our bosses have filled their pockets with money: over $250 million in stock grants was paid out over the past two years! This is an outrage! We work harder, but only they get richer. It's time to take action!

Q: What is the main idea of the speech?
(a) Employees have not received any stock grants.
(b) Executives are threatening workers' job security.
(c) Some employees deserve raises more than others.
(d) Airline executives profit at the expense of their workers.

50

As president of the Engineering Association, I am pleased to announce a new competition to combat the problem of arsenic in drinking water. Arsenic contamination of well water is a serious problem and can cause vomiting, skin ailments, nerve damage, cancer, and organ failure when consumed. So we are inviting member engineers to design a cheap water treatment system for removing arsenic. The winner will be rewarded full funding to implement the design.

Q: What is the announcement mainly about?
(a) A new finding on the dangers of arsenic in water.
(b) A contest for removing arsenic from drinking water.
(c) The results of a competition to design a water system.
(d) The humanitarian work of the Engineering Association.

51

I now want to talk about the various techniques astronomers use for discovering planets beyond our solar system. One technique is the wobble method. It deduces the presence of a planet by the gravitational tug it gives the star it orbits. The more massive and closer the planet, the greater the wobble of its star. Another technique is the winking method, where a planet is detected by the way it slightly dims a star's light when it passes in front of it.

Q: What is the main topic of the lecture?
(a) Methods for locating planets orbiting stars.
(b) How astronomers distinguish types of stars.
(c) Astronomers' hopes for discovering new planets.
(d) How successful the wobble and winking methods are.

52

As drama students, you should not confuse the Stanislavski system with method acting. The Stanislavski system is an approach to acting where performers analyze characters' emotions and motivations. On the other hand, method acting, which was actually developed by one of Stanislavski's protégés, involves actors using their own memories and experiences to create an authentic, "real" performance.

Q: What is the lecture mainly about?
(a) How actors actually use the Stanislavski system.
(b) The contrast between Stanislavski and his protégé.
(c) How the Stanislavski system differs from method acting.
(d) The superiority of method acting over the Stanislavski system.

53

Do you want to learn English? Then English World is for you! English World is a computer game in which you play a visitor to an English-speaking country. You can choose to visit Australia, the UK, Canada, or the US. While playing, you select English phrases to communicate with various characters, and you can only move up levels by successfully completing harder and harder tasks, such as buying a meal or asking for directions. Try English World today!

Q: Which is correct about English World according to the advertisement?
(a) Users can make a choice of which country to visit.
(b) Users must create their own English phrases.
(c) Users progress up levels by making money.
(d) Users compete on a plastic game board.

54

Members of the board, I'll be blunt. I am worried about our company's proposed merger. First, there is no guarantee that we will profit from such a merger. What can we gain from joining with a failing company? We risk weakening, not strengthening, our organization. Second, we would need a new management structure, and no doubt that will incur job losses, not only in management but at all levels of the company. Frankly, I can't see the merger as worth it.

Q: Which is correct about the merger according to the talk?
(a) It will guarantee more profit for the company.
(b) It will strengthen the company's organization.
(c) It will result in companywide job losses.
(d) It is worth the risk in the long run.

55

Eastern and central parts of New Zealand experienced prolonged sunny periods today. Other parts of the country have been overcast, with occasional showers. During the evening though, showers will ease and become less frequent. Tomorrow, scattered showers are likely throughout the country, followed by heavy showers and thunderstorms in the afternoon.

Q: Which is correct according to the New Zealand weather report?
(a) Today eastern parts had showers.
(b) There will be no rain this evening.
(c) Tomorrow rain is expected in the west.
(d) It will be partly sunny tomorrow afternoon.

56

I'd like to announce that our research team now believes that chronic overeating is a substance abuse disorder and an addiction. You might think there is a substantial difference between someone who's lost control over alcohol and someone who's lost control over food. But the brain responses of such individuals show minor differences. In fact, overeaters display many of the characteristics of addicts, such as denial and delusional thinking.

Q: Which is correct according to the research findings?
(a) Overeating was proven unique among all other addictions.
(b) Overeaters share similar brain responses with alcoholics.
(c) Overeaters have negligible addiction characteristics.
(d) Overeating is not linked to irrational thoughts.

57

The future environmental trend I'll discuss next is what I call the leveling of the world. What I mean is a global rise of middle-class citizens. This, I believe, will have a huge impact. Economically, it is likely to be beneficial. But it will create enormous resource complications and environmental stresses, if all these people consume as rampantly as Americans. And it is not only the rising middle-classes in China and India who pose a threat. Population growth is increasing middle-class numbers in the West, too.

Q: Which is correct according to the speaker?
(a) Economic gains will come from a rising middle-class.
(b) American consumers are not in the least excessive.
(c) China does not represent a big threat to resources.
(d) The middle-class is receding in the West.

58

I would now like to talk about the social upheaval caused by the Bubonic Plague in 14th century Europe. One huge effect it had was to weaken the authority of the Catholic Church. People turned from the Church when they saw it could offer them no protection from the plague. They also witnessed Christian ideals vanish from society. As plague victims were abandoned in the struggle for survival, people died in large numbers and no amount of faith or hope could stop it.

Q: What can be inferred from the lecture?
(a) The churches helped the rich rather than the poor.
(b) People embraced other religions besides Catholicism.
(c) The plague spread quicker through church gatherings.
(d) People were profoundly disillusioned with Christianity.

59

Inspired by ancient Inuit goggle design, Yeti winter sport goggles come with the best in technological advances—the best design, the best materials, and the best production quality. With 90 percent UV protection, outstanding peripheral vision, anti-fogging technology, and guaranteed durability against snow, wind, ice, and rocks, no other winter sport goggles on the market today compare to Yeti. Want to keep your eyes extra-safe? Choose Yeti.

Q: What can be inferred about Yeti goggles from the advertisement?
(a) They do not compete well in the marketplace.
(b) They are made by an innovative new company.
(c) They barely improve on the original Inuit design.
(d) They are targeted at sports enthusiasts.

60

Good afternoon, everyone. Thanks for attending this impromptu employee meeting. The subject I mainly want to address today is sexual harassment, since a recent incident has raised concerns. I want to make it clear that there will be zero tolerance for this sort of conduct at this company. And I want to reiterate what I touched on at a meeting we had last month: any allegations received will be dealt with aggressively but fairly.

Q: What can be inferred about the company from the talk?
(a) It is lax in enforcing sexual harassment policies.
(b) It considers sexual harassment as a serious issue.
(c) It is confident its workplace is free of sexual harassment.
(d) It regards sexual harassment as an employee's private problem.

서울대 최신기출 **4**

Listening Comprehension **Scripts**

1

M Pardon me. Which way is Central Hospital?

W _____

(a) Sorry, I'm new here.
(b) I hope you're all right.
(c) You'd better call a doctor.
(d) It's the best hospital in town.

2

W Sir, do you have anything to declare?

M _____

(a) No, nothing at all.
(b) It was a long flight.
(c) Yes, I'm on vacation.
(d) I'll take the shuttle bus.

3

M How come you didn't call me back?

W _____

(a) I'll be back shortly.
(b) I lost your number.
(c) I'll call you later.
(d) I missed the bus.

4

W Do you want to see a movie on Saturday night?

M _____

(a) I didn't think it was great.
(b) Actually, I already have plans.
(c) OK, I'll be with you in ten minutes.
(d) I wanted to ask how you liked the movie.

5

M Do you mind if I turn off the fan?

W _____

(a) Go right ahead.
(b) But it's my turn.
(c) It's cooled down.
(d) That's hard to say.

6

W Send me an email when you arrive.

M _____

(a) Yes, please do.
(b) I will. Take care.
(c) Thanks. You too.
(d) It won't take long.

7

M Too bad you missed Peggy's party last night.

W _____

(a) I love parties.
(b) I missed her, too.
(c) Yeah, I had to work late.
(d) Well, everyone seemed happy.

8

W Hello. This is Room 805. I need a wake-up call tomorrow at seven.

M _____

(a) OK. We'll give you a call then.
(b) We'll send one up shortly.
(c) I can, but not today.
(d) Call me anytime.

9

M How are you finding the Italian literature course?

W _____

(a) I'd love to visit Italy.
(b) I can't find the classroom.
(c) I've just finished the book.
(d) So far, it's pretty interesting.

10

W It's been raining for days. I wonder when it'll stop.

M _____

(a) I'm feeling much better.
(b) I would rather not stop.
(c) No wonder you hate rain.
(d) Soon, according to the forecast.

11

M Melanie, are you going to accept John's marriage proposal?

W _____

(a) No, I haven't read it yet.
(b) Sure, I know it'll be over soon.
(c) Of course I want to stay married.
(d) I'm taking some time to think about it.

12

W I got a ticket for running a red light this morning.

M _____

(a) I'll save you a seat.
(b) Well, I'll pay you later.
(c) I hope the fine isn't too high.
(d) Next time, wear your seat belt.

13

M Who do you work for now?

W _____

(a) I'm busy now.
(b) I'm self-employed.
(c) I trained as an accountant.
(d) I work for about 40 hours a week.

14

W Don't you think Mr. Johnson is the best teacher here?

M _____

(a) Yeah, he should try harder.
(b) I can't think of anyone better.
(c) I'll believe him when I see the evidence.
(d) No, his performance has been underrated.

15

M Good news! I finally negotiated a raise.

W _____

(a) That payment was long overdue.
(b) You've deserved one for ages.
(c) Yes, prices are rising.
(d) I'm so sorry.

16

W I'd love some coffee right now.
M Me too. Should I make some?
W Why don't we go out?
M _____

(a) Sounds great! I'll get my bag.
(b) I'd like a cappuccino, please.
(c) But I've already prepared it.
(d) OK. See you tonight, then.

17

M Hi. I'm calling about the car you advertised.
W OK. Do you want to have a look at it?
M Sure, but the price seems a little high.
W _____

(a) It's parked over there.
(b) I think we've bargained enough.
(c) Really? I didn't notice that.
(d) Well, I can lower it a little.

18

W George, we should leave soon. Are you ready?
M No, I can't decide what to wear.
W Oh, come on. Just choose something.
M _____

(a) It's at seven-thirty.
(b) I'd like to take it slow.
(c) OK, you can go without me.
(d) But I want to look my best.

19

M The more I read, the better this book gets.

W Really? I didn't think you'd be interested in non-fiction.

M There's more to this one than I expected.

W _____

(a) I knew you'd like it.

(b) Maybe I'll read it later.

(c) I guessed how you'd feel.

(d) I wonder what will happen next.

20

W When did you say your mom was coming?

M Friday. I need to be at the airport by 5.

W Does she plan to stay long?

M _____

(a) It's been quite some time.

(b) The flight may be delayed.

(c) Just under a week, I think.

(d) Five hours seems too long.

21

M So, where should we eat breakfast?

W How about the Big Egg café? They have great omelets.

M What else do they have?

W _____

(a) Their omelets are really big.

(b) Just all kinds of egg dishes.

(c) There is a place downtown.

(d) I think they're open till 11.

22

W Welcome back! How was your trip?

M Hectic, but I had a good time.

W So, how is everyone back home?

M _____

(a) I met all my family.

(b) Pretty much the same.

(c) I wish I could stay longer.

(d) My family's still out of town.

23

M Hello. Can I help you find something?

W Yes, I want to rent a dress for my graduation.

M Oh, we have some nice black ones over here.

W _____

(a) Renting would be cheaper than buying.

(b) I'm paying the rent after graduation.

(c) I need a new dress as well.

(d) I'd prefer a lighter color.

24

W I think I'll order the curry today.

M I wouldn't recommend it.

W You don't think it's a good idea?

M _____

(a) It's on me this time.

(b) I'll order the same thing.

(c) The curry's not great here.

(d) It wasn't a good idea to come here.

25

M How was your camping trip?

W Ugh. The campgrounds were all wet and muddy from the rain.

M Oh, no! So, where did you sleep?

W _____

(a) The animals kept us awake.

(b) We stayed at a motel nearby.

(c) I didn't get much sleep anyway.

(d) We walked all the way back.

26

W How do you pronounce this name written here?

M Gwyneth. It's Welsh.

W Oh, how do you know it's Welsh?

M _____

(a) I'm pretty sure that's right.

(b) That's the language of Wales.

(c) Some people say it differently.

(d) I read about it online the other day.

27

M What're you doing on Thursday night?

W Why? What do you have in mind?

M The Moscow Circus is in town.

W _____

(a) I've never been there before.

(b) I saw the movie before.

(c) I agree. Leave it for later.

(d) That's not my kind of thing.

28

W I was really impressed with the new art gallery.

M Me too. The renovations looked great.

W If only the same firm could do the city hall.

M _____

(a) Wow! They must be popular.

(b) No, that was a different decorator.

(c) I don't think that'd be hard to arrange.

(d) Many people have visited the new gallery.

29

M Guess what! I won the raffle at the company party!

W Congratulations! You must be happy.

M Yes. I've never won anything before.

W _____

(a) I know. It's a bargain.

(b) You did work hard for it.

(c) That's no reason to try it.

(d) Well, you got lucky this time.

30

W How could you crash my car?

M Sorry, I thought the parking brake was on.

W That's the last time I let you drive it!

M _____

(a) Watch where you're going.

(b) It's OK. I'm not worried about it.

(c) The other driver had the right of way.

(d) Oh, but I promise to be more careful next time.

31

W Are you going to Ralph's birthday party this weekend?

M Yeah, but I haven't bought a gift yet.

W We could buy him something together.

M Good idea. What should we get?

W Why don't we get a CD? He loves listening to music.

M OK, let's go look for one today.

Q: What are the speakers mainly talking about?

(a) A friend who loves music.

(b) A CD they enjoyed listening to.

(c) A birthday present for a friend.

(d) A birthday party they will go to.

32

W Bob, have you filed your income tax return yet?

M Yeah, I did it a month ago. How about you?

W Not yet. I don't know the first thing about taxes.

M Well, if you don't do it on time, you'll have to pay interest.

W Right. I guess I'll have to hire an accountant to help me.

M Make sure to get one soon. Time's running out.

Q: What is the main idea of the conversation?

(a) The man hired a new accountant.

(b) The woman needs to file her taxes.

(c) The man received a large tax return.

(d) The woman dislikes paying income tax.

33

M Hey, Amy. I have an invitation for you.

W An invitation? What's it for?

M My daughter's getting married next month. Here.

W Oh, thank you very much. What's the date?

M Sunday, October 5th. I hope you can come.

W Don't worry about that. I'll definitely be there.

Q: What is the man mainly doing in the conversation?

(a) Asking the woman out on a date.

(b) Inviting the woman to a wedding.

(c) Accepting the woman's invitation.

(d) Proposing marriage to the woman.

34

W Hello. I need to change my flight.

M Certainly. What is your reservation number, please?

W Oh, just a second. I have it here somewhere. Umm, it's 2911A.

M OK, that's for Helsinki on the 25th. Is that right?

W Yes. I need to change it to the 31st, if possible.

M That's no problem, but I'm afraid there will be a 50-dollar charge.

Q: What is the woman mainly doing in the conversation?

(a) Buying an airline ticket to Helsinki.

(b) Checking in at an airline counter.

(c) Changing her scheduled flight.

(d) Paying a $50 penalty.

35

M I'm so excited that we're finally going to see a Broadway show tomorrow.

W I know! And we should do something before the show, too.

M How about lunch on Fifth Avenue? There are lots of good places there.

W Sure. And after that we can visit the Empire State Building.

M OK by me. I'd also like to see Central Park.

W That's a lot in one day. But let's give it a try.

Q: What are the man and woman mainly doing?

(a) Looking at a map.

(b) Planning tomorrow's itinerary.

(c) Booking a sightseeing tour.

(d) Deciding which show to see.

36

M What are you reading?

W I think you'd like it. It's a book on surviving in the wilderness.

M Hmm, that does sound kind of interesting. Are you learning much?

W Yeah. For example, eating plants that look like carrots can be dangerous.

M Really? Why is that?

W Because they might be hemlock, which is very poisonous.

Q: What is the conversation mainly about?

(a) What to do to survive in nature.

(b) Which plants are dangerous to eat.

(c) What the woman learned from a book.

(d) Why the man should read survival books.

37

M I can't believe we lost another game.

W Yeah, it was a tough loss, but we did our best.

M If I'd scored that last basket, we'd have won.

W Maybe, but everyone makes mistakes. You played really well.

M Thanks, but it's frustrating because we almost won.

W Look, try to forget about it. We still played a good game.

Q: What are the man and woman mainly talking about?

(a) Mistakes made by other players.

(b) The man's poor performance.

(c) A ball that the man lost.

(d) Losing a close game.

38

W My computer is giving me a lot of problems.

M Not again. You should've gotten a new one a long time ago.

W I know, but can I borrow your laptop for now?

M OK, but I need it back later. I'm not done with my paper yet.

W That's fine. I just need it for an hour to finish an assignment.

M Sure. Here you go.

Q: Which is correct according to the conversation?

(a) The man needs his computer now.

(b) The woman does not have a computer.

(c) The woman needs to finish an assignment.

(d) The man is going to lend the woman his textbook.

39

M I didn't see you at work yesterday. Where were you?

W Oh, I stayed in bed for most of the day.

M Were you sick or something?

W I had a bad cold.

M How do you feel now—better?

W Yeah, a day of rest did me good.

Q: Which is correct about the woman according to the conversation?

(a) She worked hard yesterday.

(b) She took a day off work.

(c) She is feeling quite sick.

(d) She thinks she needs more rest.

40

M Did you know that Jim is retiring?

W Really? I hadn't heard that. What a shame for us!

M Yeah, they're having a really hard time finding a replacement.

W I wonder if they'll ask him to stay a bit longer.

M Maybe. Or they might just promote someone from within the company.

W I wish we could convince him to stay somehow.

Q: Which is correct according to the conversation?

(a) Jim is planning to move to a new job.

(b) The woman wishes that Jim would stay.

(c) The woman knew about Jim's retirement.

(d) The company has found Jim's replacement.

41

W I just joined the campus gym. Are you a member?

M Yeah, as of two weeks ago. Are you going to sign up for aerobics?

W No. The classes look really good, but they cost extra.

M True, but I take them, and I think they're worth it.

W Do you work out in the mornings? I'm planning to go before class.

M Yes, me too. I guess we'll be seeing each other more often, then.

Q: Which is correct according to the conversation?

(a) The man joined the campus gym two months ago.

(b) The woman is going to take an aerobics class.

(c) The woman plans to work out in the evenings.

(d) The man exercises in the mornings.

42

M Oh, no! What's this on my windshield?

W Uh oh, it looks like you got a ticket.

M Darn. I thought it was OK to park here.

W Me too—I'm the one who suggested it. How much is it?

M It's a fifty-dollar fine. That's going to hurt.

W Look, I'll split it with you. It's partly my fault.

Q: Which is correct according to the conversation?

(a) The man got a ticket for speeding.

(b) The man knew he had parked illegally.

(c) The woman advised the man where to park.

(d) The woman thinks the man should pay the entire fine.

43

W Steve is here to pick me up. I've got to run, Dad.

M You be home by 11, young lady.

W There's no need to worry. I will.

M Well, we'll be waiting for you when you get home.

W Oh, you don't have to wait up.

M We don't mind. Remember, home by 11.

Q: What will the woman most likely do next?

(a) Head out on a date.

(b) Ask what time it is.

(c) Leave to go to school.

(d) Start arguing with her father.

44

M Margaret, did you see that a letter came for you today?

W Yes, it was from another publishing house.

M What did they think of your manuscript?

W Well, they just made a few useful comments.

M So, there's no reason to celebrate?

W Not yet. We'll have to wait for the next one.

Q: What can be inferred from the conversation?
(a) The man is happy about the letter.
(b) The man and woman are both authors.
(c) The woman's manuscript was rejected.
(d) The woman works for a publishing house.

45

W Sorry you didn't get promoted to assistant manager.

M Me too. Why did they hire someone from outside?

W I have no idea. I was expecting them to choose you.

M Yeah, I'm thinking about quitting over it.

W I don't know; it's not easy to find work these days.

M True. I guess I should bide my time.

Q: What can be inferred from the conversation?
(a) The woman is the man's superior.
(b) The woman will be promoted soon.
(c) The man will probably not quit his job.
(d) The man knows the new assistant manager.

46

It is my opinion that genetic science is overly concerned with getting rich from new discoveries. This leaves genetic research in a tangle of overlapping and fragmented patent rights. It is slowing the great adventure of further genetic discoveries and the possibility of medical cures. This is an intolerable exploitation of science.

Q: What is the main idea of the talk?
(a) Genetics poses a threat to ethical living.
(b) Desire for profits is hindering genetic research.
(c) Scientists ought to focus more on medical cures.
(d) Scientists are making errors in genetic research.

47

If you are worried about future medical bills, look no further than State Health for help. We can provide you with a daily budget in the event of hospitalization, and with compensation for reduced paychecks if you ever have to take time off due to an accident or illness. With the rising costs of hospitalization and prescriptions, why take the risk? Call State Health now for a quote.

Q: What is the advertisement mainly about?
(a) Coping with the cost of health insurance.
(b) Ways to budget for future hospitalizations.
(c) Avoiding medical expenses by staying healthy.
(d) Reasons to obtain health insurance coverage.

48

Is the work force changing in America? According to statistics, the answer is yes. America's white-collar work force has overtaken the ranks of blue-collar workers for the first time in history. Those who worry that America is becoming a nation of lawyers may not be wrong: there are now 1.4 lawyers for every farmer, whereas 25 years ago there were 4.5 farmers for every lawyer. Other occupations on the rise are computer analysts, doctors and psychologists.

Q: What is the main topic of the news report?
(a) The reason for a decrease in blue-collar workers.
(b) The most popular new career choices.
(c) The increase in white-collar workers.
(d) The growing number of lawyers.

49

As we all know, there is a considerable market for our products in Southeast Asia, but even though our company is doing extremely well there, we are concerned about the situations in Indonesia and Malaysia. We are currently seeing virtually no profits from these two countries. I propose, therefore, that we pull our staff out of these two countries and bolster our sales force in other markets, such as Thailand and Singapore.

Q: What is the main point of the talk?
(a) The market in Southeast Asia is yielding no profits.
(b) The company should expand to include Thailand and Singapore.
(c) The economic outlook for Indonesia and Malaysia is worsening.
(d) The company should focus on areas besides Indonesia and Malaysia.

50

Most of you have probably heard of the African-American civil rights leader Malcolm X. He was someone about whom opinions varied and still vary. Although he worked for social change and civil rights, he was labeled a closet conservative, a Black Power extremist and a religious fanatic. Some even called him a menace to society. This is mainly because we don't have much information about his life. Interpretations of his legacy are still constantly being rewritten today.

Q: What is the speaker's main point about Malcolm X?
(a) His speeches were poorly understood.
(b) He was involved in a wide range of actions.
(c) He means different things to different people.
(d) His historical significance has been exaggerated.

51

Today, you will be learning about a very accurate earthquake prediction technique. The technique relies on data analysis of past statistics and the physics of sliding blocks. Out of 11 earthquakes of magnitude 5 or greater in the California area since 2002, 10 took place on or near the hotspots predicted by this new technique. Its developer, John Rundle at the University of Colorado, has also used the technique to predict that by 2010 a magnitude 7 earthquake will hit California's Imperial Valley.

Q: What is the main topic of the talk?
(a) The accuracy of current earthquake prediction methods.
(b) The likely location of the next major earthquake.
(c) A promising advance in earthquake forecasting.
(d) A new theory about the cause of earthquakes.

52

I'd like to talk to you about the influence native cultures have had on the Americas and beyond. You have probably heard of the Native American names applied to nations, provinces, states, cities, rivers and lakes in the Americas. For example, Mississippi, Illinois, Wyoming, Mexico and Peru. But did you also know that Native Americans invented the snowshoe, toboggan and canoe? Chocolate, tobacco and quinine were also first used by Native Americans before being discovered by the rest of the world.

Q: What is the main topic of the talk?
(a) Influential Native Americans in American history.
(b) Native American contributions to global culture.
(c) The creativity of America's native peoples.
(d) Word origins of many places and tools.

53

The Sultan Travel Pack is now available at Simpsons! This versatile bag is small enough to use as a carry-on, but has an expandable bottom. It is made of lightweight, water-resistant material, with zippered exterior pockets. A padlock and two keys are included to secure the main zipper. The Sultan Travel Pack is normally priced at 200 dollars, but for a limited time only, you can save 40 percent on this quality product.

Q: Which is correct about the Sultan Travel Pack according to the advertisement?
(a) It can be used as a carry-on.
(b) It can be expanded on the sides.
(c) It comes with a combination lock.
(d) It is currently priced at 40 dollars.

54

Hello, everyone! We are scheduled to start our tour of the Newport Botanical Gardens at 10:30, in about ten minutes, but before we begin, we need to go over a few things. First, please refrain from smoking for the duration of the tour. And second, please do not pick any of the flowers or plants. Also, we will break for lunch at noon for an hour, before starting the second part of the tour through the park.

Q: Which is correct according to the instructions?
(a) The tour is being delayed.
(b) Smoking is allowed in certain areas.
(c) Visitors should not pick any flowers.
(d) The tour will continue after a 30-minute lunch.

55

The new Coffee Select 12-cup coffee maker from JavaKing is as reliable as they come. With our newly developed patented brewing system, Coffee Select will deliver coffee just the way you like it every single time. You can even set the timer up to 24 hours ahead. That means Coffee Select can have your coffee ready when you wake up. Order online today to receive free shipping for a limited time only.

Q: Which is correct about the coffee maker according to the advertisement?
(a) It makes up to ten cups of coffee at a time.
(b) It runs on a standard brewing system.
(c) It can be shipped for free anytime.
(d) It can be set a day in advance.

56

Ladies and gentlemen, you have all seen the data on our division's net profits from last year. Although we started off the year well, third quarter sales dropped dramatically. Something similar seems to be happening again this year. We would like to have an open discussion about this problem. Each of you is expected to present your thoughts on possible reasons for this pattern, as well as propose possible solutions.

Q: Which is correct according to the talk?
(a) The discussion will focus on the performance of last year.
(b) The division's sales fell in the third quarter of last year.
(c) The head of the board will propose solutions.
(d) This year's sales had a very poor start.

57

This fall construction sites across Eastern Canada are expected to be busy. The value of building permits, which is a key indicator of construction activity, rose to its highest level in July. A total of 6.8 billion dollars' worth of building permits were issued. That's a 20.6 percent increase over the June total and it is 7.5 percent higher than the previous record set in October of 2007.

Q: Which is correct according to the news report?
(a) June saw a record high in permit sales.
(b) Permit sales usually exceed $7 billion each month.
(c) Permits worth 6.8 billion dollars were issued in July.
(d) Permit values increased by 7.5 percent over the June total.

58

Our research on the effectiveness of man-made reefs has found that they are having a positive environmental impact. One particularly successful example is the Red Bird Reef. Since several old New York City subway cars were dropped into the sea, the barren ocean floor 80 feet down has transformed into a carpet of sea grasses, walled thick with blue mussels and sponges and is teeming with fish of all kinds.

Q: What can be inferred about the Red Bird Reef from the talk?
(a) It has attracted many fish species.
(b) Its success has surprised scientists.
(c) Some of its materials negatively affect sea life.
(d) It is one of the oldest artificial reefs in the world.

59

As university administrators, it's our job to advance the globalization of higher education. To do this, we must dispel the brain drain myth— the idea that developing countries are losing their most talented citizens. Consider the many Indian graduate students that have entered the US education system, mostly in science and engineering, and are now helping to modernize the Indian economy. Clearly the notion of a brain drain is nothing more than a myth, and something that we can now move past.

Q: What does the speaker imply about graduate students from India?
(a) Many who study in the US eventually return home.
(b) American universities are actively recruiting them.
(c) Many have made important advances in engineering.
(d) They should be encouraged to pursue degrees in India.

60

In *New Books on Radio* this week, we revisit the war zones of the Balkans in the 1990s when Raymond Morris speaks to writer David Kosta about his new book *The Confessionals*. Kosta, a soldier during the Balkans conflict, writes about the confessions of his fellow soldiers, uncovering their truths, deceptions and psychoses. He explores their mental states now as Serbian citizens, attempting to live a normal life.

Q: What is most likely to be discussed during the radio program?
(a) Current living conditions in former war zones.
(b) The global political implications of the war.
(c) The destruction of cities in the Balkans.
(d) The psychological trauma of the war.

1

M   Hi, Jill. Thanks for coming.

W   _____

(a) Sure, I'll come.
(b) Glad to be here.
(c) I'm fine, thanks.
(d) I'd like that a lot.

2

W   When does the game start?

M   _____

(a) Two weeks ago.
(b) I'm sure you'll win.
(c) In about thirty minutes.
(d) At the stadium downtown.

3

M   Sam isn't coming to tonight's party.

W   _____

(a) He can come, too.
(b) He didn't say when.
(c) I'm glad he's coming.
(d) I'm sorry to hear that.

4

W   What would you do if you were rich?

M   _____

(a) I'd help the needy.
(b) I can't spare much.
(c) I think you're lucky.
(d) I'd have to get a job.

5

M   I can't thank you enough for all your help.

W   _____

(a) I'd appreciate that.
(b) I was happy to do it.
(c) That seems fine to me.
(d) I won't be able to help.

6

W   I hear you're teaching piano.

M   _____

(a) I practice every day.
(b) Well, I need to learn.
(c) Yeah. I tutor at home.
(d) I think I hear a piano, too.

7

M   Sorry I was so noisy moving in yesterday.

W   _____

(a) No, I didn't hear you knock.
(b) That's fine. It's understandable.
(c) I'm glad you like the neighborhood.
(d) You must have visited many places.

8

W   This looks like another rejection letter.

M   _____

(a) I won't forget to apply.
(b) That sounds promising.
(c) Don't bother sending it, then.
(d) It might not be this time, though.

9

M   Sorry, but this lot is reserved for faculty. You can't park here.

W   _____

(a) I'll try the faculty entrance over there.
(b) Really? I didn't see a sign posted.
(c) OK. I'll have one ticket, please.
(d) That's fine. I'll search later.

10

W Hello? David? I can't hear you well on this phone line.

M _____

(a) Really? It's fine on this end.
(b) Then try harder next time.
(c) I'll keep my voice down.
(d) I think a phone's ringing.

11

M Would you like to see a play with me tonight?

W _____

(a) No, I don't want to play.
(b) I can't wait till tomorrow.
(c) Well, I haven't seen it yet.
(d) I'll have to take a rain check.

12

W Isn't it too early to leave for the airport?

M _____

(a) That's OK. I'll pay the fare.
(b) We need to allow for traffic.
(c) The passengers are on board.
(d) Sometimes planes are delayed.

13

M Let's go to Europe for our summer vacation.

W _____

(a) We can't afford it at this stage.
(b) Summer jobs aren't easy to find.
(c) I can work double shifts this summer.
(d) I agree it's not the right time for that.

14

W Who would have guessed that Susan would quit work so suddenly?

M _____

(a) You could be right.
(b) She must have had her reasons.
(c) Her whereabouts have always been a mystery.
(d) I had you figured out a long time ago.

15

M Excuse me, but can I go through the checkout before you?

W _____

(a) Sure, since it's on the agenda.
(b) I've just gone through all of these.
(c) Oh, you don't have much. OK, then.
(d) The checkout counter is usually busy.

16

W Please show me your boarding pass, sir.

M Here you go.

W Are you traveling with a group?

M _____

(a) No, I'm alone.
(b) I leave tomorrow.
(c) Sorry, I don't see it.
(d) I'll fly there tomorrow.

17

M Did you see the tennis final on TV last night?

W I sure did. How about you?

M I missed it. How was it?

W _____

(a) Up until midnight.
(b) I don't watch TV.
(c) I wonder who won.
(d) It was pretty exciting.

18

W You're pale. Are you sick?

M I feel terrible, actually.

W Have you checked your temperature?

M _____

(a) I haven't seen it.
(b) It'll get warmer later.
(c) Maybe, but I didn't feel any better.
(d) Yes, it's higher than normal.

19
M Too bad it's been such a mild winter.
W What's wrong with that?
M I sell winter coats.
W _____

(a) You could try another store.
(b) It might still get colder.
(c) People love fashion.
(d) There's no need.

20
W Excuse me. Is this Derringer Avenue?
M No, Derringer is three blocks back.
W Oh, I came from there, but I didn't see it.
M _____

(a) Don't worry. I saw it.
(b) Call me if you get lost.
(c) I should've shown you.
(d) It's pretty easy to miss.

21
M Haven't we met?
W I'm not sure, but you do look familiar.
M You went to Greystone College, didn't you?
W _____

(a) Yes, I'm studying math.
(b) That also looks familiar.
(c) No, but I did live nearby.
(d) It took three whole years.

22
W I can't cook tonight. Do you mind takeout?
M Not again! That's three days in a row!
W But I have to finish this report.
M _____

(a) Well, I hope this doesn't become a habit.
(b) Please submit the report to me soon.
(c) Frankly, I don't feel like eating out.
(d) I'm getting tired of these recipes.

23
M I think Brendan would make a good goalkeeper.
W You're kidding. Dennis would be way better.
M But Dennis isn't as fast.
W _____

(a) That's the way to go.
(b) He scored a great goal.
(c) No, you're better than him.
(d) I disagree. I think he's quicker.

24
W Hi, I'm calling about the apartment. Is it still available?
M Yes, would you like to come and take a look?
W Absolutely. Would tomorrow evening be all right?
M _____

(a) No, it's already been rented.
(b) Sure, I'll be home all evening.
(c) It depends on what you can afford.
(d) Of course. Come and have a look now.

25
M Who's that talking to the boss?
W She's our new sales manager.
M They didn't let Cathy go, did they?
W _____

(a) No, she got promoted.
(b) She'll be gone by then.
(c) Yes, she'll be here soon.
(d) She got back from vacation.

26
W Why are you using this photocopier?
M Because the copier on my floor isn't working.
W Really? But it's only a year old.
M _____

(a) There's still time to fix it.
(b) I should've used this copier first.
(c) I know, but it keeps breaking down.
(d) Then, we need to buy more copiers.

27
M Did you buy the right light bulb for the lamp?
W I thought so, but now that I'm home I see it's too small.
M Why didn't you take the old one along for comparison?
W _____

(a) I would've, but I'd already thrown it away.

(b) That's true. I can compare them easily.

(c) I thought the new one wasn't that big.

(d) I'll be sure to when I turn it on.

28

W The wallpaper in the living room is in bad shape.

M Yeah, it's dirty and some ends are peeling.

W Do you think it's time we replaced it?

M _____

(a) Let's take it back to the store.

(b) That would really spruce things up.

(c) I've been wanting to study interior design.

(d) We can't hire a professional on our budget.

29

M Congratulations on your promotion.

W Thanks! It came as a big surprise.

M Why? Haven't you been anticipating it for a while?

W _____

(a) That's true. It was a big letdown.

(b) No, it's not that I'm ungrateful for it.

(c) Well, I wasn't holding out much hope.

(d) Sure, I know several strong candidates.

30

W Pete, do you have time for a meeting later?

M Sure. What's it about?

W The newsletter. I need ideas.

M _____

(a) Some just aren't feasible.

(b) A newsletter's a good idea.

(c) OK. Let's do it this afternoon.

(d) Yes, it's still under discussion.

31

W Let's have a look at that sore tooth of yours.

M Thanks Dr. Smith. It's been really painful for two days now.

W Open wide. Mmm… you've got a cavity. OK, you can relax now.

M Will you be able to fix it today?

W Yes, the cavity isn't that bad, so it won't take too long.

M Oh, good. That's a relief.

Q: What is the man mainly doing in the conversation?

(a) He is asking for medication.

(b) He is getting a tooth examined.

(c) He is worrying about his health.

(d) He is making a dentist appointment.

32

M Hello. How may I help you?

W I'd like to insure my new car, please.

M Certainly. May I see your license, please?

W I don't have it with me. Is that a problem?

M Yes. I'm sorry, but we can't proceed without it.

Q: What is mainly taking place in the conversation?

(a) The man is searching for his license.

(b) The woman is trying to insure her car.

(c) The man is trying to sell the woman a car.

(d) The woman is being told to license her car.

33

W Has anyone applied for the marketing job we advertised online?

M Actually, for some reason, only a few applications have come in.

W But the ad has been out for five days.

M I know, but so far we've only received three résumés.

W I guess it's still just the first week. It's probably too early to start worrying.

M Yeah, maybe we'll get more responses next week.

Q: What is mainly being discussed in the conversation?

(a) The requirements for a job.

(b) The number of job applicants.

(c) The difficulties of finding a job.

(d) The application deadline for a job.

34

W Hello, I'd like to change one of my classes, please.

M Which one would you like to change?

W I'd like to move my English class to third period.

M OK, I'll check. I'm sorry, but that section is full.

W Oh, no. So, what are my options?

M How about moving it to fourth period?

W Well, I guess that'll have to do.

Q: What is the woman mainly trying to do?

(a) Reschedule her English class.

(b) Study something besides English.

(c) Do a different English assignment.

(d) Be excused from her English class.

35

M Stacy, I've got really big news, but I need some advice.

W Sure, tell me what it is, and I'll let you know what I think.

M I've just been offered a position overseas in Germany.

W That's great! So, what's the problem?

M Well, it's a big step. I'd have to leave a lot behind.

W True, but I say go for it. It'll be a great experience.

Q: What is the main topic of the conversation?

(a) The advantages of working overseas.

(b) Reasons why the man should go overseas.

(c) A job opportunity the man needs advice on.

(d) The man's overseas job application process.

36

W I can't believe how long it takes to get to work now.

M I know. The roads are completely choked with tourists.

W Does this happen every summer?

M Yeah, commuting is a nightmare this time of year.

W How do you usually cope with it?

M I leave for work earlier in the morning.

Q: What is mainly being discussed in the conversation?

(a) The unexpected rise in tourism.

(b) The hectic summer schedule at work.

(c) The traffic problems tourists encounter.

(d) The difficulties with commuting in summer.

37

M Would you like to catch a movie tomorrow, Amy?

W Sorry. I told a friend I'd help her move in the afternoon.

M Then, how about seeing something later on?

W Sure. I'll be finished by six.

M When should I pick you up, then?

W Make it half past 7.

Q: What is mainly happening in the conversation?

(a) The man is helping the woman move.

(b) The woman is planning her weekend.

(c) The man is arranging a date with the woman.

(d) The woman is considering which movie to see.

38

W I don't think this new blouse is my style.

M So why did you decide to buy it?

W I thought the color was pretty and that it fit well.

M It is a nice color, but the blouse is no good if you'll never wear it.

W Yeah, but I wanted to try something trendy.

M Still, I'd return it if I were you.

Q: Why is the woman unhappy with her new blouse?

(a) It is too dark.

(b) It is out of fashion.

(c) It is too small for her.

(d) It does not suit her style.

39

M Hello, I'm calling about the boat you advertised in yesterday's paper.

W Oh, yes. Are you interested in buying it?

M Very much so. It has twin 135 horsepower engines, right?

W Yes. And they've hardly been used, so they're like new.

M Can I come over to see it tomorrow afternoon sometime?

W Sure. Any time after three is fine.

M OK. I'll call before I come. See you then.

Q: Which is correct according to the conversation?

(a) The woman is selling two boats.

(b) The man wants to buy a new engine.

(c) The woman's boat has already been sold.

(d) The man plans to look at a boat tomorrow.

40

W Have you seen Eric lately?

M No, not recently. Why do you ask?

W I was wondering whether he's still upset.

M What would he be upset about?

W His girlfriend left him last week.

M Oh, I didn't know that.

W Yeah, apparently he took it pretty badly.

Q: Which is correct according to the conversation?

(a) The woman just spoke to Eric.

(b) The man knew Eric was upset.

(c) The man has not seen Eric recently.

(d) The woman thinks Eric behaved badly.

41

M Excuse me. Do you have any rooms left?

W I'm sorry, but we're full for the next two weeks.

M Is there anywhere else I could try?

W There's another hostel nearby.

M Oh, thanks very much. Is it far?

W No, just ten minutes by bus. It's called the Charlton.

Q: Which is correct according to the conversation?

(a) The man wants a room at a hostel.

(b) The hostel will have vacancies tomorrow.

(c) The man booked a room at the Charlton.

(d) The Charlton is a ten-minute walk away.

42

M You seem distracted. Is everything OK?

W Oh, yeah. I was just thinking about my date tonight.

M Date? I didn't realize you had one.

W Yes, I'm going to dinner with a guy from work.

M So, where are you going to eat? Somewhere nice, I hope.

W That's the problem. We haven't decided yet.

Q: Which is correct according to the conversation?

(a) The woman is thinking about her date tomorrow.

(b) The man already knew about the woman's date.

(c) The woman has a lunch date with a co-worker.

(d) The woman is unsure of where to go for dinner.

43

W Have you seen my cell phone anywhere?

M Are you telling me you've lost it again?

W Yeah, I wish I could remember where I left it.

M Last time it was on our dresser.

W I already checked, but it wasn't there.

M Maybe you left it at work.

Q: What can be inferred from the conversation?

(a) The woman often misplaces her phone.

(b) The man and woman work together.

(c) The woman's phone is in her purse.

(d) The man is hiding the woman's phone.

44

W Our work conditions here need to change.

M I agree. There aren't enough incentives to stay longer.

W Maybe we can talk to our boss about it.

M That's a great idea. Why don't we do that right now?

W But first we have to decide on the changes we really want to see.

M I guess you're right. Let's make a list and then go see him.

Q: What can be inferred about the man and woman from the conversation?

(a) They really want a new boss.

(b) They think changes are unlikely to happen.

(c) They are not happy with their work conditions.

(d) They are reluctant to bring matters to their boss.

45

W I heard the company is opening a branch overseas.

M Do you think they'll ask any of us to move there?

W I don't know. I also heard they're hiring a new manager.

M What about James? He'll stay here, won't he?

W My guess is he'll go to manage the new branch office.

M I sure hope not.

Q: What can be inferred from the conversation?

(a) The man wants to see the woman go overseas.

(b) The woman will choose the new manager.

(c) The woman would like to work overseas.

(d) The man does not want James to go.

46

My talk on religions in India turns now to Indian gods. Hindu deities are usually depicted as human figures, but they often appear in vivid and unnatural colors. This is because, in India, colors have meanings attached to them and are often associated with gods according to each supreme being's nature. As an example, one of the most important goddesses, Durga, is red because that color symbolizes both power and purity.

Q: What is the lecturer's main point about Indian gods?

(a) They are depicted in meaningful colors.

(b) They are portrayed in human forms.

(c) Their coloring is primarily reddish.

(d) Their classification is complex.

47

One tip for those of you trying to quit smoking for good is to exercise more often after you quit. Exercising will decrease the likelihood of gaining weight in the early weeks after giving up cigarettes. It will also give you more energy and make you feel more positive about yourself. So remember: being active can help you remain a nonsmoker.

Q: What is the speaker's main point?

(a) Smoking can lead to fatal lung disease.

(b) Weight gain can be reduced by exercising.

(c) Be sure to exercise after you quit smoking.

(d) Quit smoking to enjoy the full benefits of exercise.

48

Stay at any Merilux Hotel this month and earn free air miles on your Supersavers Miles Card. Simply use your credit card to pay for a qualifying room rate, and you'll receive 500 miles on any Seaton Transatlantic, Intercontinental United or Eastwood flight. It's that easy. For reservations, contact your local travel professional or just give us a call at 1-800-MERILUX.

Q: What is the Merilux Hotel advertisement mainly about?
(a) Getting a discount with airlines.
(b) Receiving air miles with room bookings.
(c) Paying for a hotel room with a credit card.
(d) Saving money on rooms at a special business rate.

49

In today's lecture, I want to discuss William Harvey, the 17th-century English physiologist. Harvey discovered that blood was pumped by the heart, and not, as was believed, moved by pulsing arteries. He conducted research by observing patients and experimenting with animals, and in 1628 he published his findings on how the heart works.

Q: What is mainly being discussed about William Harvey?
(a) He experimented with human beings.
(b) He invented the idea of heart transplants.
(c) He uncovered the heart's role in circulation.
(d) He was the first to discover what blood does.

50

When diagnosed with a disease, it's advisable to verify the diagnosis by getting a second opinion. This precaution, however, is not foolproof. That's what Jennifer Jones found out when she was diagnosed with breast cancer. Her first doctor told her she had breast cancer after mistakenly reading another patient's test results as Jennifer's. Then, her second doctor made the same misdiagnosis because he read the same incorrect test results. Unfortunately, this led to her getting a breast removed when she didn't need to.

Q: What is the speech mainly about?
(a) The best treatment for breast cancer patients.
(b) What double-checking a doctor's diagnosis entails.
(c) The occasional failure of a second-opinion diagnosis.
(d) What mistakes are most often made by incompetent doctors.

51

Before tomorrow's parent-teacher conference, I want to remind all participating teachers to stick to the facts about each student, but at the same time be encouraging when it comes to students who are not doing well. Parents are paying a lot of money to send their children here, and I want them assured that their money is being well spent. Now, I'm not instructing you to bend the truth. I am simply asking you to maintain positive attitudes.

Q: What is the main idea of the talk?
(a) Teachers need to treat poor students better.
(b) Teachers must not lie to parents of bad students.
(c) Teachers have to focus more on telling the truth.
(d) Teachers should give student results in a positive light.

52

Today I want to talk about something that has been highly influential in the development of Canada's literary canon: the landscape. Canada's vast and remote terrain is a predominant feature in the novels of numerous Canadian writers, such as Margaret Atwood, renowned for her literary fiction, and Douglas Coupland, famous for his explorations of pop culture. Regardless of their genres and styles, most Canadian authors would agree that geography has greatly influenced their imaginations and their writing.

Q: What is the main topic of the lecture?
(a) The influence of environmental issues on writers in Canada.
(b) The current diversity of writing in Canada's literary world.
(c) The dominance of peculiar settings in Canadian literature.
(d) The impact geography has had upon Canadian writers.

53

The whales we're going to see on today's tour are humpbacks, named for their rounded backs. They are black with white throats and have long, wing-like flippers. Because they swim close to the shore, humpbacks were once an easy target for whalers, and their numbers were drastically reduced. However, in 1972, a law prohibiting hunting humpbacks for oil was passed, and their numbers have since recovered, making them visible from the shoreline.

Q: Which is correct about humpbacks according to the talk?
(a) They have short flippers.
(b) They are decreasing in number.
(c) They are now protected by a hunting law.
(d) They no longer swim near the shore.

54

Northern Queensland's tropical rainforests are home to some of the most unique animal species on earth. One such animal is the tree kangaroo, which lives high up in the trees and eats leaves and fruit. They are extremely agile up among the treetops but are surprisingly clumsy on the ground. The tree kangaroo looks more like a small bear with a long tail than a kangaroo, but the two kangaroos actually evolved from a common ancestor.

Q: Which is correct about tree kangaroos according to the lecture?
(a) They resemble small bears.
(b) They live on the forest floor.
(c) They are swift on the ground.
(d) They have short but strong tails.

55

I'd like to mention one final thing before class finishes. Please remember that next week is your final oral testing period. A blank schedule is posted on my office door. Before the end of the week, make sure you write your name in a time slot on the schedule indicating when you'd like to be tested. Also, instructions for your final assignment are posted on the class webpage. It is very important to have that in by the due date.

Q: What should students do before the end of the week?
(a) Take the final oral test.
(b) Pick a time to be tested.
(c) Change an assignment topic.
(d) Submit their final assignment.

56

Bhutan is a country that has pursued a unique political and economic path. It was run by Buddhist priests until the 20th century, when a monarchy was established. That monarchy, currently headed by the world's youngest hereditary ruler, has seen its power gradually eroded. Curiously enough, even though Bhutan is the second poorest country in the world, there is no unemployment, no begging, and almost no crime.

Q: Which is correct about Bhutan according to the lecture?
(a) Its crime rate has increased rapidly.
(b) Its ruler has recently been displaced.
(c) It is run by a group of Buddhist priests.
(d) Its poverty has not caused unemployment.

57

An official with China's space program said last night that China's first female astronauts will embark on a space mission before 2010. On China's next mission female astronauts will fly with male counterparts as flight commanders or on-board engineers. According to the deputy chief of China's space program, four female astronauts will be chosen for the mission, and China's air force has reportedly selected 30 female pilots to be trained as astronauts.

Q: Which is correct according to the news report?
(a) China will send women into space before 2010.
(b) China's next space mission will have an all-female crew.
(c) Thirty female pilots will be sent on China's next mission.
(d) Female astronauts will function only as on-board engineers.

58

Baseball star Roderick Standes is being sued for making false claims about weight-loss pills he endorsed. A consumer advocacy group has accused Standes of grossly misrepresenting the effectiveness of Diet-Easy pills manufactured by the Florel Company. Independent researchers have consistently shown the pills to have little effect on weight loss. Standes, who signed an endorsement contract with Florel last year, has denied he knowingly did anything wrong.

Q: What can be inferred about Diet-Easy pills from the news report?
(a) They actually cause people to gain weight.
(b) Standes claims he had no idea they were ineffective.
(c) Florel has a history of making similarly harmful drugs.
(d) Standes has been sued before for endorsing other products.

59

We should do more than just negotiate agreements about the world's climate problems. Until the major polluters of the world, including the United States and China, substantially cut their greenhouse gas emissions, international agreements like the Kyoto treaty will remain irrelevant. Such treaties, partnerships and negotiations amount to a lot of legal mumbo-jumbo and technical talk while nothing happens on the ground.

Q: What is the speaker's view of present international climate negotiations?
(a) They are ineffective and little more than a waste of time.
(b) They produce more conflict than peace among nations.
(c) They pressure major polluters to change overnight.
(d) They are mainly of interest to climate experts.

60

While it's true that the Aztecs had an advanced culture among ancient American tribes, many of those advances were borrowed. For centuries, the Aztecs were a barbarous nomadic tribe struggling to survive in northern Mexico. In the 12th century, they migrated to central Mexico, where they built their capital city on a swamp. From there, they absorbed the already advanced cultures of existing inhabitants and embarked on expansion through conquest. It was only through this absorption and acquisition that the Aztecs emerged as a power in the 14th century.

Q: What can be inferred about the Aztecs from the lecture?
(a) They sold technology to neighboring tribes.
(b) They were widespread and influential as nomads.
(c) They were not responsible for many cultural innovations.
(d) They found central Mexico was better for growing crops.

서울대 최신기출 **6**

Listening Comprehension **Scripts**

1

M How far is the public library from here?

W _____

(a) I'll see you there.
(b) It's open until 5 pm.
(c) I have to return a book.
(d) It's only nine blocks away.

2

W Oh, sorry, I spilt coffee on your desk.

M _____

(a) I'll use my computer.
(b) I don't need any help.
(c) This coffee is quite good.
(d) That's OK. No harm done.

3

M I'm afraid I can't join you on your road trip.

W _____

(a) Why not?
(b) I will, instead.
(c) Then let me drive.
(d) I'm leaving tomorrow.

4

W Is there a direct flight to Pittsburgh from this airport?

M _____

(a) Yes, I've driven to Pittsburgh once.
(b) Upgrade your flight for more comfort.
(c) No, you need to transfer at JFK airport.
(d) Don't take an express bus to Pittsburgh.

5

M I was really surprised when I won the math award.

W _____

(a) Math is my favorite subject.
(b) I hope you're right this time.
(c) You deserve it. You worked hard.
(d) I went through a lot of trouble to get it.

6

W Would you like to exchange this or get a refund?

M _____

(a) It depends on the price.
(b) Do you have the receipt?
(c) Yes, please, in fives and tens.
(d) I'd like my money back, please.

7

M How are you doing today, Cathy?

W _____

(a) Not really.
(b) Couldn't be better!
(c) You look great today.
(d) You're quite welcome.

8

W I've been working out every day for a week but haven't lost any weight!

M _____

(a) That's almost twice my size.
(b) You'll have to start exercising.
(c) I guess I'll look for an alternative.
(d) At least you look fitter than before.

9

M What's the weather going to be like tomorrow?

W _____

(a) I hope so.
(b) That's not good.
(c) I like cloudy days.
(d) I hear it'll be sunny.

10

M How can I reach Mr. Miller? It's really urgent.

W _____

(a) You'd better hurry up.
(b) Try calling his cell phone.
(c) I'm sure it'll arrive eventually.
(d) It's OK. I don't want to bother you.

11

W The food was terrible at that restaurant.

M _____

(a) I know how you feel about eating out.
(b) Next time we should try to get there earlier.
(c) I hope there's a table for us near the window.
(d) We won't be going there again, that's for sure.

12

M The exam schedule looks horrible this semester.

W _____

(a) Right. Our teachers grade so hard.
(b) Yeah, I wish it were better organized.
(c) I didn't do so well on my exam, either.
(d) I'll make copies of the schedule for you.

13

W How did you meet your wife?

M _____

(a) I'd like you to meet her.
(b) Through a matchmaker.
(c) She was sincere and optimistic.
(d) We've been married for a long time.

14

M This is the best movie so far this year.

W _____

(a) It's about time.
(b) How fast time flies!
(c) You can say that again!
(d) It's too far away to tell.

15

W Are these paintings all genuine?

M _____

(a) Yes, everything is here.
(b) No, they're oil paintings.
(c) One or two are reproduced.
(d) They're all very delightful.

16

M Is Bill there?
W Yes. Who's calling?
M It's Sam from the drugstore.
W _____

(a) Wait for me.
(b) OK, just a minute.
(c) I need some aspirin.
(d) May I leave a message?

17

W What do you plan to study in college?
M Medicine. I want to become a doctor.
W Why a doctor?
M _____

(a) I'll do my best.
(b) Call the nurse, then.
(c) I want to help sick people.
(d) Because I'm feeling sick.

18

W How can I help you today, sir?
M Do you have this shirt in a larger size?
W No, I'm sorry. That's the largest size.
M _____

(a) Oh, I see. Thanks anyway.
(b) I don't see it, either.
(c) I've finished now.
(d) Great, it'll suit me better.

19

M I'm thinking of buying an apartment this month.

W That isn't a very good idea.

M Why do you say that?

W _____

(a) I'll help you find a good one.

(b) Prices are too high right now.

(c) I'm tired of moving around, too.

(d) It's too far from where you work.

20

W Any special plans for this weekend?

M Well, I'm going to plant a small garden.

W Really? What kind of plants?

M _____

(a) Mostly herbs.

(b) That's not my plan.

(c) It's not a big garden.

(d) Maybe in a year or two.

21

M Hi, Mandy. How are you this morning?

W Not good. I have a splitting headache.

M Sorry to hear that. What do you think caused it?

W _____

(a) It's probably from stress.

(b) I'll get some pills for you.

(c) I'll try and get some sleep.

(d) Yes, that could be the reason.

22

W Are you still coming to the tennis match with me?

M I wish I could, but I don't have the time.

W But you said you would come this time.

M _____

(a) I had a good time.

(b) I don't play tennis.

(c) Sorry, I have to study.

(d) It's going to be a tough match.

23

M Let me carry that bag for you.

W No thanks, I'm all right.

M But it looks really heavy.

W _____

(a) It's all I can do.

(b) Here, I'll carry it then.

(c) Don't worry. I can manage.

(d) Actually, I gained a few kilos.

24

W Oh, no, the computer crashed again!

M Not again! This is the fourth time! We need a new one.

W But we can't afford one right now.

M _____

(a) Here, I'll install it for you.

(b) Well, I'll give you a discount.

(c) That's OK. It won't happen again.

(d) Maybe we can put it on our credit card.

25

M Have you read *White Noise*?

W Of course. I love Don DeLillo.

M Me too. He's a great novelist.

W _____

(a) Sure, I know him.

(b) I've heard of him, too.

(c) The best, in my opinion.

(d) An excellent book, I've heard.

26

M Hey, you look great in that dress!

W Thanks. I was worried that I might look silly in it.

M No! It fits you perfectly.

W _____

(a) I'm relieved to hear that.

(b) And I lost a matching purse.

(c) Then what would you worry about?

(d) I've been asking myself the same question.

27

W I heard you had a blind date last night. How was it?

M Great. Everything went well.

W Who arranged it for you?

M _____

(a) A colleague of mine set it up.
(b) No plans yet. We've just met.
(c) I don't know her well enough.
(d) It was arranged at a restaurant.

28

W Hey, where've you been? I haven't seen you for a while.

M I just got back from my trip to Spain.

W I didn't know you went to Spain.

M _____

(a) I'll see you at the airport.
(b) You're welcome to join us.
(c) Really? I thought I'd mentioned it.
(d) We stayed there longer than I thought.

29

W Beijing Takeout. How may I help you?

M I'd like to order wonton soup and shrimp with mixed vegetables, please.

W Would you like that delivered?

M _____

(a) That's alright. I'll come by in an hour.
(b) I'll just have a stir fry dish instead.
(c) Let me check the yellow pages.
(d) I'd like it extra spicy, thanks.

30

W Mr. Smith, the tiles in the restaurant bathroom need to be replaced.

M Why? There's nothing wrong with them.

W Yes, but they're starting to look old.

M _____

(a) I don't think that warrants the expense.
(b) Then, we need to think about an interior.
(c) It's unlikely to change things around here.
(d) That's what I was trying to explain to you.

31

M Have you started your term project yet?

W Not yet. But I will soon.

M Which topic did you choose?

W I haven't decided yet.

M Me neither. They all seem really difficult.

Q: What is the conversation mainly about?

(a) Passing an exam.
(b) Beginning a new class.
(c) Choosing a good school.
(d) Doing a project assignment.

32

M Are you busy Saturday night?

W I haven't made any plans yet.

M Do you want to have dinner with me?

W Sure. And how about watching a movie after?

M Sounds good. What time shall we meet?

W Let's meet at 5:30.

Q: What are the speakers mainly talking about?

(a) Which movie to watch.
(b) What to do on Saturday.
(c) What to have for dinner.
(d) When to meet for the movie.

33

W Dan! What's wrong? You look upset.

M I'm worried about my son.

W Why? What's the problem?

M He can't seem to find a job.

W How long has he been out of work?

M Almost a year. He says there aren't any good jobs out there.

Q: What is Dan's main concern?

(a) His son's being out of work.
(b) Giving his family a good life.
(c) Moving out and getting a job.
(d) Confronting his son's behavior.

34

M Well, we have to re-do all our vacation plans.

W What do you mean? What happened?

M The airline has changed some of our flight times.

W You're kidding! Will that mess up our itinerary?

M Yeah, we're going to have to rearrange hotel bookings.

W And is it going to cost us extra?

M No, but we'll lose a day in Paris.

Q: What are the speakers mainly talking about?

(a) How their vacation budget has changed.

(b) How their bookings were made incorrectly.

(c) How their flight to Paris has been cancelled.

(d) How their travel schedule has been changed.

35

W Hi, Tom. Sorry to bother you at home.

M No, that's alright. Is this Glenda?

W Yes, I'm calling from the office.

M The office? What are you doing at the office on a Saturday?

W I have some work that needs to be done before Monday.

M Oh, I see. What can I do for you?

W I was wondering where you put the Johnson file.

Q: What is the purpose of the woman's phone call?

(a) To see if the man could help out at the office.

(b) To ask the man where a certain file is located.

(c) To explain why she is working on Saturday.

(d) To inform the man of a change of schedule.

36

M Have you heard about that new store at the Fashion Trends Mall?

W Heard about it? I've already shopped there twice. They have the newest styles!

M Really? I heard the clothes are totally expensive.

W Some of them are, but actually, the majority is reasonably priced.

M I don't know. I kind of hate spending a lot on my outfits.

W Well, you should check it out anyway. You might be surprised.

Q: What is the couple mainly discussing?

(a) A trendy new clothing store.

(b) The location of a new casual store.

(c) The best clothing store at the mall.

(d) Expensive outfits at the shopping mall.

37

W Are you doing much tomorrow?

M Not that much. Why?

W I need some help carrying lots of old books.

M Sure, I can help. Where are you taking them?

W To a second-hand book shop downtown.

M OK. We can use my car.

W Great! That'll make it quick and easy.

Q: What are the man and woman mainly talking about?

(a) Visiting a library on the weekend.

(b) Arranging to move some old books.

(c) Selling a car at a second-hand auto shop.

(d) Throwing out books that are no longer wanted.

38

W Excuse me? I think you're in my seat.

M Are you sure? I have seat #23.

W Can I see your ticket, please?

M My ticket? Sure. Here it is.

W Your ticket is for row A. This is row B.

M What? Let me see... Oh, you're right. I'm sorry.

Q: Which is correct according to the conversation?

(a) The woman has lost her ticket.

(b) The woman's ticket is not valid.

(c) The man had the woman's ticket.

(d) The man was not in the right seat.

39

M Do you need help finding a particular book?

W No thanks. I'm just going to browse the best-sellers section.

M OK. But some best-sellers were moved to alphabetical shelves recently.

W Which ones got moved?

M Those over six months old.

W Oh, OK. I'll keep that in mind.

Q: Which is correct according to the conversation?

(a) The store has been redecorated.

(b) The store opened six months ago.

(c) The woman needs help in finding a book.

(d) The woman wants to look at best-sellers.

40

W I'm breaking up with Tim.

M Why? You two seemed great together.

W He's not for me. He's always late for everything.

M Come on, you can't break up over such a trivial thing.

W Well, to be honest, there's another, more serious problem.

M What? Is he seeing someone else?

W No, he says he's not ready for marriage.

Q: What is the main reason the woman wants to break up with Tim?

(a) He gets upset over trivial things.

(b) He is always late for everything.

(c) He does not want to get married.

(d) He has been dating someone else.

41

M Hi, Susan!

W Where have you been? You're a day late.

M What do you mean?

W You were supposed to pick the furniture up yesterday.

M Was I? I thought it was today.

W No, it was supposed to be yesterday. Didn't you read my text messages?

M Oh, I think I must have gotten the days mixed up, sorry.

Q: What did the man do wrong?

(a) He did not fix the woman's furniture.

(b) He forgot to visit the woman last week.

(c) He failed to turn up at an appointed time.

(d) He did not have any excuse for being late.

42

M How are your new neighbors upstairs?

W Unbelievable. They make so much noise.

M Why, is it a large family?

W There must be at least three kids up there.

M Do they run around and bang things a lot?

W All the time. It's driving me crazy.

Q: Which is correct according to the conversation?

(a) The woman's children are driving her crazy.

(b) The woman's neighbor asked her to be quiet.

(c) The woman has a noisy family living above her.

(d) The woman does not agree with the man's suggestion.

43

M Which DVD did you choose?

W I got *Gone with the Wind*.

M *Gone with the Wind*? That's too long and too old.

W Well, you pick one, then.

M I will. I'm going to look at the new releases.

W OK. I'll put this back.

Q: What will the man and woman probably do next?

(a) See a movie at the theater.

(b) Watch the film the woman has chosen.

(c) Go home and watch *Gone with the Wind*.

(d) Rent a movie other than *Gone with the Wind*.

44

W Acme stocks have fallen again.

M They must be pretty low now.

W You know, it could be a good time to buy.

M Are you sure they'll go up again?

W Not immediately, perhaps, but they will in the long run.

M But the company hasn't done very well recently.

W I know, but they're sure to bounce back.

M I'm not sure I want to take that kind of risk.

Q: What can be inferred from the conversation?

(a) The man is less sure of investing in Acme than the woman.

(b) The man has bought more stocks than the woman.

(c) The woman will make a lot of money on her stocks.

(d) The woman will probably wait before buying stocks.

45

W I just found this old photo. Look how long your hair was!

M And check out your clothes. They're so old-fashioned!

W That was the style everyone wore.

M We sure were wild and crazy back then.

W Those were the good old days, though, weren't they?

M I'll say.

Q: What can be inferred from the conversation?

(a) The man and woman are throwing away old photos.

(b) The man and woman do not regret their past.

(c) The woman prefers the man with long hair.

(d) The woman still likes hippie fashion.

46

Most TVs have much the same basic design. But at Ryo Electronics we believe customers want to look at something more interesting than a box. That's why we make TVs that come in different shapes and sizes. We make TVs shaped like animals for kids and others in antique or art-deco styles for adults. Choose a TV that fits your décor: don't just buy a TV, buy a Ryo TV.

Q: What is mainly being advertised?

(a) TVs that come in uncommon shapes.

(b) A company that makes electronic toys.

(c) New TVs designed with extra functions.

(d) A TV service offering unusual programs.

47

Before we examine the development of the aqualung, I'll give you a brief talk on the origins of scuba diving. They go further back than you might think, to around 4500 BC. Scuba diving all began with what is called free-diving, when humans simply held their breath underwater to hunt for food or to gather pearls and coral. Later, in ancient Greece, soldiers were trained to hold their breath underwater to attack enemy ships.

Q: What is the main topic of the talk?

(a) Different methods of diving.

(b) Military uses of free-diving.

(c) The popularity of free-diving.

(d) The beginnings of scuba diving.

48

In tonight's program, I'll show you how to start growing fruit inside your house. Some fruit trees, like grapefruit, orange, and lemon, can be grown indoors in the traditional way by simply planting a seed in a pot. Others, like the avocado, require a little more work. To grow an avocado tree, suspend the seed in a cup of water with the pointy end up. Use toothpicks stuck in the seed to suspend it in the water. Put it in a warm place out of direct sunlight and remember to add water as needed.

Q: What is the show mainly about?

(a) Proper materials for gardening.

(b) Growing fruits in an indoor setting.

(c) Methods for planting avocados in a pot.

(d) Techniques for growing plants without sunlight.

49

When I first started lecturing on health some years ago, nutritionists believed that fat consumption was linked to the development of cancers. This is still true, and fats should be avoided whenever possible. However, according to the latest findings, eating more fruits and vegetables is even better than avoiding fats. Researchers now say that if you regularly eat fruits and vegetables, you can reduce the risk of contracting cancer by about 30 to 40 percent.

Q: What is the lecture mainly about?
(a) How often you need to eat fruits.
(b) What to eat to reduce the risk of cancer.
(c) How fat consumption is linked to cancer.
(d) What one of the main causes of cancer is.

50

By the end of the 17th century, Britain primarily traded with two regions: one was comprised of its colonies in present-day America and the other was comprised of its West African coastal stations. These regions formed a "triangular" network of trade routes to distribute raw materials, labor, and finished goods. Ships from England visited Africa to exchange goods for slaves, then transported the slaves to plantations in the New World. There they exchanged the slaves for tobacco, sugar and other colonial produce to bring back to England.

Q: What is the main topic of the lecture?
(a) Britain's major trade routes in the 17th century.
(b) Intercontinental trade between Africa and America.
(c) The growth of Britain's economy in the 17th century.
(d) The profitability of the slave trade in the British Empire.

51

Now that you know some of the basics of Swahili culture, I want to focus specifically on how Swahili art is influenced by Islam, the faith that most Swahilis practice. Its influences are evident in the geometric designs and patterns that appear in Swahili art, in the decorations of pottery and furniture, and in the artwork and in the structures of Swahili architecture. Because Islam discourages the representation of living beings in art, such geometric patterns are everywhere.

Q: What is the main idea of the lecture?
(a) Swahili culture reveals diverse artistic influences.
(b) Islamic beliefs have influenced Swahili art and culture.
(c) Swahilis are adverse to portraying living things in their art.
(d) Geometric patterns in Swahili art are unique in Islamic culture.

52

The issue I'd like to highlight at this pharmaceuticals conference is how the news media can move drugs, almost instantaneously, from medical research to miracle cures. Too often, the nation's media seems more interested in hype than in critically appraising new drugs; in effect they are assisting the drug-industry's marketing drives. The problem has grown dramatically in recent years, as drug advertising has increased, delivering higher ad revenues to the media. I'm not saying it's a conspiracy, but it sure looks like one.

Q: What is the speaker's main topic?
(a) Why false reports about drugs occur in the media.
(b) How the media's practices benefit the drug industry.
(c) Why tighter controls are needed in the drug industry.
(d) How the drug industry has manipulated the media in the past.

53

Thanks for coming to our school's Parent-Teacher Night. Before we start, I just want to remind parents about our attendance policy. Regular and punctual attendance is very important, so please call the school office if your child is too sick to come to school. On the day your child returns to school, he or she must bring a hand-written note explaining the reasons for absence. The note needs to be written, dated and signed by you. A doctor's note can be brought instead, if you have one, but still requires the date and your signature.

Q: Which is correct about the written note of absence?
(a) It must be accompanied by a doctor's note.
(b) It should be handed in by the child's parent.
(c) It must be dated and signed by a child's doctor.
(d) It should explain why the child was not at school.

54

The exhibit in the nautical wing of the museum features items retrieved from sunken ships. This exhibit includes a candle that was taken out of the *Royal George*, a ship that sank in 1782. Naturally, it was exposed to salt water for many years, but this example illustrates how durable and resistant candles are, as it would still burn if it were lit. Eighteenth-century candles like this were made by combining beeswax and animal fat. The wick was usually made of woven cotton.

Q: Which is correct according to the speaker?
(a) The *Royal George* carried a cargo of salt.
(b) The cotton wick was invented soon after 1782.
(c) Candles left in water lose their capacity to burn.
(d) Animal fat was used in making candles in the 1700s.

55

The Bank of England raised its interest rates early this week, the first time since September. The move was prompted by the continuing upswing in housing prices and an overheating economy. Bank officials expect the move will curtail rapidly rising inflation rates. Critics of the move, however, say that it will likely strengthen the pound and that this in turn will ultimately hurt exports.

Q: Which is correct according to the news report?
(a) A stronger currency is expected to hurt imports.
(b) Critics complain that the pound will be weakened.
(c) Economists predict that interest rates will decline.
(d) The rate increase resulted from rising house prices.

56

This summer the Royal Armories Museum is holding an exhibition to celebrate the life of Tokugawa, the shogun who ruled Japan's army in the early 17th century. Two suits of armor that Tokugawa presented to James I of England in 1613 will be included in the display. These were the first oriental items added to the Tower of London's Royal Armories collection. You can view them along with other precious Japanese artifacts from the period at our Tokugawa Exhibition from October 10 to November 21.

Q: Which is correct according to the announcement?
(a) Tokugawa was ruler of Japan in the 1700s.
(b) The two suits of armor were given to James I.
(c) James I donated royal items to Japan's shogun.
(d) The Tokugawa Exhibition is being held in Japan.

57

J&R Solutions specializes in creating business solutions for small and mid-size organizations, supplying integration technologies that will meet your needs. Working with educational and legal industries since 1992, J&R Solutions has the insight and experience to provide you with superior information technology services. We can help you incorporate technology to fit your business strategy. Call 976-882-2121 today to schedule a consultation.

Q: Which is correct about J&R Solutions?

(a) It manufactures information technology equipment.

(b) It has worked with technology companies since 1992.

(c) It utilizes technology to meet an organization's needs.

(d) It helps large organizations with financial consultation.

58

In today's lecture, I'm going to concentrate on a modern example of the social influence of literature and how powerful it can be. About 15 years ago, a book called *The Satanic Verses* by Salmon Rushdie upset millions of the Islamic faith. While critical opinion varies on the book's quality, there is no question that it had a tremendous impact on culture. Why did a book like that have such a social impact? That's what I intend to explore today.

Q: What can be inferred from the lecture?

(a) Rushdie's book contained controversial content for Muslims.

(b) Islamic societies regularly criticize Western books.

(c) Islamicists were angry at Rushdie's poor writing.

(d) Rushdie's writings have often been against Islam.

59

A key problem in our culture is the desire to be young. This can be traced back to the Baby-Boomer generation. They grew up believing that youth was meant to conquer the older generations, but now the Boomers are the older generation. Growing old is not something they are accepting gracefully—and why should they, since the culture they helped create equated being young with success, and rejected the elderly? The problem is that it's still like that today for the generation that follows.

Q: What is the speaker likely to agree with?

(a) Youthfulness no longer guarantees success.

(b) Looking young is what the elderly should strive for.

(c) Younger generations accept growing old gracefully.

(d) Today's generation suffers the legacy of the baby-boomers.

60

In the news today, officials at the UN say international pressure is urgently needed to end the war in northern Uganda, where nearly 2 million people have been displaced. Dennis McNamara, special UN adviser on refugees, said on Friday that a humanitarian crisis is developing in Uganda as a result of neighboring countries closing their borders to refugees fleeing the fighting. Mr. McNamara stated that the crisis is exacerbated by Ugandan rebel leaders refusing to admit aid agencies into the country.

Q: What can be inferred from the news report?

(a) The mortality rate is unprecedented in Uganda's history.

(b) The UN is coordinating current relief efforts within Uganda.

(c) The war in Uganda was caused by its neighboring countries.

(d) The Ugandan refugees have tried to cross the border of their country.

Listening Comprehension

1	(c)	**2**	(d)	**3**	(b)	**4**	(a)	**5**	(d)	**6**	(d)	**7**	(a)	**8**	(c)	**9**	(c)	**10**	(a)
11	(c)	**12**	(d)	**13**	(b)	**14**	(b)	**15**	(a)	**16**	(b)	**17**	(b)	**18**	(b)	**19**	(a)	**20**	(a)
21	(b)	**22**	(a)	**23**	(c)	**24**	(b)	**25**	(a)	**26**	(d)	**27**	(d)	**28**	(d)	**29**	(d)	**30**	(c)
31	(c)	**32**	(c)	**33**	(a)	**34**	(d)	**35**	(c)	**36**	(a)	**37**	(c)	**38**	(b)	**39**	(d)	**40**	(d)
41	(c)	**42**	(c)	**43**	(c)	**44**	(b)	**45**	(d)	**46**	(b)	**47**	(a)	**48**	(d)	**49**	(d)	**50**	(b)
51	(d)	**52**	(d)	**53**	(a)	**54**	(a)	**55**	(c)	**56**	(d)	**57**	(b)	**58**	(a)	**59**	(d)	**60**	(b)

Grammar

1	(a)	**2**	(c)	**3**	(d)	**4**	(b)	**5**	(b)	**6**	(b)	**7**	(c)	**8**	(c)	**9**	(d)	**10**	(d)
11	(c)	**12**	(c)	**13**	(c)	**14**	(d)	**15**	(d)	**16**	(d)	**17**	(a)	**18**	(d)	**19**	(b)	**20**	(d)
21	(b)	**22**	(b)	**23**	(c)	**24**	(d)	**25**	(c)	**26**	(c)	**27**	(b)	**28**	(b)	**29**	(c)	**30**	(d)
31	(a)	**32**	(c)	**33**	(d)	**34**	(c)	**35**	(d)	**36**	(b)	**37**	(d)	**38**	(d)	**39**	(b)	**40**	(b)
41	(c)	**42**	(b)	**43**	(b)	**44**	(a)	**45**	(c)	**46**	(c)	**47**	(c)	**48**	(d)	**49**	(d)	**50**	(d)

Vocabulary

1	(a)	**2**	(b)	**3**	(b)	**4**	(a)	**5**	(b)	**6**	(b)	**7**	(b)	**8**	(a)	**9**	(a)	**10**	(b)
11	(a)	**12**	(b)	**13**	(a)	**14**	(a)	**15**	(d)	**16**	(a)	**17**	(a)	**18**	(a)	**19**	(c)	**20**	(b)
21	(c)	**22**	(b)	**23**	(a)	**24**	(a)	**25**	(b)	**26**	(a)	**27**	(b)	**28**	(c)	**29**	(d)	**30**	(c)
31	(b)	**32**	(b)	**33**	(a)	**34**	(d)	**35**	(d)	**36**	(b)	**37**	(b)	**38**	(a)	**39**	(b)	**40**	(a)
41	(b)	**42**	(c)	**43**	(a)	**44**	(b)	**45**	(a)	**46**	(b)	**47**	(c)	**48**	(a)	**49**	(c)	**50**	(d)

Reading Comprehension

1	(d)	**2**	(a)	**3**	(c)	**4**	(a)	**5**	(b)	**6**	(d)	**7**	(a)	**8**	(d)	**9**	(d)	**10**	(d)
11	(d)	**12**	(c)	**13**	(d)	**14**	(d)	**15**	(a)	**16**	(c)	**17**	(c)	**18**	(b)	**19**	(a)	**20**	(d)
21	(c)	**22**	(a)	**23**	(c)	**24**	(a)	**25**	(a)	**26**	(d)	**27**	(c)	**28**	(c)	**29**	(a)	**30**	(d)
31	(c)	**32**	(d)	**33**	(b)	**34**	(c)	**35**	(d)	**36**	(a)	**37**	(d)	**38**	(b)	**39**	(a)	**40**	(c)

Answer Keys

Listening Comprehension

1	(a)	**2**	(c)	**3**	(a)	**4**	(d)	**5**	(d)	**6**	(c)	**7**	(c)	**8**	(d)	**9**	(a)	**10**	(a)
11	(d)	**12**	(b)	**13**	(d)	**14**	(c)	**15**	(a)	**16**	(a)	**17**	(c)	**18**	(d)	**19**	(c)	**20**	(d)
21	(a)	**22**	(b)	**23**	(a)	**24**	(d)	**25**	(c)	**26**	(b)	**27**	(c)	**28**	(a)	**29**	(b)	**30**	(c)
31	(a)	**32**	(b)	**33**	(a)	**34**	(d)	**35**	(d)	**36**	(b)	**37**	(c)	**38**	(d)	**39**	(b)	**40**	(b)
41	(b)	**42**	(a)	**43**	(b)	**44**	(c)	**45**	(d)	**46**	(b)	**47**	(c)	**48**	(b)	**49**	(b)	**50**	(a)
51	(c)	**52**	(c)	**53**	(b)	**54**	(c)	**55**	(d)	**56**	(b)	**57**	(a)	**58**	(c)	**59**	(c)	**60**	(b)

Grammar

1	(c)	**2**	(a)	**3**	(a)	**4**	(b)	**5**	(c)	**6**	(b)	**7**	(d)	**8**	(c)	**9**	(b)	**10**	(c)
11	(b)	**12**	(b)	**13**	(d)	**14**	(d)	**15**	(d)	**16**	(c)	**17**	(b)	**18**	(b)	**19**	(d)	**20**	(c)
21	(c)	**22**	(c)	**23**	(c)	**24**	(d)	**25**	(a)	**26**	(b)	**27**	(c)	**28**	(d)	**29**	(b)	**30**	(d)
31	(d)	**32**	(b)	**33**	(d)	**34**	(b)	**35**	(a)	**36**	(c)	**37**	(a)	**38**	(d)	**39**	(a)	**40**	(c)
41	(d)	**42**	(d)	**43**	(d)	**44**	(d)	**45**	(b)	**46**	(c)	**47**	(a)	**48**	(b)	**49**	(d)	**50**	(c)

Vocabulary

1	(c)	**2**	(c)	**3**	(a)	**4**	(b)	**5**	(b)	**6**	(b)	**7**	(a)	**8**	(c)	**9**	(c)	**10**	(b)
11	(d)	**12**	(a)	**13**	(d)	**14**	(c)	**15**	(c)	**16**	(b)	**17**	(c)	**18**	(b)	**19**	(d)	**20**	(a)
21	(a)	**22**	(a)	**23**	(c)	**24**	(a)	**25**	(d)	**26**	(a)	**27**	(b)	**28**	(a)	**29**	(c)	**30**	(b)
31	(a)	**32**	(b)	**33**	(c)	**34**	(a)	**35**	(d)	**36**	(a)	**37**	(a)	**38**	(b)	**39**	(b)	**40**	(a)
41	(c)	**42**	(c)	**43**	(a)	**44**	(b)	**45**	(d)	**46**	(a)	**47**	(a)	**48**	(d)	**49**	(c)	**50**	(d)

Reading Comprehension

1	(a)	**2**	(b)	**3**	(a)	**4**	(d)	**5**	(b)	**6**	(d)	**7**	(d)	**8**	(c)	**9**	(d)	**10**	(b)
11	(b)	**12**	(a)	**13**	(b)	**14**	(c)	**15**	(b)	**16**	(c)	**17**	(d)	**18**	(c)	**19**	(d)	**20**	(b)
21	(c)	**22**	(b)	**23**	(b)	**24**	(d)	**25**	(b)	**26**	(d)	**27**	(b)	**28**	(d)	**29**	(a)	**30**	(a)
31	(d)	**32**	(a)	**33**	(c)	**34**	(d)	**35**	(a)	**36**	(d)	**37**	(c)	**38**	(b)	**39**	(c)	**40**	(d)

Listening Comprehension

1 (b)	**2** (c)	**3** (a)	**4** (a)	**5** (b)	**6** (c)	**7** (b)	**8** (b)	**9** (d)	**10** (d)
11 (b)	**12** (c)	**13** (d)	**14** (d)	**15** (d)	**16** (a)	**17** (d)	**18** (d)	**19** (b)	**20** (c)
21 (a)	**22** (d)	**23** (d)	**24** (a)	**25** (d)	**26** (a)	**27** (d)	**28** (c)	**29** (a)	**30** (d)
31 (a)	**32** (c)	**33** (b)	**34** (d)	**35** (c)	**36** (b)	**37** (b)	**38** (c)	**39** (b)	**40** (d)
41 (c)	**42** (c)	**43** (a)	**44** (a)	**45** (d)	**46** (a)	**47** (a)	**48** (b)	**49** (d)	**50** (b)
51 (a)	**52** (c)	**53** (a)	**54** (c)	**55** (c)	**56** (b)	**57** (a)	**58** (d)	**59** (d)	**60** (b)

Grammar

1 (a)	**2** (c)	**3** (c)	**4** (c)	**5** (b)	**6** (d)	**7** (b)	**8** (d)	**9** (b)	**10** (b)
11 (a)	**12** (d)	**13** (b)	**14** (d)	**15** (b)	**16** (d)	**17** (c)	**18** (d)	**19** (d)	**20** (c)
21 (c)	**22** (a)	**23** (b)	**24** (b)	**25** (c)	**26** (d)	**27** (b)	**28** (a)	**29** (d)	**30** (d)
31 (d)	**32** (b)	**33** (d)	**34** (b)	**35** (d)	**36** (b)	**37** (b)	**38** (c)	**39** (c)	**40** (c)
41 (c)	**42** (c)	**43** (d)	**44** (c)	**45** (c)	**46** (a)	**47** (d)	**48** (c)	**49** (a)	**50** (b)

Vocabulary

1 (b)	**2** (b)	**3** (c)	**4** (d)	**5** (a)	**6** (b)	**7** (a)	**8** (b)	**9** (a)	**10** (b)
11 (c)	**12** (b)	**13** (b)	**14** (b)	**15** (c)	**16** (b)	**17** (b)	**18** (a)	**19** (d)	**20** (a)
21 (d)	**22** (d)	**23** (a)	**24** (c)	**25** (c)	**26** (c)	**27** (a)	**28** (a)	**29** (c)	**30** (d)
31 (d)	**32** (c)	**33** (b)	**34** (a)	**35** (a)	**36** (a)	**37** (d)	**38** (c)	**39** (a)	**40** (c)
41 (d)	**42** (b)	**43** (d)	**44** (a)	**45** (d)	**46** (a)	**47** (b)	**48** (d)	**49** (b)	**50** (a)

Reading Comprehension

1 (b)	**2** (a)	**3** (a)	**4** (c)	**5** (c)	**6** (a)	**7** (c)	**8** (c)	**9** (d)	**10** (a)
11 (a)	**12** (c)	**13** (a)	**14** (b)	**15** (c)	**16** (d)	**17** (d)	**18** (a)	**19** (b)	**20** (d)
21 (a)	**22** (d)	**23** (c)	**24** (c)	**25** (b)	**26** (b)	**27** (d)	**28** (d)	**29** (c)	**30** (b)
31 (c)	**32** (a)	**33** (d)	**34** (d)	**35** (c)	**36** (b)	**37** (d)	**38** (c)	**39** (c)	**40** (c)

Listening Comprehension

1	(a)	2	(a)	3	(b)	4	(b)	5	(a)	6	(b)	7	(c)	8	(a)	9	(d)	10	(d)
11	(d)	12	(c)	13	(b)	14	(b)	15	(b)	16	(a)	17	(d)	18	(d)	19	(b)	20	(c)
21	(b)	22	(b)	23	(d)	24	(c)	25	(b)	26	(d)	27	(d)	28	(c)	29	(d)	30	(d)
31	(c)	32	(b)	33	(b)	34	(c)	35	(b)	36	(c)	37	(d)	38	(c)	39	(b)	40	(b)
41	(d)	42	(c)	43	(a)	44	(c)	45	(c)	46	(b)	47	(d)	48	(c)	49	(d)	50	(c)
51	(c)	52	(b)	53	(a)	54	(c)	55	(d)	56	(b)	57	(c)	58	(a)	59	(a)	60	(d)

Grammar

1	(b)	2	(a)	3	(b)	4	(b)	5	(d)	6	(c)	7	(c)	8	(d)	9	(d)	10	(b)
11	(d)	12	(c)	13	(a)	14	(d)	15	(c)	16	(c)	17	(a)	18	(d)	19	(d)	20	(c)
21	(d)	22	(a)	23	(d)	24	(c)	25	(c)	26	(a)	27	(c)	28	(d)	29	(c)	30	(a)
31	(d)	32	(c)	33	(c)	34	(b)	35	(d)	36	(c)	37	(c)	38	(c)	39	(a)	40	(b)
41	(a)	42	(d)	43	(c)	44	(d)	45	(d)	46	(b)	47	(b)	48	(b)	49	(a)	50	(b)

Vocabulary

1	(a)	2	(b)	3	(b)	4	(b)	5	(c)	6	(c)	7	(c)	8	(a)	9	(c)	10	(a)
11	(a)	12	(d)	13	(a)	14	(b)	15	(c)	16	(d)	17	(d)	18	(b)	19	(b)	20	(d)
21	(c)	22	(b)	23	(a)	24	(b)	25	(a)	26	(c)	27	(a)	28	(c)	29	(b)	30	(b)
31	(a)	32	(b)	33	(c)	34	(b)	35	(b)	36	(a)	37	(b)	38	(a)	39	(a)	40	(d)
41	(a)	42	(a)	43	(c)	44	(d)	45	(d)	46	(d)	47	(a)	48	(b)	49	(b)	50	(b)

Reading Comprehension

1	(c)	2	(d)	3	(a)	4	(a)	5	(a)	6	(b)	7	(c)	8	(b)	9	(b)	10	(d)
11	(d)	12	(c)	13	(d)	14	(d)	15	(d)	16	(c)	17	(b)	18	(d)	19	(c)	20	(c)
21	(c)	22	(d)	23	(c)	24	(c)	25	(b)	26	(c)	27	(d)	28	(b)	29	(d)	30	(c)
31	(d)	32	(c)	33	(d)	34	(a)	35	(b)	36	(d)	37	(d)	38	(c)	39	(a)	40	(a)

Answer Keys

Listening Comprehension

1 (b)	**2** (c)	**3** (d)	**4** (a)	**5** (b)	**6** (c)	**7** (b)	**8** (d)	**9** (b)	**10** (a)
11 (d)	**12** (b)	**13** (a)	**14** (b)	**15** (c)	**16** (a)	**17** (d)	**18** (d)	**19** (b)	**20** (d)
21 (c)	**22** (a)	**23** (d)	**24** (b)	**25** (a)	**26** (c)	**27** (a)	**28** (b)	**29** (c)	**30** (c)
31 (b)	**32** (b)	**33** (b)	**34** (a)	**35** (c)	**36** (d)	**37** (c)	**38** (d)	**39** (d)	**40** (c)
41 (a)	**42** (d)	**43** (a)	**44** (c)	**45** (d)	**46** (a)	**47** (c)	**48** (b)	**49** (c)	**50** (c)
51 (d)	**52** (d)	**53** (c)	**54** (a)	**55** (b)	**56** (d)	**57** (a)	**58** (b)	**59** (a)	**60** (c)

Grammar

1 (b)	**2** (a)	**3** (c)	**4** (b)	**5** (c)	**6** (b)	**7** (a)	**8** (a)	**9** (b)	**10** (b)
11 (d)	**12** (d)	**13** (c)	**14** (b)	**15** (a)	**16** (c)	**17** (a)	**18** (c)	**19** (d)	**20** (b)
21 (c)	**22** (d)	**23** (c)	**24** (a)	**25** (d)	**26** (d)	**27** (d)	**28** (a)	**29** (d)	**30** (c)
31 (d)	**32** (b)	**33** (d)	**34** (b)	**35** (d)	**36** (c)	**37** (d)	**38** (b)	**39** (c)	**40** (d)
41 (c)	**42** (b)	**43** (b)	**44** (a)	**45** (c)	**46** (a)	**47** (b)	**48** (c)	**49** (b)	**50** (c)

Vocabulary

1 (a)	**2** (c)	**3** (b)	**4** (b)	**5** (b)	**6** (b)	**7** (c)	**8** (c)	**9** (b)	**10** (c)
11 (d)	**12** (b)	**13** (d)	**14** (d)	**15** (c)	**16** (b)	**17** (a)	**18** (a)	**19** (a)	**20** (d)
21 (c)	**22** (a)	**23** (d)	**24** (a)	**25** (a)	**26** (c)	**27** (d)	**28** (b)	**29** (d)	**30** (a)
31 (a)	**32** (a)	**33** (a)	**34** (c)	**35** (b)	**36** (a)	**37** (d)	**38** (a)	**39** (a)	**40** (b)
41 (c)	**42** (b)	**43** (d)	**44** (a)	**45** (d)	**46** (c)	**47** (c)	**48** (c)	**49** (a)	**50** (a)

Reading Comprehension

1 (a)	**2** (d)	**3** (c)	**4** (c)	**5** (d)	**6** (b)	**7** (d)	**8** (c)	**9** (d)	**10** (a)
11 (b)	**12** (c)	**13** (a)	**14** (b)	**15** (b)	**16** (d)	**17** (b)	**18** (b)	**19** (a)	**20** (b)
21 (a)	**22** (a)	**23** (d)	**24** (d)	**25** (c)	**26** (d)	**27** (d)	**28** (d)	**29** (d)	**30** (d)
31 (b)	**32** (b)	**33** (b)	**34** (d)	**35** (a)	**36** (c)	**37** (a)	**38** (c)	**39** (d)	**40** (d)

Answer Keys

Listening Comprehension

1 (d)	**2** (d)	**3** (a)	**4** (c)	**5** (c)	**6** (d)	**7** (b)	**8** (d)	**9** (d)	**10** (b)
11 (d)	**12** (b)	**13** (b)	**14** (c)	**15** (c)	**16** (b)	**17** (c)	**18** (a)	**19** (b)	**20** (a)
21 (a)	**22** (c)	**23** (c)	**24** (d)	**25** (c)	**26** (a)	**27** (a)	**28** (c)	**29** (a)	**30** (a)
31 (d)	**32** (b)	**33** (a)	**34** (d)	**35** (b)	**36** (a)	**37** (b)	**38** (d)	**39** (d)	**40** (c)
41 (c)	**42** (c)	**43** (d)	**44** (a)	**45** (b)	**46** (a)	**47** (d)	**48** (b)	**49** (b)	**50** (a)
51 (b)	**52** (b)	**53** (d)	**54** (d)	**55** (d)	**56** (b)	**57** (c)	**58** (a)	**59** (d)	**60** (d)

Grammar

1 (d)	**2** (a)	**3** (b)	**4** (b)	**5** (a)	**6** (d)	**7** (b)	**8** (b)	**9** (a)	**10** (a)
11 (b)	**12** (d)	**13** (d)	**14** (b)	**15** (b)	**16** (c)	**17** (b)	**18** (a)	**19** (d)	**20** (a)
21 (b)	**22** (b)	**23** (a)	**24** (d)	**25** (b)	**26** (d)	**27** (d)	**28** (d)	**29** (a)	**30** (c)
31 (c)	**32** (a)	**33** (a)	**34** (d)	**35** (d)	**36** (a)	**37** (b)	**38** (c)	**39** (a)	**40** (a)
41 (d)	**42** (b)	**43** (a)	**44** (c)	**45** (d)	**46** (c)	**47** (c)	**48** (a)	**49** (d)	**50** (c)

Vocabulary

1 (c)	**2** (a)	**3** (b)	**4** (c)	**5** (c)	**6** (b)	**7** (c)	**8** (a)	**9** (a)	**10** (b)
11 (c)	**12** (d)	**13** (c)	**14** (a)	**15** (b)	**16** (c)	**17** (b)	**18** (b)	**19** (a)	**20** (a)
21 (c)	**22** (d)	**23** (a)	**24** (b)	**25** (a)	**26** (c)	**27** (a)	**28** (c)	**29** (c)	**30** (c)
31 (d)	**32** (a)	**33** (a)	**34** (a)	**35** (d)	**36** (a)	**37** (c)	**38** (d)	**39** (b)	**40** (b)
41 (b)	**42** (a)	**43** (d)	**44** (c)	**45** (d)	**46** (b)	**47** (c)	**48** (b)	**49** (c)	**50** (c)

Reading Comprehension

1 (c)	**2** (c)	**3** (d)	**4** (b)	**5** (d)	**6** (c)	**7** (b)	**8** (c)	**9** (a)	**10** (a)
11 (b)	**12** (b)	**13** (a)	**14** (c)	**15** (c)	**16** (a)	**17** (c)	**18** (a)	**19** (d)	**20** (b)
21 (b)	**22** (d)	**23** (d)	**24** (b)	**25** (b)	**26** (b)	**27** (c)	**28** (d)	**29** (a)	**30** (d)
31 (d)	**32** (b)	**33** (d)	**34** (a)	**35** (b)	**36** (d)	**37** (d)	**38** (a)	**39** (c)	**40** (c)

i-TEPS Review 🗨

국내 최초 통합 영어능력 평가
integrated-TEPS

⇨ 의사소통에 필요한 듣기, 말하기, 읽기, 쓰기 능력을 통합하여 평가한다.

듣기, 말하기, 읽기, 쓰기 능력은 서로 밀접한 관계를 가진 요소로 듣기, 읽기 능력 혹은 말하기, 쓰기 능력만을 단순히 측정해서는 정확한 영어능력을 평가하기 어렵다. *i*-TEPS는 유기적인 연관성을 지닌 이 네 가지 의사소통 능력을 통합적으로 측정하여 수험자의 영어능력을 정확하게 평가한다.

⇨ 변별력과 신뢰도가 있는 시험이다.

i-TEPS는 국내 최고 권위의 영어능력 평가로 듣기, 읽기 분야에서 탁월한 변별력을 인정받은 TEPS와 국내 최초 CBT 방식의 영어 말하기·쓰기 시험인 TEPS-Speaking & Writing의 성공 노하우를 바탕으로 개발되었다. 실전 영어능력을 보다 정밀하게 측정할 수 있도록 세분화된 채점 요소를 적용하고 있으며, 출제자와 채점자를 어학 분야의 최고 전문가들로 선정하여 높은 신뢰도와 탁월한 변별력을 지니고 있다.

⇨ 실전 영어능력을 측정한다.

간단한 대화를 할 수 있는 능력부터 도표를 보고 발표하는 분석력과 구성력까지, 접하는 상황에 따라 필요한 영어능력도 다양하다. *i*-TEPS는 유학이나 비즈니스 등 특정한 분야에서의 영어 활용 능력을 집중적으로 평가하는 타 시험과는 달리, 비즈니스 상황을 포함한 다양한 영어 사용 환경을 재현하여 실질적으로 활용 가능한 영어능력을 평가한다.

⇨ 경제성과 효율성을 갖춘 시험이다.

i-TEPS는 타 통합 영어능력 평가시험에 비해 응시료가 저렴하다. 한 번의 시험으로 듣기, 말하기, 읽기, 쓰기 능력을 종합적으로 평가하여 각각의 영역을 별도로 평가해야 하는 타 시험과 비교해도 응시료 부담이 적다. *i*-TEPS는 최소의 시간과 비용으로 수험자의 영어능력을 정확히 측정하는 높은 효율성을 갖춘 시험이다.

i-TEPS 영역별 유형 및 설명

i-TEPS는 기존의 TEPS와 TEPS-Speaking & Writing 시험을 토대로 듣기, 말하기, 읽기, 쓰기 능력을 종합적으로 측정하는 통합형 시험으로 개발되었다. Listening, Grammar & Vocabulary, Reading, Speaking, Writing의 5개 영역에 걸쳐 약 3시간 동안 진행되며, 총 143문항, 400점 만점으로 구성되어 있다.

영역		문제유형	문항수	시간		총점
Listening	Part 1	짧은 대화를 듣고 이어질 대화로 가장 적절한 답 고르기	15	35분		80점
	Part 2	긴 대화를 듣고 질문에 가장 적절한 답 고르기	15			
	Part 3	담화를 듣고 질문에 가장 적절한 답 고르기	10			
Grammar & Vocabulary	Part 1	대화문의 빈칸에 가장 적절한 답 고르기	15	20분		20점
	Part 2	단문의 빈칸에 가장 적절한 답 고르기	15			
	Part 3	대화문의 빈칸에 가장 적절한 어휘 고르기	15			20점
	Part 4	단문의 빈칸에 가장 적절한 어휘 고르기	15			
Reading	Part 1	지문을 읽고 빈칸에 가장 적절한 답 고르기	10	40분		80점
	Part 2	지문을 읽고 질문에 가장 적절한 답 고르기 (1지문 1문항)	19			
	Part 3	지문을 읽고 질문에 가장 적절한 답 고르기 (1지문 2문항)	6			
Speaking	Part 1	간단한 질문에 대답하기	1(3)		답변 10초	100점
	Part 2	소리내어 읽기	1	준비 30초	답변 45초	
	Part 3	일상 대화 상황에서 질문에 답하기	1(5)	준비 15초	답변 10초	
	Part 4	그림 보고 연결하여 이야기하기	1	준비 60초	답변 60초	
	Part 5	도표 보고 발표하기	1	준비 120초	답변 90초	
Writing	Part 1	받아쓰기	1	10분		100점
	Part 2	이메일 쓰기	1	15분		
	Part 3	의견 쓰기	1	30분		
계						400점

TEPS 등급표 🔊

등급	점수	영역	능력검정기준(Description)
1+급 Level 1+	901~990	전반	**외국인으로서 최상급 수준의 의사소통 능력** 교양 있는 원어민에 버금가는 정도로 의사소통이 가능하고 전문분야 업무에 대처할 수 있음. (Native Level of Communicative Competence)
1급 Level 1	801~900	전반	**외국인으로서 거의 최상급 수준의 의사소통 능력** 단기간 집중 교육을 받으면 대부분의 의사소통이 가능하고 전문분야 업무에 별 무리 없이 대처할 수 있음. (Near-Native Level of Communicative Competence)
2+급 Level 2+	701~800	전반	**외국인으로서 상급 수준의 의사소통 능력** 단기간 집중 교육을 받으면 일반분야 업무를 큰 어려움 없이 수행할 수 있음. (Advanced Level of Communicative Competence)
2급 Level 2	601~700	전반	**외국인으로서 중상급 수준의 의사소통 능력** 중장기간 집중 교육을 받으면 일반분야 업무를 큰 어려움 없이 수행할 수 있음. (High Intermediate Level of Communicative Competence)
3+급 Level 3+	501~600	전반	**외국인으로서 중급 수준의 의사소통 능력** 중장기간 집중 교육을 받으면 한정된 분야의 업무를 큰 어려움 없이 수행할 수 있음. (Mid Intermediate Level of Communicative Competence)
3급 Level 3	401~500	전반	**외국인으로서 중하급 수준의 의사소통 능력** 중장기간 집중 교육을 받으면 한정된 분야의 업무를 다소 미흡하지만 큰 지장 없이 수행할 수 있음. (Low Intermediate Level of Communicative Competence)
4+급 Level 4	201~400	전반	**외국인으로서 하급 수준의 의사소통 능력** 장기간의 집중 교육을 받으면 한정된 분야의 업무를 대체로 어렵게 수행할 수 있음. (Novice Level of Communicative Competence)
5+급 Level 5	10~200	전반	**외국인으로서 최하급 수준의 의사소통 능력** 단편적인 지식만을 갖추고 있어 의사소통이 거의 불가능함. (Near-Zero Level of Communicative Competence)

앞면(Side1)

TEPS

Test of English Proficiency
developed by
Seoul National University

수험번호
Registration No.

성명
Name
한글
한자

문제지번호
Test Booklet No.

감독관확인란

청해 Listening Comprehension (questions 1–60, each with options a b c d e)

문법 Grammar (questions 1–50, each with options a b c d e)

어휘 Vocabulary (questions 1–50, each with options a b c d e)

독해 Reading Comprehension (questions 1–40, each with options a b c d e)

주민등록번호
National ID No.

수험번호
Registration No.

비밀번호
Password

고사실란
Room No.

좌석번호
Seat No.

서 약

본인은 필기구 및 기재오류와 답안지 훼손으로 인한 책임을 지고, 부정행위 처리규정을 준수할 것을 서약합니다.

답안작성시 유 의 사 항

1. 답안 작성은 반드시 **컴퓨터용 싸인펜**을 사용해야 합니다.
2. 답안을 정정할 경우 **수정테이프**(수정액 불가)를 사용해야 합니다.
3. 본 답안지는 컴퓨터로 처리되므로 인되며, 답안지 하단의 타이밍마크(∥∥)를 찢거나, 낙서 등으로 인한 체순서 붙이의 불응할 수 있습니다.

4. 답안은 문항당 정답을 1개만 골라 ● 위 같이 정확히 기재해야 하며, 잘못 표기한 경우에는 당 관리위원회의 OMR관독기의 관독결과에 따르며, 그 결과는 본인이 책임집니다.

Good ●   Bad ◑ ◐ ✕ ✓

5. 감독관의 확인이 없는 답안지는 무효처리됩니다.

TEPS

Test of English Proficiency developed by Seoul National University

뒷면 (Side2)

응시일자 : 20 년 월 일

성명	영문
	서명

학력

학 력	재졸/학업			
초등학교	○	○	○	
중 학 교	○	○	○	
고등학교	○	○	○	
전문대학	○	○	○	
대 학 교	○	○	○	
대 학 원	○	○	○	

전공

전 공	
인 문 학	○
사회과학·법학	○
경제·경영학	○
자 연 과 학	○
의학·약학·간호학	○
공 학	○
교 육 학	○
음악·미술·체육	○
기 타	○

직업

직 업	
공 무 원	○
고시준비	○
교 사	○
군 인	○
의 료 인	○
자 영 업	○
학 생	○
회 사 원	○
직 무	○
기 타	○

직종

직 종	
그 래 픽	○
사 무 직	○
전문직(과학·공학)	○
전 문 직 (그 외)	○
전문직(법률·회계·금융)	○
기 술	○
영 업	○
홍 보	○
인 사	○
경 리	○
기 획	○
연 구	○

직책

직 책	
임 원	○
부 장	○
차 장	○
과 장	○
대 리	○
계 장	○
사 원	○
인 턴	○
기 타	○

단체 구분

학생	일반
○	○

질문란

1. 귀하의 TEPS 응시목적은?
   - (a) 입사지원
   - (b) 인사고과
   - (c) 개인실력측정
   - (d) 입시
   - (e) 국가고시 지원
   - (f) 기타

2. 귀하의 영어권 체류 경험은?
   - (a) 없다
   - (b) 6개월 미만
   - (c) 6개월 이상 1년 미만
   - (d) 1년 이상 3년 미만
   - (e) 3년 이상 5년 미만
   - (f) 5년 이상

3. 귀하께서 응시하고 계신 고사장에 대한 만족도는?
   - (a) 0점
   - (b) 1점
   - (c) 2점
   - (d) 3점
   - (e) 4점
   - (f) 5점

4. 최근 2년내 TEPS 응시횟수는?
   - (a) 없다
   - (b) 1회
   - (c) 2회
   - (d) 3회
   - (e) 4회
   - (f) 5회 이상

성명 (성·이름순으로 기재)

	성 HONG	명 GIL DONG

EX | A B C D E F G H I J K L M N O P Q R S T U V W X Y Z

(성명 마킹란: A B C D E F G H I J K L M N O P Q R S T U V W X Y Z)

〈부정행위 및 규정위반 처리규정〉

1. 모든 부정행위 및 규정위반 적발 및 이에 대한 조치는 TEPS관리위원회의 처리규정에 따라 이루어집니다.

2. 부정행위 및 규정위반 행위는 현장 적발 뿐만 아니라 사후에도 적발될 수 있으며 모두 동일한 조치가 취해집니다.

3. 부정행위 적발 시 당해 성적은 무효 처리되며 사안에 따라 최대 5년까지 TEPS관리위원회에서 주관하는 모든 시험의 응시자격이 제한됩니다.

4. 문제지 이외에 메모를 하는 행위와 시험 문제의 일부 또는 전부를 유출하거나 공개하는 경우 부정행위로 처리됩니다.

5. 각 파트별 시간을 준수하지 않거나, 시험 종료 후 답안 작성을 계속할 경우 규정위반으로 처리됩니다.

TEPS

Test of English Proficiency developed by
Seoul National University

수험번호 Registration No.

성명 Name
영문
한글
한자

문제지번호 Test Booklet No.

감독관확인란

청해 Listening Comprehension

(answer bubble grid, questions 1–60, options a/b/c/d)

문법 Grammar

(answer bubble grid, questions 1–50, options a/b/c/d)

어휘 Vocabulary

(answer bubble grid, questions 1–50, options a/b/c/d)

독해 Reading Comprehension

(answer bubble grid, questions 1–40, options a/b/c/d)

주민등록번호 National ID No.

수험번호 Registration No.

비밀번호 Password

좌석번호 Seat No.

고사실란 Room No.

서약

본인은 필기구 및 기재오류와 답안지 훼손으로 인한 책임을 지고, 부정행위 처리규정을 준수할 것을 서약합니다.

답안작성시 유의사항

1. 답안 작성은 반드시 **컴퓨터용 싸인펜**을 사용해야 합니다.
2. 답안을 정정할 경우 **수정테이프**(수정액 불가)를 사용해야 합니다.
3. 본 답안지는 컴퓨터로 처리되므로 훼손해서는 안되며, 답안지 하단의 타이밍마크(▮▮▮)를 찢거나, 낙서 등으로 인한 훼손시 불이익을 받을 수 있습니다.

4. 답안은 문항당 정답을 1개만 골라 ● 와 같이 정확히 기재해야 하며, 잘못 표기한 경우에는 당 관리위원회의 OMR판독기의 판독결과에 따르므로, 그 결과는 본인이 책임집니다.

   Good ●   Bad ◐ ◑ ⊗ ◓

5. 감독관의 확인이 없는 답안지는 무효처리됩니다.

뒷면(Side2)

TEPS
Test of English Proficiency
developed by
Seoul National University

응시일자 : 20   년   월   일

<부정행위 및 규정위반 처리규정>

1. 모든 부정행위 및 규정위반 적발 및 이에 대한 조치는 TEPS관리위원회의 처리규정에 따라 이루어집니다.

2. 부정행위 및 규정위반 행위는 현장 적발 뿐만 아니라 사후에도 적발될 수 있으며 모두 동일한 조치가 취해집니다.

3. 부정행위 적발 시 당해 성적은 무효 처리되며 사안에 따라 최대 5년까지 TEPS관리위원회에서 주관하는 모든 시험의 응시자격이 제한됩니다.

4. 문제지 이외에 메모를 하는 행위와 시험 문제의 일부 또는 전부를 유출하거나 공개하는 경우 부정행위로 처리됩니다.

5. 각 파트별 시간을 준수하지 않거나, 시험 종료 후 답안 작성을 계속할 경우 규정위반으로 처리됩니다.

성 명 (성·이름순으로 기재)

EX HONG GIL DONG

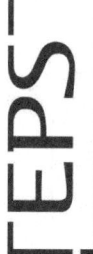

A B C D E F G H I J K L M N O P Q R S T U V W X Y Z

단체 구분

학생	일반
◯	◯

질 문 란

1. 귀하의 TEPS 응시목적은?
(a) 입사지원 (b) 인사고과
(c) 개인실력측정 (d) 입시
(e) 국가고시 자점 (f) 기타

2. 귀하의 영어권 체류 경험은?
(a) 없다 (b) 6개월 미만
(c) 6개월 이상 1년 미만 (d) 1년 이상 3년 미만
(e) 3년 이상 5년 미만 (f) 5년 이상

3. 귀하에서 응시하고 계신 고사장에 대한 만족도는?
(a) 0점 (b) 1점
(c) 2점 (d) 3점
(e) 4점 (f) 5점

4. 최근 2년내 TEPS 응시횟수는?
(a) 없다 (b) 1회
(c) 2회 (d) 3회
(e) 4회 (f) 5회 이상

성명

성	영문
명	서명

학력 (재학/졸업)
초등학교, 중학교, 고등학교, 전문대학, 대학교, 대학원

전공
인문학, 사회과학·법학, 경제학·경영학, 자연과학, 의학·약학·간호학, 공학, 어학, 음악·미술·체육, 기타

직업
공무원, 고시준비, 교사, 군인, 의료인, 자영업, 학생, 회사원, 무직, 기타

직 업
공무원, 교사준비, 사, 인, 의료인, 영업, 생, 회사원, 무직, 기타

직종
군무, 역무, 자무, 공무, 의료, 품질관리, 전산, 생산관리, 서비, 기타

직책
임원, 부장, 차장, 과장, 대리, 계리, 사원, 인턴, 기타

TEPS

Test of English Proficiency
developed by
Seoul National University

청 해
Listening Comprehension

문 법
Grammar

어 휘
Vocabulary

독 해
Reading Comprehension

수험번호
Registration No.

성명
Name
한글
한자

문제지번호
Test Booklet No.

감독관확인란

주 민 등 록 번 호
National ID No.

수 험 번 호
Registration No.

비 밀 번 호
Password

고사실란
Room No.

좌석번호
Seat No.

서 약

본인은 필기구 및 기재오류와 답안지 훼손으로 인한 책임을 지고, 부정행위 처리규정을 준수할 것을 서약합니다.

답안작성시
유 의 사 항

1. 답안 작성은 반드시 **컴퓨터용 싸인펜**을 사용해야 합니다.

2. 답안을 정정할 경우 수정테이프(수정액 불가)를 사용해야 합니다.

3. 문 답안지는 컴퓨터로 처리되므로 인되며, 답안지 하단의 타이밍마크(▮▮▮)를 찢거나, 낙서 등으로 인한 체손시 불이익을 받을 수 있습니다.

4. 답안은 문항당 정답을 1개만 골라 ● 와 같이 정확히 기재해야 하며, 필기구 오류나 본인의 부주의로 잘못 표기한 경우에는 답 관리위원회의 OMR판독기의 판독결과에 따르며, 그 결과는 본인이 책임진다.

정확 표기
Good ●
Bad ◐ ◑ ⊗ ◎

5. 감독관의 확인이 없는 답안지는 무효처리됩니다.

성	영문	
명	서명	

학력

학 력	졸업(업)	재학(휴학)
초등학교	○	○
중 학 교	○	○
고등학교	○	○
전문대학	○	○
대 학 교	○	○
대 학 원	○	○

전공

전 공	
인 문 학	○
사회과학·법학	○
경제학·경영학	○
자 연 과 학	○
의학·약학·간호학	○
공 학	○
교 육	○
음악·미술·체육	○
기 타	○

직업

직 업	
공 무 원	○
고시준비	○
교 사	○
군 인	○
의 료 인	○
자 영 업	○
학 생	○
회 사 원	○
전 문 직	○
기 타	○

종사 직종

직 종	
기 타	○
가 정 주 부	○
의 료	○
자 영 업	○
공 무	○
의료 품질 관리	○
진 단 직	○
행정 관 리	○
생 산 직	○
서 비 스	○
기 타	○

직책

직 책	
임 원	○
부 장	○
차 장	○
과 장	○
대 리	○
계 장	○
사 원	○
인 턴	○
기 타	○

단체 구분

학생	일반
○	○

질문란

1. 귀하의 TEPS 응시목적은?
   (a) 입사지원   (b) 인사정책
   (c) 개인실력측정   (d) 입시
   (e) 국가고시 지원   (f) 기타

2. 귀하의 영어권 체류 경험은?
   (a) 없다   (b) 6개월 미만
   (c) 6개월 이상 1년 미만   (d) 1년 이상 3년 미만
   (e) 3년 이상 5년 미만   (f) 5년 이상

3. 귀하께서 응시하고 계신 고사장에 대한 만족도는?
   (a) 0점   (b) 1점
   (c) 2점   (d) 3점
   (e) 4점   (f) 5점

4. 최근 2년내 TEPS 응시횟수는?
   (a) 없다   (b) 1회
   (c) 2회   (d) 3회
   (e) 4회   (f) 5회 이상

성 명 (성·이름순으로 기재)

	EX	H	O	N	G		G	I	L		D	O	N	G							
A	Ⓐ																				
B	Ⓑ																				
C	Ⓒ																				
D	Ⓓ																				
E	Ⓔ																				
F	Ⓕ																				
G	Ⓖ																				
H	Ⓗ																				
I	Ⓘ																				
J	Ⓙ																				
K	Ⓚ																				
L	Ⓛ																				
M	Ⓜ																				
N	Ⓝ																				
O	Ⓞ																				
P	Ⓟ																				
Q	Ⓠ																				
R	Ⓡ																				
S	Ⓢ																				
T	Ⓣ																				
U	Ⓤ																				
V	Ⓥ																				
W	Ⓦ																				
X	Ⓧ																				
Y	Ⓨ																				
Z	Ⓩ																				

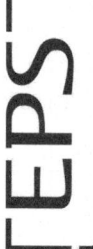

응시일자 : 20   년   월   일

〈부정행위 및 규정위반 처리규정〉

1. 모든 부정행위 및 규정위반 적발 및 이에 대한 조치는 TEPS관리위원회의 처리규정에 따라 이루어집니다.

2. 부정행위 및 규정위반 행위는 현장 적발 뿐만 아니라 사후에도 적발될 수 있으므로 모두 동일한 조치가 취해집니다.

3. 부정행위 적발 시 당해 성적은 무효 처리되며 사안에 따라 최대 5년까지 TEPS관리위원회에서 주관하는 모든 시험의 응시자격이 제한됩니다.

4. 문제지 이외에 메모를 하는 행위와 시험 문제의 일부 또는 전부를 유출하거나 공개하는 경우 부정행위로 처리됩니다.

5. 각 파트별 시간을 준수하지 않거나, 시험 종료 후 답안 작성을 계속할 경우 규정위반으로 처리됩니다.

TEPS

Test of English Proficiency
developed by
Seoul National University

수험번호 Registration No.

성명 Name
한글
한자

문제지번호 Test Booklet No.

감독관확인란

청해 Listening Comprehension

(OMR answer grid, questions 1–60)

문법 Grammar

(OMR answer grid, questions 1–50)

어휘 Vocabulary

(OMR answer grid, questions 1–50)

독해 Reading Comprehension

(OMR answer grid, questions 1–40)

주민등록번호 National ID No.

수험번호 Registration No.

비밀번호 Password

좌석번호 Seat No.

고사실란 Room No.

Good ▮   Bad ⦸ Ⓧ ◐ Ⓥ

서약

본인은 필기구 및 기재오류와 답안지 훼손으로 인한 책임을 지고, 부정행위 처리규정을 준수할 것을 서약합니다.

답안작성시 유의사항

1. 답안은 작성은 반드시 **컴퓨터용 싸인펜**을 사용해야 합니다.

2. 답안을 정정할 경우 수정테이프(수정액 및 풀기)를 사용해야 합니다.

3. 본 답안지는 컴퓨터로 처리되므로 훼손해서는 안되며, 답안지 하단의 타이밍마크(▮▮▮)를 찢거나, 낙서 등으로 인한 훼손시 불이익을 받을 수 있습니다.

4. 답안은 문항당 정답을 1개만 골라 ① 와 같이 정확히 기재해야 하며, 필기구 오류나 본인의 부주의로 잘못 표기한 경우에는 답 관리위원회의 OMR판독기의 판독결과에 따르며, 그 결과는 본인이 책임집니다.

5. 감독관의 확인이 없는 답안지는 무효처리됩니다.

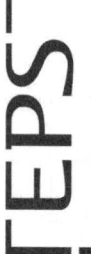

TEPS
Test of English Proficiency
developed by
Seoul National University

뒷면 (Side2)

응시일자 : 20___년 ___월 ___일

성 명 (성·이름순으로 기재)

성: EX HONG GIL DONG

| | A | B | C | D | E | F | G | H | I | J | K | L | M | N | O | P | Q | R | S | T | U | V | W | X | Y | Z |

단체구분
학생 ☐   일반 ☐

성 명
영문
서명

학력
최종학력   초등학교 / 중학교 / 고등학교 / 전문대학 / 대학교 / 대학원

전공
인문학 / 사회과학·법학 / 경제학·경영학 / 자연과학 / 의학·약학·간호학 / 공학 / 교육학 / 음악·미술·체육 / 기타

직업
공무원 / 교사(교수)·강사 / 군인 / 의료인 / 자영업 / 학생 / 회사원 / 기타

직종
기획 / 인사·총무 / 재무·회계 / 영업·판매 / 홍보 / 생산·품질관리 / 연구개발 / 정보처리 / 자산관리 / 구매·자재 / 비서 / 기타

직책
연구직 / 임원 / 부장 / 차장 / 과장 / 대리 / 계장 / 사원 / 인턴 / 기타

TEPS

Test of English Proficiency
developed by
Seoul National University

수험번호 Registration No.

성명 Name
한글
한자

문제지번호 Test Booklet No.

감독관확인란

청해 Listening Comprehension

(문항 1–60, 보기 ⓐ ⓑ ⓒ ⓓ)

문법 Grammar

(문항 1–50, 보기 ⓐ ⓑ ⓒ ⓓ)

어휘 Vocabulary

(문항 1–50, 보기 ⓐ ⓑ ⓒ ⓓ)

독해 Reading Comprehension

(문항 1–40, 보기 ⓐ ⓑ ⓒ ⓓ)

수험번호 Registration No.

주민등록번호 National ID No.

비밀번호 Password

좌석번호 Seat No.

고사실란 Room No.

서약

본인은 필기구 및 기재오류와 답안지 훼손으로 인한 책임을 지고, 부정행위 처리규정을 준수할 것을 서약합니다.

답안작성시 유의사항

1. 답안 작성은 반드시 **컴퓨터용 싸인펜**을 사용해야 합니다.
2. 답안을 정정할 경우 수정테이프(수정액 불가)를 사용해야 합니다.
3. 본 답안지는 컴퓨터로 처리되므로 훼손해서는 안되며, 답안지 하단의 타이밍마크(‖‖)를 찢거나, 낙서 등으로 인한 훼손시는 무효처리됩니다.
4. 답안은 문항당 정답을 1개만 골라 ● 와 같이 정확히 기재해야 하며, 필기구 오류나 본인의 부주의로 잘못 표기한 경우에는 당 관리위원회의 OMR판독기의 판독결과에 따르므로, 그 결과는 본인이 책임집니다.

   정확한 표기: ●   잘못된 표기: ◐ ◔ ✕ ⊘
5. 감독관의 확인이 없는 답안지는 무효처리됩니다.

성 영문
명 서명

TEPS
Test of English Proficiency
developed by
Seoul National University

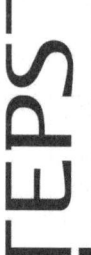

직업

직업		
공무원		직원
교사·강사		군인
의료인		자영업
회사원		학생
무직		기타

전공

학력	전공	직업
초등학교	인문	공무원
중학교	사회과학·법학	교사준비
고등학교	경제학·경영학	교사
전문대학	자연·의학·간호학	군인
대학교	외국어·어학	의료인
대학원	공학	자영업
	음악·미술·체육	학생
	기타	회사원
		무직
		기타

직종

직종		직위
금융	회장
기계·금속	부회장
전문직(법률회계금융)	사장
기술	부사장
예술	전무
유통	상무
종합	이사
서비스	부장
경영	차장
기타	과장
구매	계장
	사원
	인턴
	기타

단체 구분

학생	일반
○	○

질문란

1. 귀하의 TEPS 응시목적은?
   ⓐ 입사지원 ⓑ 인사정책
   ⓒ 개인실력측정 ⓓ 입시
   ⓔ 국가고시 지원 ⓕ 기타

2. 귀하의 영어권 체류 경험은?
   ⓐ 없다 ⓑ 6개월 미만
   ⓒ 6개월 이상 1년 미만 ⓓ 1년 이상 3년 미만
   ⓔ 3년 이상 5년 미만 ⓕ 5년 이상

3. 귀하께서 응시하고 계신 고사장에
   대한 만족도는?
   ⓐ 0점 ⓑ 1점
   ⓒ 2점 ⓓ 3점
   ⓔ 4점 ⓕ 5점

4. 최근 2년내 TEPS 응시횟수는?
   ⓐ 없다 ⓑ 1회
   ⓒ 2회 ⓓ 3회
   ⓔ 4회 ⓕ 5회 이상

성

EX	H	O	N	G

명 (성·이름순으로 기재)

G	I	L		D	O	N	G

(성명 마킹표: A B C D E F G H I J K L M N O P Q R S T U V W X Y Z)

응시일자 : 20   년   월   일

〈부정행위 및 규정위반 처리규정〉

1. 모든 부정행위 및 규정위반 적발 및 이에 대한 조치는 TEPS관리위원회의 처리규정에 따라 이루어집니다.

2. 부정행위 및 규정위반 행위는 현장 적발 뿐만 아니라 사후에도 적발될 수 있으며 모두 동일한 조치가 취해집니다.

3. 부정행위 적발 시 당해 성적은 무효 처리되며 사안에 따라 최대 5년까지 TEPS관리위원회에서 주관하는 모든 시험의 응시자격이 제한됩니다.

4. 문제지 이외에 메모를 하는 행위와 시험 문제의 일부 또는 전부를 유출하거나 공개하는 경우 부정행위로 처리됩니다.

5. 각 파트별 시간을 준수하지 않거나, 시험 종료 후 답안 작성을 계속할 경우 규정위반으로 처리됩니다.

앞면(Side1)

TEPS

Test of English Proficiency
developed by
Seoul National University

청 해
Listening Comprehension

문 법
Grammar

어 휘
Vocabulary

독 해
Reading Comprehension

서 약

본인은 필기구 및 기재오류와 답안지 체순으로 인한 책임을 지고, 부정행위 처리규정을 준수할 것을 서약합니다.

답안작성시 유의사항

1. 답안 작성은 반드시 **컴퓨터용 싸인펜**을 사용해야 합니다.
2. 답안을 정정할 경우 **수정테이프(수정액 불가)**를 사용해야 합니다.
3. 본 답안지는 컴퓨터로 처리되므로 인되며, 답안지 하단의 타이밍마크(III)를 찢거나, 낙서 등으로 인한 체순시 불이익이 발생할 수 있습니다.

4. 답안은 문항당 정답을 1개만 골라 ● 와 같이 정확히 기재해야 하며, 필기구 오류나 본인의 부주의로 잘못 표기한 경우에는 답 관리위원회의 판독결과에 따르며, 그 결과는 본인이 책임집니다.

정묫 표기한			
Good	●	Bad	◐ ◑ ⊗ ⊘

5. 감독관의 확인이 없는 답안지는 무효처리됩니다.

수험번호
Registration No.

성명
Name
한글
한자

문제지번호
Test Booklet No.

감독관확인란

주민등록번호
National ID No.

수험번호
Registration No.

비밀번호
Password

좌석번호
Seat No.

고사실란
Room No.

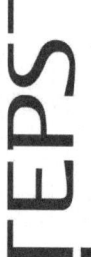

뒷면(Side2)

TEPS
Test of English Proficiency
developed by
Seoul National University

응시일자 : 20　　년　　월　　일

〈부정행위 및 규정위반 처리규정〉

1. 모든 부정행위 및 규정위반 적발 및 이에 대한 조치는 TEPS관리위원 회의 처리규정에 따라 이루어집니다.

2. 부정행위 및 규정위반 행위는 현장 적발 뿐만 아니라 사후에도 적발될 수 있으며 모두 동일한 조치가 취해 집니다.

3. 부정행위 적발 시 단체 성적은 무효 처리되며 사안에 따라 최대 5년까지 TEPS관리위원회에서 주관하는 모든 시험의 응시자격이 제한됩니다.

4. 문제지 이외에 메모를 하는 행위와 시험 문제의 일부 또는 전부를 유출 하거나 공개하는 경우 부정행위로 처리됩니다.

5. 각 파트별 시간을 준수하지 않거나, 시험 종료 후 답안 작성을 계속할 경우 규정위반으로 처리됩니다.

성	명 (성·이름순으로 기재)
성 HONG	명 GIL DONG

EX

A B C D E F G H I J K L M N O P Q R S T U V W X Y Z

(letter bubble grid A–Z for each column)

단 체 구 분
학생	일반
◯	◯

질 문 란

1. 귀하의 TEPS 응시목적은?
 ⓐ 입사지원　ⓑ 인사정책
 ⓒ 개인실력측정　ⓓ 입시
 ⓔ 국가고시 지원　ⓕ 기타

2. 귀하의 영어권 체류 경험은?
 ⓐ 없다　ⓑ 6개월 미만
 ⓒ 6개월 이상 1년 미만　ⓓ 1년 이상 3년 미만
 ⓔ 3년 이상 5년 미만　ⓕ 5년 이상

3. 귀하에서 응시하고 계신 고사장에 대한 만족도는?
 ⓐ 0점　ⓑ 1점
 ⓒ 2점　ⓓ 3점
 ⓔ 4점　ⓕ 5점

4. 최근 2년내 TEPS 응시횟수는?
 ⓐ 없다　ⓑ 1회
 ⓒ 2회　ⓓ 3회
 ⓔ 4회　ⓕ 5회 이상

성	영문
명	서명

학 력
학 력	재중 학업
초등학교	◯
중 학 교	◯
고등학교	◯
전문대학	◯
대 학 교	◯
대 학 원	◯

전 공
인문
사회과학·법학
경제학·경영학
자 연 과 학
의학·약학·간호학
공 학
교 육
음악·미술·체육
기 타

직 업
공 무 원
교 사 준 비
교 사
군 인
의 료 인
자 영 업
학 생
회 사 원
무 직
기 타

직 종
무 역
여 행
자 금
공 무 원
영 업 관 리
품 질 관 리
진 산
행 정
생 산 관 리
서 비 스
기 타

직 책
회 원
임 부 장
차 장
과 장
대 리
계 장
사 원
인 턴
기 타

직 위
고 위 직 공 무 원
전문직(과학·공학)
전 문 직 (의 약)
전문직(법률회계금융)
기 술 공
기 능 공
사 무 직
영 업 직
서 비 스 직
농 어 업
생 산 직
단 순 노 무
기 타

TEPS
Test of English Proficiency
developed by
Seoul National University

앞면(Side1)

수험번호 Registration No.
성명 Name 한글
한자

문제지번호 Test Booklet No.

감독관확인란

청해 Listening Comprehension	문법 Grammar	어휘 Vocabulary	독해 Reading Comprehension

유의작성시
유의사항

서약

본인은 필기구 및 기재오류와 답안지 훼손으로 인한 책임을 지고, 부정행위 처리규정을 준수할 것을 서약합니다.

1. 답안 작성은 반드시 **컴퓨터용 싸인펜**을 사용해야 합니다.
2. 답안을 정정할 경우 수정테이프(수정액 사용불가)를 사용해야 합니다.
3. 본 답안지는 컴퓨터로 처리되므로 인되며, 답안지 하단의 타이밍마크(▐▐▐)를 찢거나, 낙서 등으로 인한 훼손시 발생할 수 있습니다.

4. 답안은 문항당 정답을 1개만 골라 ❶와 같이 정확히 기재해야 하며, 필기구 오류나 본인의 부주의로 잘못 표기한 경우에는 답 관리위원회의 OMR판독기의 판독결과에 따르며, 그 결과는 본인이 책임집니다.

정답 표기한
Good ❶   Bad ⓐ ⓘ ⓧ ⓨ

5. 감독관의 확인이 없는 답안지는 무효처리됩니다.

수험번호 Registration No.
주민등록번호 National ID No.
비밀번호 Password
좌석번호 Seat No.
고사실란 Room No.

TEPS

Test of English Proficiency
developed by
Seoul National University

밑면(Side2)

응시일자 : 20 ___ 년 ___ 월 ___ 일

성명 / 서명

성명	영문
	서명

직업

직 업		전 공		학 력		

학력: 초등학교 / 중학교 / 고등학교 / 전문대학 / 대학교 / 대학원

전공: 인문 / 사회과학·법학 / 경제학·경영학 / 자연과학 / 의학·약학·간호학 / 공학 / 교육 / 음악·미술·체육 / 어학 / 기타

직업: 공무원 / 교사·준비 / 교수 / 군인 / 의료 / 자영업 / 학생 / 회사원 / 사무직 / 기타

직종

직: 고위임직원 / 전문직(과학·공학) / 전문직(교육) / 전문직(법률·회계·금융) / 기술·준전문직 / 사무 / 서비스 / 판매 / 농림어업 / 기능 / 장치·기계조작 / 단순노무 / 군인 / 기타

종: 농업 / 어업 / 광업 / 제조업 / 전기·가스·수도 / 건설업 / 도소매업 / 숙박·음식점업 / 운수·통신업 / 금융·보험업 / 부동산·임대업 / 공공행정·국방 / 교육서비스업 / 보건·사회복지 / 오락·문화·운동 / 기타서비스업 / 가사서비스 / 국제·외국기관 / 기타

단체구분

학생 ◯	일반 ◯

질문란

1. 귀하의 TEPS 응시목적은?
   @ 입사지원 ⓑ 인사정책
   ⓒ 개인실력측정 ⓓ 입시
   ⓔ 국가고시 지원 ⓕ 기타

2. 귀하의 영어권 체류 경험은?
   @ 없다 ⓑ 6개월 미만
   ⓒ 6개월 이상 1년 미만 ⓓ 1년 이상 3년 미만
   ⓔ 3년 이상 5년 미만 ⓕ 5년 이상

3. 귀하께서 응시하고 계신 고사장에
   대한 만족도는?
   @ 0점 ⓑ 1점
   ⓒ 2점 ⓓ 3점
   ⓔ 4점 ⓕ 5점

4. 최근 1년내 TEPS 응시횟수는?
   @ 없다 ⓑ 1회
   ⓒ 2회 ⓓ 3회
   ⓔ 4회 ⓕ 5회 이상

성명 (성·이름순으로 기재)

성: HONG
명: GIL DONG

EX A B C D E F G H I J K L M N O P Q R S T U V W X Y Z
(각 행마다 ⒶⒷⒸⒹⒺⒻⒼⒽⒾⒿⓀⓁⓂⓃⓄⓅⓆⓇⓈⓉⓊⓋⓌⓍⓎⓏ)

〈부정행위 및 규정위반 처리규정〉

1. 모든 부정행위 및 규정위반 적발 및 이에 대한 조치는 TEPS관리위원회의 처리규정에 따라 이루어집니다.

2. 부정행위 및 규정위반 행위는 현장 적발 뿐만 아니라 사후에도 적발될 수 있으며 모두 동일한 조치가 취해집니다.

3. 부정행위 적발 시 당해 성적은 무효 화되며 사안에 따라 최대 5년까지 TEPS관리위원회에서 주관하는 모든 시험의 응시자격이 제한됩니다.

4. 문제지 이외에 메모를 하는 행위와 시험 문제의 일부 또는 전부를 유출 하거나 공개하는 경우 부정행위로 처리됩니다.

5. 각 파트별 시간을 준수하지 않거나, 시험 종료 후 답안 작성을 계속할 경우 규정위반으로 처리됩니다.

TEPS

Test of English Proficiency
developed by
Seoul National University

수험번호
Registration No.

성명
Name
한글
한자

문제지번호
Test Booklet No.

감독관확인란

청해 Listening Comprehension

(문항 1~60, 각 문항 ⓐ ⓑ ⓒ ⓓ)

문법 Grammar

(문항 1~25, 각 문항 ⓐ ⓑ ⓒ ⓓ)

어휘 Vocabulary

(문항 1~50, 각 문항 ⓐ ⓑ ⓒ ⓓ)

독해 Reading Comprehension

(문항 1~40, 각 문항 ⓐ ⓑ ⓒ ⓓ)

주민등록번호
National ID No.

수험번호
Registration No.

비밀번호
Password

좌석번호
Seat No.

고사실란
Room No.

서약

본인은 필기구 및 기재오류와 답안지 훼손으로 인한 책임을 지고, 부정행위 처리규정을 준수할 것을 서약합니다.

답안작성시 유의사항

1. 답안 작성은 반드시 **컴퓨터용 싸인펜**을 사용해야 합니다.
2. 답안을 정정할 경우 **수정테이프**(수정액 및 풀기)를 사용해야 합니다.
3. 본 답안지는 컴퓨터로 처리되므로 훼손해서는 안되며, 답안지 하단의 타이밍마크(┃┃┃)를 찢거나, 낙서 등으로 인한 훼손시 불이익을 받을 수 있습니다.
4. 답안은 문항당 정답을 1개만 골라 ● 와 같이 정확히 기재해야 하며, 필기구 오류나 본인의 부주의로 잘못 표기한 경우에는 답 관리위원회의 OMR판독기의 판독결과에 따르며, 그 결과는 본인이 책임집니다.

   Good ●   Bad ⊙ ◐ ⊗ ⊘

5. 감독관의 확인이 없는 답안지는 무효처리됩니다.

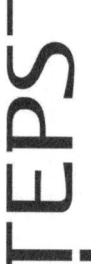

뒷면(Side2)

TEPS
Test of English Proficiency
developed by
Seoul University

응시일자 : 20   년   월   일

〈부정행위 및 규정위반 처리규정〉

1. 모든 부정행위 및 규정위반 적발 및 이에 대한 조치는 TEPS관리위원회의 처리규정에 따라 이루어집니다.

2. 부정행위 및 규정위반 행위는 현장 적발 뿐만 아니라 사후에도 적발될 수 있으며 모두 동일한 조치가 취해 집니다.

3. 부정행위 적발 시 당해 성적은 무효 화되며 사안에 따라 최대 5년까지 TEPS관리위원회에서 주관하는 모든 시험의 응시자격이 제한됩니다.

4. 문제지 이외에 메모를 하는 행위와 시험 문제의 일부 또는 전부를 유출 하거나 공개하는 경우 부정행위로 처리됩니다.

5. 각 파트별 시간을 준수하지 않거나, 시험 종료 후 답안 작성을 계속할 경우 규정위반으로 처리됩니다.

단체구분

학생	일반
◯	◯

질문란

1. 귀하의 TEPS 응시목적은?
   - ⓐ 입사지원 ⓑ 인사정책
   - ⓒ 개인실력측정 ⓓ 입시
   - ⓔ 국가고시 지원 ⓕ 기타

2. 귀하의 영어권 체류 경험은?
   - ⓐ 없다 ⓑ 6개월 미만
   - ⓒ 6개월 이상 1년 미만 ⓓ 1년 이상 3년 미만
   - ⓔ 3년 이상 5년 미만 ⓕ 5년 이상

3. 귀하께서 응시하고 계신 고사장에 대한 만족도는?
   - ⓐ 0점 ⓑ 1점
   - ⓒ 2점 ⓓ 3점
   - ⓔ 4점 ⓕ 5점

4. 최근 2년내 TEPS 응시횟수는?
   - ⓐ 없다 ⓑ 1회
   - ⓒ 2회 ⓓ 3회
   - ⓔ 4회 ⓕ 5회 이상

성	명 (성·이름순으로 기재)

	성	명	

EX HONG GIL DONG

A B C D E F G H I J K L M N O P Q R S T U V W X Y Z

(각 문자열마다 Ⓐ Ⓑ Ⓒ Ⓓ Ⓔ Ⓕ Ⓖ Ⓗ Ⓘ Ⓙ Ⓚ Ⓛ Ⓜ Ⓝ Ⓞ Ⓟ Ⓠ Ⓡ Ⓢ Ⓣ Ⓤ Ⓥ Ⓦ Ⓧ Ⓨ Ⓩ)

성	명
영문	
서명	

학력

	자졸업	
졸업	재학	
초등학교	◯ ◯	
중학교	◯ ◯	
고등학교	◯ ◯	
전문대학	◯ ◯	
대학교	◯ ◯	
대학원	◯ ◯	

전공

- 인문·어학 ◯
- 사회과학·법학 ◯
- 경제학·경영학 ◯
- 자연·공과 ◯
- 의학·약학·간호학 ◯
- 교육 ◯
- 음악·미술·체육 ◯
- 기타 ◯

직업

- 공무원 ◯
- 고시준비 ◯
- 교사 ◯
- 군인 ◯
- 의료인 ◯
- 자영업 ◯
- 학생 ◯
- 회사원 ◯
- 무직 ◯
- 기타 ◯

직책

- 임원 ◯
- 부장 ◯
- 차장 ◯
- 과장 ◯
- 대리 ◯
- 계장 ◯
- 사원 ◯
- 인턴 ◯
- 기타 ◯

종사직종

- 금융 ◯
- 무역 ◯
- 유통 ◯
- 건설 ◯
- 서비스 ◯
- 제조 ◯
- 언론 ◯
- 정보통신 ◯
- 화학 ◯
- 전기·전자 ◯
- 기타 ◯

Memo

TEPS

Test of English Proficiency
developed by
Seoul National University

  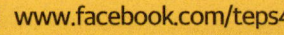

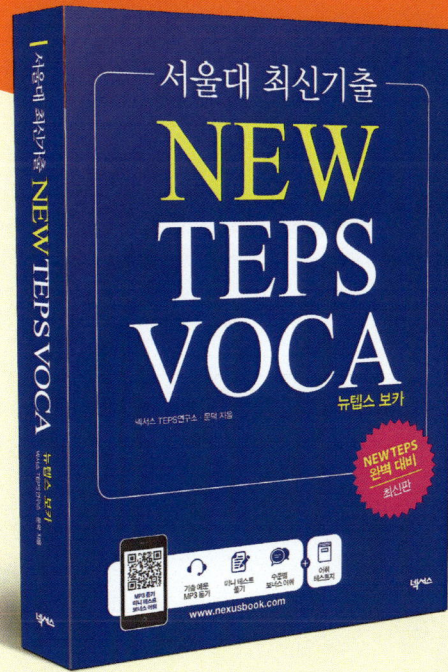

NEW TEPS 실전 모의고사 3회분

김무룡 · 넥서스 TEPS 연구소 지음 | 12,000원

(정답 및 해설 무료 다운로드)

YES 24 〈국어 외국어 사전〉 베스트셀러 ※2018년 5월 기준